Here She Comes Now

Here She Comes Now

WOMEN IN MUSIC WHO HAVE CHANGED OUR LIVES

EDITED BY JEFF GORDINIER AND MARC WEINGARTEN

ICON

This edition published in the UK in 2016 by
Icon Books Ltd, Omnibus Business Centre,
39–41 North Road, London N7 9DP
email: info@iconbooks.com
www.iconbooks.com

First published in the United States in 2015 by Barnacle Book | Rare Bird Books

Sold in the UK, Europe and Asia
by Faber & Faber Ltd, Bloomsbury House,
74–77 Great Russell Street,
London WC1B 3DA or their agents

Distributed in the UK, Europe and Asia
by TBS Ltd, TBS Distribution Centre, Colchester Road,
Frating Green, Colchester CO7 7DW

Distributed in South Africa
by Jonathan Ball, Office B4, The District
41 Sir Lowry Road, Woodstock 7925

Distributed in Australia and New Zealand
by Allen & Unwin Pty Ltd,
PO Box 8500, 83 Alexander Street,
Crows Nest, NSW 2065

ISBN: 978-1-78578-060-8

Typeset in Minion

Printed and bound in the UK by Clays Ltd, St Ives plc

CONTENTS

Live Through This

Jeff Gordinier

"First I was afraid, I was petrified…"

There is a boy sitting in the audience at a television studio.

The year is 1978, and the boy's family has just moved to Southern California from the East Coast. Back on Long Island, the boy tended to spend his days in a seventies version of a Wordsworthian reverie, wandering through the woods for hours in tie-dyed blue jeans and green high-top sneakers, adrift in his thoughts. But there are no forests here in the smoggy suburbs of Los Angeles, and it's hard to make friends, and the kid feels alienated and lonely, as kids often do.

Back east, it would have been customary for the boy and his classmates to go on a field trip to, say, a modern art museum in Manhattan or the summer estate of Theodore Roosevelt, but this is Southern California in the seventies, and things are weird. Here the students go on field trips to watch the taping of TV shows. Which is why he finds himself in the studio audience of a program called *Kids Are People Too.*

Kids Are People Too resembles a late-night talk show, except that it airs in the afterschool hours, and its target audience is tweens. Among the celebrity guests on this strange afternoon are Ricardo Montalbán, the actor who plays a kind of cornball Prospero on *Fantasy Island,* a series that to this day rivals *Twin Peaks* in the category of Craziest Thing Ever to Appear in Prime Time; and F. Lee Bailey, a lawyer who will, years later, go onto dubious fame as a member of the legal team defending O. J. Simpson against accusations of murder.

To repeat: *Yes, this was a school field trip.*

I was that kid, and decades later I have no memory of what the attorney and the actor blathered about on *Kids Are People Too.*

All I remember is how an electric current of don't-fuck-with-me disco empowerment—a surge of uncrushable, sacramental, stand-up-for-yourself symphonic boogie—whipped through the room when Gloria Gaynor took the stage to lip-synch her way through a hit song called "I Will Survive."

How strong a song was "I Will Survive"? The word "anthem" gets thrown around way too profligately these days, but "I Will Survive" remains, to this day, strong enough not only to outlast and outclass its time-capsule associations with disco, but also to rise above the act of lip-synching. It didn't matter that Gloria Gaynor wasn't really singing on the set of *Kids Are People Too.* It didn't matter that she didn't have a band. It didn't matter that "I Will Survive" was almost certainly *not* composed with suburban white boys like me in mind. The message of the song felt universal enough to relieve me, momentarily, of my preteen loneliness and insecurity. In that instant, on that ridiculous Burbank soundstage, "I Will Survive" raced through my adolescent system the way pilfered spoonfuls of vitamin-and-mineral-dense malt syrup raced through Billy Pilgrim's veins in Kurt Vonnegut's *Slaughterhouse-Five*: "A moment went by, and then every cell in Billy's body shook him with ravenous gratitude and applause."

Applause. For whatever reason, in the decades that followed, female performers and songwriters would often be the ones whose music buoyed up my spirits. I'm talking about a very wide range of talents here—Martha Argerich and Mitsuko Uchida, Billie Holiday and Dinah Washington, Heart and the Pretenders, Blondie and Nico, Dionne Warwick and Patti Smith, Emmylou Harris and Rosanne Cash, Donna Summer and Diana Ross, Joni Mitchell and Janis Joplin, Exene Cervenka and Siouxsie Sioux, Natalie Merchant and Tracy Chapman, Fiona Apple and Cat Power, Lauryn Hill and Amy Winehouse, Gillian Welch and Lucinda Williams, Katell Keineg and Feist, Neko Case and Roberta Flack. Sometimes I'll pack up a bunch of CDs for a long road trip—yes, I'm a child of the seventies and eighties, and I still use CDs—and along the way I'll reach into the stack and realize that almost every album I have chosen as a traveling companion has a woman at the center of it.

For years, the royal outlets of the rock press had a habit, now and then, of publishing special packages celebrating "women in rock." As welcome as that recognition might have been, it also wound up looking pretty predictable. There seemed to be this compulsion, back then, to toast women who could "hold their own" with their cock-rocking compatriots in, say, Led Zeppelin. (Meanwhile, those of us who loved Heart's "Barracuda" and the Pretenders' "Precious" and Hole's "Violet" never had the slightest doubt that the Wilson sisters and Chrissie Hynde and Courtney Love owned the department of ass kicking.) It seems crazy now, during a post-Madonna era in which the pop charts are dominated by Beyoncé and Taylor Swift and Lady Gaga, but for a few decades loyal readers of certain magazines came away with the impression that female musicians were marginalized—viewed, strangely, as a separate camp.

Our goal with this book was to do something altogether different. Instead of striving to establish a canon, we wanted to pull together personal stories of how female singers and songwriters can, to put it bluntly, save our lives. I have no idea whether Gloria Gaynor ever saw her name carved into Italian marble as part of some *Rolling Stone* list, but I do know that she ranks high in my own private pantheon. So do Laurie Anderson's *Big Science,* Cat Power's *The Greatest,* the first Tracy Chapman album, the Fiona Apple album with the really long title—when a group of songs happens to pull you out of a pit of confusion and oblivion, you don't worry too much about whether it measures up to Derek & the Dominos.

Our objective here was to honor the mysterious connection between voice and listener. So instead of compiling a checklist of artists who needed to make an appearance in these pages in order to qualify the book for Library of Congress-sanctioned approval, we opted for a more indirect route. We simply went to novelists, poets, bloggers, songwriters, and journalists (most of them women) whose work we admire, and we asked them to weigh in. It didn't take long. Susan Choi on Stevie Nicks, Allison Glock on Dolly Parton, Rosie Schaap on Sandy Denny, Dael Orlandersmith on Patti Smith, Alina Simone on Sinead O'Connor, Katell Keineg on Nina Simone, Bart Blasengame on Liz Phair, Phyllis Grant on Madonna and Miley Cyrus, Ada Limón on Aretha Franklin and Loretta Lynn and the soul-cleansing art of karaoke—these provocative, engrossing testimonials poured forth with very little prompting.

We apologize in advance. The result that you hold in your hands is a book that never pays explicit tribute to Joni Mitchell— even though we agree with you that her genius is crucial and unquestionable—but does make room for Poly Styrene, the force at the front of X-ray Spex. Mary J. Blige and Kate Bush and Björk and Kathleen Hanna are here; Joan Jett and Dionne Warwick and Cat Power and Suzanne Vega and Etta James, alas, are not. Even though many of these omissions caused us wincing regret, Marc Weingarten and I sought to exert minimal influence and interference when it came to the choices. The driving force with each one, ultimately, had to be story: not hagiography, but real, raw stories about lives changed and charged up by the greatness of female artistry.

And story managed to intervene as we (slowly, slowly) put this book together. Marital crises, life-threatening illnesses, professional derailments—some of our contributors (and editors) found themselves caught up in the struggle of life at the very moment that they were trying to write about music that can soothe the pain and illuminate a safe way home. Heroically, most of them powered through. Some, in spite of equally heroic efforts, never made it to the finish line. (Hey, we're saving Annie Lennox for the sequel.) All of us, we'd like to think, reconnected with the gospel that got beamed into my head back when I was a kid in Southern California watching Gloria Gaynor pantomime her way through her shining moment in the pop culture sun.

Survive.
You will survive.
Just fucking survive.

Diamond in
a Rhinestone World

Allison Glock

t started with *Nine to Five*.

Certainly, I would have heard Dolly Parton before then. As a southerner, her voice would have been in the air around me, like cicadas, like chorus frogs. I would have noted her tremulous soprano sailing from a passing truck or my grandmother's kitchen radio, and it would have lodged in my brain, so peculiar and particular a sound that were I ever to hear it again I would recognize and respond to it immediately, almost primally, a dinner bell for the soul. Which is likely what happened as I viewed *Nine to Five*, a winning, cheese puff of a film released in 1980, when I was twelve, and had yet to grasp the singularity of so many things.

As I watched Dolly sashay around, outfitted in goofy, coiled white wigs and layers of feathery eyelashes, shimmying, and squealing, and stealing every scene, I understood immediately that this was someone worth paying attention to. It was less a conscious decision than a reflex, as is inevitable in matters of the heart. Even though the movie was her acting debut (and she was costarring alongside seasoned greats Lily Tomlin and Jane Fonda), Dolly stood out. Not simply because she was sexy. Which she was, edibly so. Or funny. Which she was, a modern Mae West without the disdain. But because she existed at all.

A cornpone confection of outsized *everything* that somehow managed to radiate dignity, Dolly was unlike anything I (or anyone) had seen before. She was the drag queen that could make you cry. The clown you wanted to sleep with. So clearly her own invention, so happily inhabiting the merry house she'd built, Dolly made it hopeless to resist her campy, cartoon charms.

Smitten, I saw *Nine to Five* at least a half-dozen times, my adolescent tomboy self fascinated by Dolly's cultivation of overt, kitchen sink femininity. The abundant bosom. The ski-jump bum. The dresses cinched at the waist like sausage cording. There was a playful absurdity to Dolly that made sexuality seem less terrifying, like a gag all we gals could be in on. She was playing a character, of course. But inherent in that performance was palpable integrity. The same way Jack Nicholson was never not Jack, Dolly was never not Dolly. Some personalities arrive so fully formed, are such forces of nature, that there is no such thing as pretend. (And, as I would come to understand, it is Dolly's genius that in her conspicuous fakery she is more genuine than any entertainer in the business.)

The best part was the theme song, which Dolly wrote and sang, and became a Platinum-selling, multiple Grammy winner. Dolly composed the number while on the set using her lengthy acrylic nails for percussion. It was a jaunty tune, folksy, inclusive. But with—like all things Dolly—a hidden depth that snuck up on you.

> *Tumble outta bed and I stumble to the kitchen*
> *Pour myself a cup of ambition…*

It begins, a working woman's blues, all sing-songy sweetness, until the next verse.

> *They let you dream, just to watch 'em shatter*
> *You're just a step on the boss man's ladder*
> *But you got dreams he'll never take away...*

When she sings the dream line, her voice breaks slightly, then recovers just as quickly to assert the finish.

> *He'll never take away.*

It is in that tiny moment that Dolly reveals how much she understands the world her listeners live in, and she with them, an intimacy you don't expect or need in a blockbuster comedy theme song, but she inserts nonetheless, because she wants you to know that she sees you, that she feels your pain, shares your longing. Because, unlike most performers, Dolly never sings at you. She sings *for* you.

Dolly accomplishes this to much deeper effect in less frolicsome tunes. Her considerable canon—she's penned more than 3,000 songs—includes iconic gut punchers like "Jolene" and "Coat of Many Colors," which unpack hard realities about poverty, shame, fear, and loss. Still, it is her peerless gift to subvert something that, on the outside, appears slight, and fill it with an unexpected center of meaningful goodness. Her songs, in this way, much like her premeditated appearance, are so much more than meets the ear.

After *Nine to Five,* I became obsessed with Dolly. I say "obsessed," but with Dolly, obsession is relative. Her fans are known for their unbridled fidelity, many building their lives around Dolly's as one would a guru or church (*For the Love of Dolly,* a documentary filmed in 2006, attests to this phenomenon). Unlike garden-variety fandom, Dolly inspires *devotion*. Defensiveness, even. As if she were kin. As if someone were shit-talking your mama.

Her supporters are diverse. Gays. Bluehairs. Rednecks. Christians. Pageant girls. Feminists. Lesbians. Mountain folk. Fellow musicians. Old-timey country lovers. Hipsters. Tweens. All drawn by her extraordinary voice and her message of inclusion. When she is confronted by her more conservative base that can't reconcile her faith with her liberal personal politics, Dolly punctures their bigotry with wit, explaining, "God and I have a great relationship, but we both see other people."

Dolly understands life is serious business. Which is why she cracks wise so often. It is this squeaky joy—a Dolly signature—that allows many cynics to underestimate her, to dismiss her penetrating optimism as stupidity, an error she is generally happy to let stand.

"I don't mind being called a dumb blonde," she often quips, "because I know I'm not dumb and I know I'm not blonde."

Dolly craved high heels before she knew she'd be short. She pined for blinding glamour from the dank shade of a holler. Hers was restless blood, looking for outlets. She found several, not the least of which was what she calls "looking ridiculous." A deliberate choice that served the twin purposes of calling attention to herself and allowing her to hide; her enormous breasts disarming Trojan horses, obscuring multitudes.

In that way, Dolly is a litmus test. People who love her tend to understand that life is a huge, hot mess of contradictions and struggle, but that is no reason not to enjoy yourself while you're here. People who don't love her? Well, to bad-mouth Dolly is to reveal the worst about yourself. That you don't get the joke. That you see only what's in front of you. That you wouldn't know seminal talent if it fell like a wrecking ball into your lap. Basically, if you hate Dolly, you're probably an asshole.

***

IN 1946, DOLLY REBECCA Parton was born dirt-floor poor into a large Appalachian family. A dozen children in a one-room cabin nestled in the Great Smoky Mountains. Her father farmed tobacco. Her grandfather was a holy roller in the Pentecostal church, where like so many Southern greats, Dolly learned the value of song, and how faith and art are pretty much the same thing.

By the time she was nine, Dolly was already performing for audiences on *The Cas Walker Show*—a Knoxville, Tennessee radio and television program run by Walker, a hillbilly populist straight out of an O'Connor novel, who once buried a man alive in a parking lot for publicity. Walker cottoned to Dolly—saw her as kin by hardscrabble circumstance—and put her in his lineup alongside folks like The Everly Brothers (whom, in a fit of pique, he once kicked off the stage). By age thirteen, Dolly had left Walker and graduated to the Grand Ole Opry, where she met Johnny Cash, an encounter she later described, saying, "I was just a young girl from the Smokies, but I would gladly have given it up for Mr. Cash in the parking lot."

Instead, he walked the line and told her to trust herself when it came to her music career. (This was no small thing. A decade later Dolly refused none other than Elvis Presley the rights to "I Will Always Love You," against the advice of almost everyone in the business, a decision that ended up netting her millions after Whitney Houston used the tune for yet another blockbuster movie theme song, making Dolly the only artist to ever earn a number one record twice with the same song as a singer and three times as a writer.)

The day after her high school graduation in 1964, Dolly moved to Nashville. There she played guitar, mandolin, banjo, fiddle, auto harp, and harmonica, and penned songs for Kitty Wells, Hank Williams Jr., and Skeeter Davis. She also got married to a fella she met outside the Wishy Washy Laundromat her first day in town.

(She and Carl Dean remain married today.) At twenty-one, Dolly became a featured act on Porter Wagoner's weekly variety show. Their collaboration was a famously fruitful one, netting a six-year streak of top ten singles for the pair and high exposure for Dolly, who Wagoner routinely infantilized even as her talents began to outshine his own. Ten years later, eager to launch a bigger solo career, Dolly bid Wagoner adieu with "I Will Always Love You," a ballad not of a failed romance, but of a codependent partnership that needed severing. It was a classy move, a gesture of fidelity and forgiveness. It was also one of the best love songs ever written, Dolly penning it in 1974, at only twenty-eight years old.

Wagoner had at times been critical of Dolly's writing, insisting she would never get radio play with the lyrics she chose in songs like 1969's "Down From Dover," a mournful ballad about a pregnant teenager who is exiled by her family. Wagoner may have been right about the short term. But Dolly, legacy-minded and unabashed in her ambitions, understood that if she wrote from the belly of truth, audiences would respond forever, and songs like "Dover" would resonate and evolve into classics.

Which is exactly what happened. As the decades have passed, "Dover" (along with many of her other, darker numbers) has received its due critical props, largely because of the storytelling certain folks initially found objectionable.

"When I wrote [Dover]—Lord, so many years ago, the mid-sixties, I guess—I knew a lot of young girls getting pregnant, and usually in the mountains people would pretty much turn you out. You were trash and a whore and your daddy and mama wouldn't let you come home," Dolly explained in a 2008 interview. "I'm touched by everything, and that used to bother me...how awful that must be."

Dolly said the song came to her "like a movie," and the account is relentlessly tragic, its devastation resting not solely in the naive girl's exclusion and humiliation, but in her clinging hope that the child's father will "hurry down from Dover," and return to her.

> *My mama said I was a fool and she did not believe it when I told her that everything would be alright 'cause soon he would be coming down from Dover.*

The song continues, tracking the heartrending erosion of her convictions, and concludes with a stillborn birth, a fate the narrator believes she deserves.

> *It's lonely in this place where I'm a lyin'*
> *Our baby has been born but something's wrong, it's too still, I hear no cryin'*
> *I guess in some strange way she knew she'd never have a father's arms to hold her*
> *So dying was her way of telling me he wasn't coming down from Dover.*

At root, "Dover" is less a chronicle of teen pregnancy than the universal story of the end of youth, of the excruciating transition we all go through when we are shown the consequences of belief, and the limitless cruelty of others. Dolly takes something painfully specific and delivers it in such a way that it blossoms in your head without you even knowing how, an emotional smart bomb. Everyone cries after listening to "Dover," because everyone has felt regret, has played the fool, has suffered betrayal, has been the betrayer. Dolly writes often of "the beautiful lie," the games we all play with ourselves, the ceaseless waltz between reality and what we wish were real. It is natural territory for her.

Though she is familiar with life's dark passengers—"I prefer rocky road to vanilla"—Dolly doesn't dwell in shadow. She focuses on connection. *Every* connection. Even after sixty years in the business, you'd be hard-pressed to find one person who has a bitchy Dolly Parton story. She works with the same crew. Travels with the same band. Talks to strangers like they're family. If she appears in the tabloids, it's because of her figure, not because she's left a crappy tip. Dolly remains grounded, forever the farmer's daughter.

It is this empathy that makes it impossible for her to write a frivolous song. Even her poppiest confections hold a line or turn of phrase that acts as a haiku of wisdom. This bedrock of knowledge Dolly attributes to her kinfolk and impecunious upbringing, where missing the signs or not knowing how the world works could get you killed.

"Most of my people were not that educated, but they had horse sense," she explained to Barbara Walters in a 1977 sit down, after Walters condescendingly asked if Parton's people would be considered "hillbillies." In the same interview, Walters makes Dolly stand up and give a twirl, marveling at her clothing and her appearance while simultaneously telling her she "doesn't need" to look the way she does. (Walters also wonders aloud how she managed to find common ground with someone so manifestly common.)

Dolly gamely rolls with every punch, "I would never stoop so low as to be fashionable," she says cheekily, even showing Walters her collection of wigs and "machine washable" costumes; never betraying even a hint of annoyance, though she does tease Walters once, warning she might have to kick her in the shin if she did call the Parton clan hillbillies, a benevolent redirect Walters misses completely as she is: 1) not Southern, and 2) talking over her subject.

These were the years when Dolly was consciously making her transition from Nashville celebrity to household name, a goal she met in record time with minimal blowback. (The only grumbling came from a few country diehards who felt she was abandoning them for greener pastures, a gross misread of the light she would ultimately come to cast on the genre).

"I would like to be a superstar," Dolly explained to Walters matter-of-factly. "In order to be a superstar, you have to appeal to a majority of people. And that's what I'm trying to do."

Ahead of her time, Dolly was one of the first crossover artists who ushered in the mainstreaming of country music. She was also one of the first women bold enough to chase goals previously permissible only to men.

"I'm not going to limit myself just because people won't accept the fact that I can do something else," she said. And she didn't.

No other artist has been *Ms.* magazine's Woman of the Year, a Kennedy Center Honoree, and the first *person* ever awarded the Good Housekeeping Seal of Approval. To date, Dolly boasts forty-five Grammy nominations (eight wins), one hundred million in record sales, and fistfuls of songs that are considered classics in any genre. She also built a theme park outside her hometown in Pigeon Forge, Tennessee. Dollywood is the area's largest employer and a much-needed boon to the local economy. When you visit, you can see the Partons' original Tennessee mountain home, as well as Dolly's coat of many colors. The roller coasters aren't too shabby, either.

Dolly is not one for half-assing. Unlike other music legends, she never got tangled up in drugs, booze, or no-good men. Instead, she worked harder than a lumberjack, kept her knickers on (turning down *Playboy* multiple times), and her hair high. She managed her own career with supreme success, believing quite rightly that, when it came to her business, she knew best.

"We are really like products whether we like it or not," she discerned early in the game (decades before Madonna), and decided then and there that she alone would be in charge of quality control. This, too, was unnaturally forward thinking—recognizing that all her legitimate artistic merit would mean nothing if no one saw fit to buy. "Show biz is a money-making joke," she surmised, wisely, "and I like to tell jokes."

There is a clip on YouTube of Dolly's 1993 appearance on *Late Night with David Letterman*. When she steps onstage, poured into a sequined black gown, hair feathered back like a Cherokee headdress, Letterman, the original arbiter of smug detachment, is conspicuously ruffled. Their pre-chat embrace lingers an uncomfortable length of time, our host rounded over and clinging to Dolly like a turtle shell. Eventually, they break apart to sit and talk, Letterman blushing and grinning throughout. Dolly pats and praises him, helps him along, but he is so taken he barely maintains, his torso rocking in and out, seduced stupid.

Later, she sings him a song—not one from the album she came to promote, but an older one, because she remembered that's what he likes best.

And so it goes. Dolly cracking us all like eggs.

Now, at sixty-seven, she continues to tour. She continues to write. Her voice older, but hardly worn for the years, is as affecting as it was in her youth, still vibrating with emotion that rattles the cage, still reminding us of our essential fragility.

People sew their hearts to hers because it feels safe. She is, in her own words, a "leaning post of life."

When she was just starting out, Dolly said she hoped when she was gone that people would remember her.

I can't imagine anyone alive who could forget.

Revenge of the Nerds

Taffy Brodesser-Akner

"I've never thought about songwriting as a weapon," Taylor Swift said with a straight face to an interviewer from *Vanity Fair* whilst the magazine was profiling her in 2013.

No, not Taylor Swift. Not the author of songs like "Forever and Always," written in the wake of her relationship with former boyfriend Joe Jonas, the better-looking Jonas brother, and featuring this lyric: "Did I say something way too honest, made you run and hide like a scared little boy?" Not her, who wrote/sang about her relationship with the actor Jake Gyllenhaal, "Fighting with him was like trying to solve a crossword/and realizing there's no right answer."

Not Taylor, who leaves the impossible-to-crack clues in her liner notes for each song by capitalizing a variety of letters that spell out the subjects in a very essential way: "TAY" for a song about ex-boyfriend Taylor Lautner; "SAG" for the Gyllenhaal one (as in Swift And Gyllenhaal, or that they're both Sagittarius. I don't know).

For Taylor Swift to pretend that her entire music career is not a tool of passive aggression toward those who had wronged her is like me pretending I'm not carbon-based: too easy to disprove, laughable at its very suggestion.

Don't get me wrong—I say all this with utter admiration. Taylor's career is, in fact, the perfected realization of every writer's narrowest dream: To get back at those who had wronged us, sharply and loudly, and then to be able to cry innocent that our intentions were anything other than poetic and pure. Most of us can only achieve this with small asides. Taylor not only publicly dates and publicly breaks up, but she then releases an achingly specific song about the relationship—and that song has an unforgettable hook—all the while swearing she won't talk about relationships that are over. Yes, date Taylor Swift, and not only will she shit on you on her album, but the song will become a single, then a hit, and then you will hear yourself shat upon by an army of young women at Staples Center. And then she'll deny that she was ever doing anything other than righteously manifesting her art. It's diabolical, and for a lifelong passive-aggressive like me, it's made her my hero.

***

LIKE A GOOD PASSIVE-AGGRESSIVE, Taylor never owns up to this behavior. In that *Vanity Fair* profile, she repeats her vow to never kiss and tell, but then refers the journalist to an anonymous friend who does have permission to tell. And tell she does: About Taylor's romance with Harry Styles from One Direction, about Jonas, about Lautner. Like a next-generation digital-age retaliator, Taylor has found a way to tell her story without telling it herself. First her friend tells *Vanity Fair,* now *Vanity Fair* tells us like it's news. Now it's not just rumor; it's from an actual news source. Don't look at me, she says. I didn't say anything. And, well, she's kind of not lying. Kind of.

"When I knew something was going on in someone's personal life and they didn't address it in their music, I was always very confused by that," Taylor told *The New York Times*.[1] "I owe it to people from letting them in from Day 1."

The songs are, after all, her art! And art isn't about anything specific. It's about human experience, and it's subject to interpretation. In fact, this song isn't about me at all, she seems to say. It's about *you.*

Consider the initial remark—"I've never thought about songwriting as a weapon"—itself a statement of roundabout, unimpeachable genius.

In fact, you can find everything you need to know about the multifaceted genius of Swift's passive-aggression—her gift for words, her understanding of exactly what she was put on this earth to do—in that sentence. Never thinking about something is not the same as not having done it. And *weapon,* a literally loaded word, is something bad. She's not being bad, or mean. She's just letting it out. She's just *processing.*

When *The New York Times* asked her about her relationship with Joe Jonas, the answer was: "He's not in my life anymore, and I have absolutely nothing to say about or to him." Except that song she wrote about him, of course. Oh, and her song "Better Than Revenge," which was aimed at Camilla Belle, the actress who ostensibly "stole" Jonas away (sample lyric: "She's an actress, whoa; She's better known for the things that she does on the mattress, whoa"). For his part, Jonas wrote his own song indicting Taylor that was heard by whomever listens to his music, but, well, lyrics just ain't his thing: "Now I'm done with superstars

---

1 Jon Caramanica, "My Music, MySpace, My Life," *The New York Times*, November 7, 2008. www.nytimes.com/2008/11/09/arts/music/09cara.html?pagewanted=all

and all the tears on her guitar"—"Teardrops on My Guitar" was an early hit of Taylor's. This was the equivalent of the urban myth dance-off that may or may not (*probably not, but let me dream!*) have taken place between Britney Spears and Justin Timberlake following their breakup. It was a fan's dream. A real brawl. Actual tween idol drama.

But still, Taylor would not own up to her song subjects. Either because she just loves getting off on a technicality, or she thinks we're idiots. I believe it's the former. Because between the liner notes and the timelines, there's really no way to doubt it: if you just broke up with Taylor Swift, that there song is most certainly about you.

***

THE MASTERSTROKE OF ALL of this passive-aggression is, of course, "Dear John," a single on her album *Speak Now*. It is the accumulation of her feints with little Disney boy Joe Jonas or *Twilight* hunk Taylor Lautner. This time, a man about twice her age came around, stole her heart, and then broke it. This is what she'd been preparing for her whole life.

Here are some of the lyrics to "Dear John," printed without permission, in full detail, since no excerpt can adequately portray what a writhing takedown the song is:

> *Well, maybe it's me and my blind optimism to blame*
> *Or maybe it's you and your sick need to give love then*
> *take it away*
> *And you'll add my name to your long list of traitors*
> *who don't understand*
> *And I'll look back and regret how I ignored when they said*
> *run as fast as you can*

Dear John, I see it all now that you're gone
Don't you think I was too young to be messed with?
The girl in the dress cried the whole way home

Dear John, I see it all now it was wrong
Don't you think nineteen's too young to be played by
Your dark twisted games when I loved you so
I should've known

You are an expert at sorry and keeping lines blurry
Never impressed by me acing your tests
All the girls that you've run dry have tired, lifeless eyes
'Cause you've burned them out

But I took your matches before fire could catch me
So don't look now
I'm shining like fireworks over
Your sad, empty town

Taylor wrote this in the aftermath of her relationship with renowned rake John Mayer, a man who committed the sin of breaking the heart of a post-Pitt Jennifer Aniston, among others (Vanessa Carlton, Jessica Simpson, Miley Cyrus—and those are just the musical ones; by the time this is published, surely his near-engagement to Katy Perry, much spoken about on the radio now, will be a thing of the past). He is a man of little variety. His type is unsuspecting, pretty, petty, and also white.

Did John Mayer deserve this? He's guilty of his own snide songwriting crimes: It was an open secret that he had written "Your Body is a Wonderland" to honor the fleshy coil of that other J. Lo., Jennifer Love Hewitt, whom he dated circa 2002. And he did write a pretty scorching post-breakup song about Taylor called

"Paper Doll," which is a basically a patronizing work of little art that sounds as loungey and un-new as his other music. The song talks about a girl who changes dresses a lot, which is not a crime as far as I know, and something about cutting cords—perhaps he felt like she was too young or too tied to the music industry trappings. Not like him. Nobody tells him what to wear or who to write soft-rock songs about!

However you feel about revenge songs, we can agree that Taylor's "Dear John" is a master class in passive-aggression. First, consider Taylor's use of the generic "Dear John" letter for this specific John—*there's that plausible deniability again!*—as if to make it sound like a goodbye letter to *anyone*, when really it's a goodbye letter to *someone*.

Then there's the viciousness. "Dear John" lays bare all that we suspected of Mayer's psyche that it's actually uncomfortable to listen to. Not since Alanis Morissette wrote the scathing "You Oughta Know," allegedly about former *Full House* star Dave Coulier (an unlikely lothario, true, but hey, Canada has its own rules), has a song about an ex been so cringe-worthy.

Of "Dear John," Taylor said: "There are things that were little nuances of the relationship, little hints. Everyone will know, so I don't really have to send out emails on this one."

And just as she had wished for, John Mayer was humiliated, and he told *Rolling Stone* as much. Mayer also takes issue with "Dear John" as a musician. "I will say as a songwriter that I think it's kind of cheap songwriting," he said. "I know she's the biggest thing in the world, and I'm not trying to sink anybody's ship, but I think it's abusing your talent to rub your hands together and go, 'Wait till he gets a load of this!' That's bullshit."

But Taylor maintains that she's innocent, having told *The Times,* "I can say things I wouldn't say in real life. I couldn't put the sentence together the way I could put the song together." It's not that she didn't want to say this to your face, John. It's just that she *couldn't.*

But John maintained she crossed some line that he didn't cross when he wrote "Paper Doll," or that Joni Mitchell didn't cross when she wrote "Free Man in Paris" about David Geffen, or Neil Diamond when he wrote "Sweet Caroline" about Caroline Kennedy (though I'm still not one hundred percent sure that's true). Using his name was not fair in love's war, but really, the objection must be to spilling details of such intimate abuse. And that's where Taylor excels.

See, Taylor was, according to lore, a chubby geek in middle school. She was abandoned by her peers in sixth grade, just when her songwriting powers were coming to fruition, and so just as her gift began to sprout, so did her ability to articulate them and, just a couple of years later, publicize them. The metabolism of this follows that of the digital age into which Taylor was born: Have a thought, post it. None of this rigorous checking with legal, followed by second thoughts, followed by self-doubt, followed by yielding to decency like a puppy dog. But more on that later.

It was a dream come true for a rejected-feeling girl who was coming into her own as a tall, dazzling blonde with a microphone and a following. Is there any one of us who kept a diary without wishing deep down that someone would find it and understand us fully, down to the ugliest detail? Is there anyone among us who didn't hope that the world would learn from that diary exactly how the world had wronged us?

She was no match for a soft-rock singer who has been getting laid his whole life on the strength of his guitar and his pillowy lips.

***

THAT'S HOW TAYLOR SWIFT became the hero to of all of us losers, of anyone humiliated in middle school, the publicly dumped in high school, or anyone who ever realized during the car ride home the perfect comeback that would now go unsaid. We don't all have the wherewithal to process what has happened to us and synthesize it into a pop song that will be broadcast to a bajillion fans. And we certainly, for the most part, lack the platform. Today's teenager can craft the perfect Tweet or Facebook update, toy with it, post it, modify it, delete it. Taylor puts it out there, and out there it stays.

In a way, she was made for this. She was born with the face of an accusation. Her eyes, which see everything and narrow naturally; upturned, judgy nose to look down past; lips that tend toward pursing. Yet she was also born lovely, with a sweet, thin voice and an engaging smile. She's smart and tall, and she's thin now. Who would not love her? In fact, for those of us who were chubby youths, who had no friends, the invention of Taylor Swift is no less than the invention of a super-robot sent through time and space to lure the mean girls and mean boys into loving us, and then break their hearts and tell the world what scum they are. We couldn't have dreamed it better.

Taylor's denials are another layer of performance art. Because has there ever been a more passive-aggressive profession than writing? Writing is first born of a need to explain oneself, and it is comorbid with the desperate loneliness of an ostracized, chubby middle-schooler, like she was and, well, like I was. The popular kids can explain themselves to each other. Only the lonely are left to their writing. It's through the tools of observation that we learn to hone an otherness…we begin to define ourselves from the way we are different. And slowly, slowly, we spend so much time pretending that someone is listening that we often don't know how to change modes once people are.

Taylor became an ambassador swan to all us ducklings who never got the opportunity to rise above our social circumstances or have relationships with men like actual Kennedys or One Direction band members. Her songs are her report back to us from the land of fantasy: here's what it's like when one of us becomes one of them. Living as Taylor Swift in her songs becomes the closest thing you—I—ever came to cool.

Because I swear I've moved on from all the heartache and all the rejection. I swear the memories of eating lunch alone don't hurt as much as they used to. I'm thirty-eight! I'm married! I have children! When I think of the phone pranks played on me, when I think of the names called out to me, when I think of the parties I wasn't invited to, the moments I realized he was cheating, or when the group of girls looked at me like I was disgusting, it doesn't sting me the way it did at the time. But something's still there, and I know it because I've concocted the thing I should have said in my head in each of those situations.

Eventually, what happens is this: things you write get published and/or sung. And that's when the people you've been writing about begin to hear what you've been thinking of them this whole time. If you're a magazine writer like I am, you hedge your bets. You count on most people not being great readers, and then you hedge further by maybe not posting this particular essay on your Facebook page. You also build in some sort of plausible deniability: If it sounds like a particular person, make sure there's an added detail—never untrue, remember I'm a journalist—that makes it so that this small story could actually apply to several people. I am always prepared with an "Oh! That's not you! I can't tell you who it is, but of course it's not *you*." Writing has taught me that you can retain friendships while still harboring a bunch of anger toward someone. Anger is not the same as not liking someone, and it's certainly not incompatible with wanting to be liked.

Alas, I've actually never had to use it. Because after about two years of writing essays, I learned about something I will hereby in these pages name the Passive-Aggressive Writer's Conundrum:

People, particularly non-writers, are an optimistic, delusional bunch. If you mention people in an unflattering way without naming them, they will never recognize themselves in your story—even if you name actual details of circumstances surrounding the stories. However, if you mention them in a flattering way without naming them—say, talk about the time they gave you water in the desert—they will immediately assume you're talking about them, even though they've never been to the desert or traveled with you.

(Taylor inherently knows about the Conundrum, and uses it to create her plausible deniability: Yeah? Prove it!)

The thing is, no matter how often I build the perfect retort into the memory of the thing that happened—and they would be "Dear John"-style retorts, designed for maximum, long-lasting psychic carnage—it never changes the fact that I never articulated things. I was walked upon and insulted, teased, and, worst, ignored. And so I chose a different kind of life, a smaller one where I could think before I spoke and then my words would be loud enough to last on a printed page. See, I do have a platform. I'm a writer. And there is so much revenge I'd like to get, so many scores to settle, but I'm older now and see so clearly the consequences of putting something in print.

There is a part of me that doesn't want to show how petty I am by naming the names of those who wronged me—years ago, I wrote an essay about how the mean girls from grade school were now my Facebook friends, and I lacked the nerve to post the essay to Facebook. Part of me doesn't want them to know that I still think about it. I should, by now, not even remember it, right? We are generally people who like to pretend that our childhoods happened to another version of us, that we don't carry the scars that we do. So I play it safe. I don't refer to people who have wronged me; I don't ever put in writing the thing I should have said, the thing I'm still kicking myself for not saying. I don't know if that makes me dumber or smarter than Taylor, and I certainly don't know if my refusal to use my work as a tool of passive-aggression makes me braver or more afraid.

I have become someone who is only perfectly vengeful in my head. The closest I've gotten is writing an essay about a man who broke my heart and changing his name from Garry to Gary. (But there's hope, isn't there? Here I just admitted what I did! Suck it, Garry!)

Taylor exists as our id. She alone posses the chutzpah to play innocent as she boldly winks at what she's done in a forum more public than even the most viral article. But it's also through her that we can continue to fantasize about a revenge most perfect, an aggression so passive that no one sees it coming, that no one can confirm it once they've been hit. That day might be around the corner, and it's Taylor who allows us to dream of it: dream of a time when the stings of the past are made better through the public hanging of dirty laundry, a time when we say the perfect thing in the moment when it most counts, a moment when we finally get the last word. It's on that day that we, too, will have our most perfect aggression realized. It's on that day you will find us shining like fireworks over their sad empty towns.

A Rock Star is a Teenager

Alina Simone

t occurred to me one day as I wondered why we say "fanboy" and "fangirl," but never "fanman" or "fanwoman." A fan is a kid, I realized. And who else does a kid worship if not the badass older sister, who calls teachers by their first names, puts a miniature harpoon through her septum, and starts dating three guys at the same time, *together*? The one who doesn't care what anyone has to say about anything, when you care so excruciatingly much what everyone thinks of everything. It's a form of hero worship that reduces you to a juvenile state of wonder. This was exactly how I felt about Sinéad O'Connor when she slashed through the shrink-wrapped monolith of eighties pop with no greater weapon than her honest wrath.

It was 1989, and for the better part of the decade, girls like me had been taught to adopt a convoluted form of postfeminist logic when contemplating the female icons of the era. By carefully folding your ideals into a tiny origami crane, you could arrive at the proscribed conclusion: that someone like Madonna—who was rarely the sole author of her songs (let's not quibble about this)—could never get by on sheer musical talent alone (ditto), and never failed to present herself as anything but maximally sexy and fashion-fit—was some kind of role model. Twenty years later, I can appreciate the ways in which Madonna broke barriers for women by reveling in her sexuality, *owning* it the way stars like Elvis had unquestioningly done for decades, but that's not how I felt when I first heard Sinéad O'Connor. Here was an artist who not only wrote and produced her own songs—ambitious, complicated, strange compositions that left you feeling both wondrous and raw—but possessed a voice of such glacial beauty that all comparisons (Kate Bush, Annie Lennox) fell away like a bunch of random, squiggly lines tacked next to her name. And the things she said! When Sinéad talked, you never got "Sinéad," but the shy, strange, one-hundred-percent human former street urchin who spoke in a quiet, lilting voice that still sounded like church music, even when the thing she was trying to so gently explain was exactly how much she hated you. Journalists interviewing Sinéad were treated with confidences usually reserved for gynecologists, and the results were predictably disastrous for her. But for the rest of us, who felt like 1987 was a lame party at the house of a popular jock who everyone secretly thinks is stupid and boring, Sinéad was the 120-proof vodka poured into lukewarm punch.

But the kicker was this: with a face that could have been torn from the pages of an illuminated manuscript, here was a woman who went to heretical lengths to make herself *less,* not more, beautiful. Sinéad could have easily gone the Madonna route—collagen implants, personal trainers, a lifetime of calling an Altoid after dinner "dessert"—instead she chose thrift-shop T-shirts and a shaved head. Every girl I'd ever met longed to be beautiful. *More beautiful.* The bravest thing a beautiful girl can ever do, in the eyes of another girl, is to make herself ugly. Paradoxically, in Sinéad's case, making herself "ugly," only made her more beautiful.

Really, nothing aside from a dioxin-and-road-salt facial could make Sinéad truly ugly, but she was trying, and that meant a lot. If you ask me, a full two years before Kurt Cobain set the freaks, geeks, and burnouts of the world free, it was Sinéad who shot the first arrow over the bow. Her live appearance at the 1989 Grammy awards, where the Song of the Year award went to Bobby McFerrin for "Don't Worry, Be Happy," was a win for the Holden Caulfields of the world. She was bald, combat-booted, and yeah, okay, lip-synching, but she did not give the tiniest shit what you thought of that. More impressively, "Mandinka," the song she so energetically mouthed, was casually studded with stomach-dropping vocal fjords that sounded like nothing else on the radio.

So I decided to take Sinéad O'Connor as my patron saint. The Patron Saint of Badassitude. For an overweight Russian girl who spent most of her summers at math camp, this was, in college-admissions speak, a "reach." Especially given that Sinéad O'Connor had already achieved more in her teenaged years than most people could given ten lifetimes.

***

A Brief History of Sinéad's Teenage Years

THIRTEEN: Sinéad applies for a summer job handing out drink tickets at a nightclub in a nearby village by putting on a "load of eyeliner and makeup" and pretending to be seventeen.[2] It works.

---

2 http://www.sineadoconnor.com/sineads_post_type/sinead-utobiography-entry-1-copyright-by-sinead-oconnor/

FOURTEEN: Sinéad becomes a "school-refuser."[3] According to an anonymous biography on a sketchy Angelfire site that projects the hostile-but-knowing tone of an estranged cousin longing for reconciliation, Sinéad spends her time skipping school to play video games in Dublin with quarters stolen from her father. Her chronic truancy also leads to a well-documented career in shoplifting.

FIFTEEN: After being arrested for stealing a pair of gold shoes for a friend to wear to a Pretenders concert, Sinéad is sent to An Grianán, a notorious reform school for pregnant teens and delinquent minors run by the Sisters of our Lady of Charity.

A sympathetic nun redeems bleak days spent "in the basement, washing priests' clothes in sinks with cold water and bars of soap"[4] by giving Sinéad her first guitar. It is while performing Barbara Streisand's "Evergreen" at her guitar teacher's wedding that Sinéad is discovered by drummer Paul Byrne of the newly-formed band, In Tua Nua.

Bryne gives her some music and Sinéad first writes the melody and lyrics for a song she calls "Take My Hand." She records the song with In Tua Nua, and even though she is later deemed too young to join the band, it is released as a single on their 1984 Island Records debut. *Melody Maker* magazine names the song "Single of the Week." Later, it will become the theme for a film, *The Doctor and the Devils*, starring Timothy Dalton.

Just to review: This is her first song. She is fifteen.

SIXTEEN: She spends eighteen months at An Grianán, before being sprung for a posh Quaker boarding school. In spite of the supportive new environment, Sinéad starts skipping school again

---

3 Melanie Wallwork, "Sinéad O'Connor's faith in music," *Bury Times*, August 2nd, 2003. www.burytimes.co.uk/leisure/the_big_interview/10589926.print/

4 Sinéad O'Connor, "To Sinead O'Connor, the pope's apology for sex abuse in Ireland seems hollow," *The Washington Post*, March 28, 2010. www.washingtonpost.com/wp-dyn/content/article/2010/03/25/AR2010032502363.html

to busk on the streets—a practice she credits with putting the propane in her voice. After less than a year at her new school, Sinéad wakes up one morning and thinks, "I can't stand any more of this."[5] She drops out of high school and moves to Dublin, where she gets a job delivering singing telegrams. She is paid six pounds a night to dress up as either a naughty French maid or a nun-in-a-mini-skirt and "sit on blokes' knees and read them lustful poems."[6] She also joins Ton Ton Macoute, which she describes as a "failing funk band." They start making the rounds on Dublin's pub circuit.

SEVENTEEN: By now, Sinéad has already written half the songs that will appear on *The Lion and the Cobra,* including the incendiary first single, "Troy." As the singer for Ton Ton Macoute, she catches the attention of Nigel Grainge, the head of Ensign Records. "They were horrible," Grainge told the *Los Angeles Times.* "Awful songs, awful playing, but she was interesting… This little student-type with a baggy jersey and torn jeans, just singing to her feet for three-quarters of an hour with this amazing voice." He sends her a plane ticket to London.

EIGHTEEN: Sinéad signs to Ensign and moves into a dingy cold water flat in London. But before she begins recording *The Lion and the Cobra,* she collaborates on a stunning song called "Heroine," with U2's David Howell Evans (better known as The Edge), for the soundtrack to the movie *Captive.*

That same year, her mother is killed in a car accident.

NINETEEN: After four months of studio work, Sinéad is appalled by the "Grace Slick" aesthetic her producer, Mick Glossop, had glossopped all over her album. "He had string lines everywhere,

5 http://archivedmusicpress.files.wordpress.com/2009/02/the-stud-brothers-interview-sinead-oconnor-12th-december-1987.jpg
6 This is how her former Kiss-o-gram boss, Ken O'Farrell, described Sinéad's job to The Sun. (Independent (London), November 29, 1992. The Life of Saint Sinéad by William Leith)

and fiddles. It was just a joke. There were like fifteen-minute jams on the ends of things. A waste of time."[7] Sinéad convinces her record company to scrap a completed album and let her produce *The Lion and the Cobra* herself. No small feat considering she also informs them that she is pregnant with the child of John Reynolds, her session drummer. When they suggest she "tart herself up a little," she responds by shaving her head.

CODA: By age twenty, Sinéad has gone from a petty criminal and high school drop out to the creator of one of the decade's most highly praised debut albums. She has also lost a mother and become one. Within three years of its release, *The Lion and the Cobra*—which Ensign expected to top out at sales of 25,000—earns Gold Record status and a Grammy nomination for Best Female Rock Vocal Performance. Put aside the shredding of Pope John Paul II, the declaration and undeclaration of lesbianism, the ordination as Mother Bernadette Mary by the Latin Tridentine Church, the anal sex booty call via Twitter, the eighteen-day marriage, and all the other media imbroglios that have obscured her musical legacy for the past twenty years, and what you have is the inspiring story of a troubled, but awesomely talented, young woman who lifted herself out of the crosshairs of a tragic and predictable fate through sheer force of will.

That much is still true.

***

7 Los Angeles Times, August 7, 1988. Sinéad O'Connor: The Pluck of the Irish by Richard Cromelin

Things I Associate With Being a Teenager

- Having sex six times in a row, even though you don't feel like it anymore
- *The Fountainhead*
- Skinny-dipping
- Dreaming about driving to Canada (substitute Mexico if you're south of Missouri)
- Swearing that you'll *never* XYZ
- Swearing that you'll *always* XYZ
- Thinking: *You don't really know me*
- The handjob-under-the-jacket-spread-over-both-of-your-laps move
- Dating people who in hindsight could be classified as psychopaths or homeless
- Eight-hour conversations with people even you're not sure you're friends with
- Writing a poem about suicide
- Being too cold or too hot almost all of the time
- Whispering: "I feel like I'm going crazy"
- Keeping a journal
- Butt-aches from sitting on asphalts, stoop, or stairs
- The statement: "(Insert Band Name) saved my life."

***

Sinéad O'Connor Saved My Life

In most cases, when a teenager says a band saved their life, what they're really saying is *This chance exposure to a transcendental piece of art gave me a better excuse to stay in my room all the time and plot my escape.* In my case it meant something very specific: I fell in love with the boy I would one day marry because of Sinéad O'Connor.

"I want to show you something," I intoned, leading a boy whose legendary mullet had earned him the nickname "Jesus" upstairs into the living room. "Sit."

I had been practicing singing "Troy" for months now, like a lonely and obsessive world-class wanker. "Troy" was the first single off Sinéad's debut album. It had also become the litmus test by which I judged the worth of all human beings. For example, I knew that I would strongly dislike anyone who called "Troy" "feisty," but would absolutely loathe the person who called it "histrionic." Counterfactually, I was positive that as long as I lived, it would only be possible for me to love someone who loved "Troy" as much as I did. I would have made blood-siblings out of a fifty-eight-year-old dishdasha-wearing goat-herder if "Troy" was his jam, I swear.

But back to "Troy." The song doesn't so much begin as emerge within your consciousness as a distant shimmer of violins. Then there it is—a voice so pure, so shivery and dangerous, it's like a thousand melted church bells have been forged into the world's most beautiful razor blade. The blood empties from your head, your fingers feel cold and tingly as that pin-perfect voice sinks its tiny fishhooks into your skin, ratcheting its way up your arms, your back, your neck. By the time it turns feral, by the time dragons are being slain and Troy is being burned and great, inhuman yowls are being unleashed from thunderclouds of strings, drums, and synths, your surrender is complete. It feels like a giant, Amazonian parasite has crawled up into your ear holes and is sucking out your brain. Best. Feeling. Ever.

Or maybe you won't feel anything. Maybe you'll think it's an inscrutable, six-and-a-half-minute exercise in melodrama. Which is totally fine. Except it means you have no soul.

When MTV's Kevin Seal asked Sinéad what the song "Troy"—whose title is a reference to the poem "No Second Troy" by Irish poet William Butler Yeats—was really about during an interview on the cult music show *120 Minutes,* her response was, "Well, it's very personal and very autobiographical and therefore one that I never explain to anyone." But the year before she explained to Seal that she never explained "Troy" to anyone, she explained it quite explicitly to the Stud Brothers when they interviewed her for *Melody Maker* magazine[8]:

"'Troy', which is the most intense love song on the album, was definitely about how I felt I was being manipulated and how I felt I was being toyed with, in that this person in particular who I madly, madly loved when I was seventeen, knew how I felt and was using that to get his way—not necessarily in sex."

Sinéad was seventeen when she wrote "Troy"; I was seventeen when I bluffed my way through it, a capella, in my parent's living room for Jesus. That even my bullshit, mimeographed, cringingly-Irish-accented version worked its magic is a great testament to the original. We both trace the real start of our relationship to that night. And it wasn't like "Troy" just happened to be the match dropped on some preexisting romantic kindling; I fell madly, madly in love with Jesus because he was the only person who understood how I could love such a messy, complicated, uncategorizable, passionate, scornful song. It's why I'd elected to barricade myself in my room, working my vocal cords halfway to nodes, overplaying junior varsity field hockey, or doing yearbook, or—God forbid—mangling blameless Aretha Franklin songs as a member of the Pitch Pipes. Because he knew exactly how I felt and didn't use that to get his way—in sex. Jesus got it. He had soul.

---

8 http://archivedmusicpress.files.wordpress.com/2009/02/the-stud-brothers-interview-sinead-oconnor-12th-december-1987.jpg

After her 1991 tour, Sinéad stopped performing "Troy" live. For seventeen years, fans' only consolation was a disturbing music video of O'Connor's naked torso rotating like a hot dog under a rotisserie lamp. Then she suddenly decided to sing "Troy" again for the first time at Night of the Proms in Belgium in 2008. I wrote Sinéad to ask why she'd stopped singing "Troy," but inquiries sent to @vampyahslayah, Sinéad's new twitter handle, and iamwonderful@me.com, her email address, went unanswered.

***

Some real quotes from my teenage diaries:

- "I just want to dance and glimmer—on and on forever."
- "He's done it again, trapped me into loving him with those terrible eyes."
- "I love him so much—it's inescapable, this frightening passion I feel only for him."
- "I tried to wash away the badness of the day in the shower. I stood there a long time under the hot drippings, hating and feeling weak."
- "I wanted to cast them all away, this lot of fake, adulterous friends."
- "I realized in a flash that none of these people mattered. They were only driftwood sailing languidly by, some lingered long, others drifted by swiftly, but singing is the anchor, the one thing that burns me like nothing else, that I love more and put above all others."
- "I hung up just as he was saying, 'I really care about you.' It was so pure, and wonderful, and satisfying, and freeing—this feeling that I didn't give a shit about whether he loved or hated me. I could do what I pleased."

- "I want to be alone to read, write, sing, and listen to Sinéad. I'll tell K. not to come tonight. Always and forever—singing is everything."
- "I'll be lonely—but it will be a strong, self-imposed loneliness."
- And my favorite: "I'm amazing!"

***

Teenagers get a bad rap

Immaturity, recklessness, stupidity, righteousness, gall, pretension, melodrama—these are all things we associate with teenagedom. In the public imagination, the ages of thirteen to nineteen have come to be seen as some kind of dystopian, if occasionally exhilarating, channel-crossing we must endure while hopped-up on a cocktail of hormones and inexperience, all for the sake of reaching the safety of adult shores. To all that, I say: bullshit.

Even now I fight the urge to lighten things up. To not get all Sturm und Drang-y about things. See? It makes one feel adult and wise to rationalize the passions of youth away. And okay, there's a lot to praise about tolerance, compassion, long-view-taking, and all the other virtues of maturity. But let's just take a moment to contemplate whether something has also been lost in the crossing—something important. Like, do you even remember what it's like to feel…real *passion*? That feeling of things really mattering. The in-the-moment sensation of life being lived. The conviction, when facing almost any decision, that huge things are at stake: your future, your integrity, your heart. The highs and lows. Unironic, unrepentant, full-blown, romantic gestures. The rage. Hating people—all those petty tyrants of youth—and being totally justified. Loving your friends. *Really loving* them as though you were parachuting the beaches of Iwo Jima together and not just two freshmen in an Earth Science class whose last names happened to both end in "W."

And here's an even scarier question: What if the teenaged you was *right?* That the one who felt angry, and lonely, and scared so much of the time, who said things too bluntly and felt them too keenly, was actually the *better* you? And what if the way you experienced and responded to things as a teenager, your hopes for yourself and your expectations for other people, was actually in some undeniable way better than the expectations that guide you now? What if, in all our adult wisdom, we've pickled our best selves in the vinegar of rationality?

Maybe that's why "rational rock star" sounds like an oxymoron. But who wants to love a rational rock star, anyway? I prefer to love Sinéad, the least rational rock star of them all. Her virtues have always been teenage virtues. And though her current, protracted war-of-words with the twenty-year-old pop star Miley Cyrus (not to mention the recent decision to tattoo the letters "B" and "Q" on her face) has left many thinking, *WTF, Sinéad?*, I would argue that self-immolation was always part of the bargain she made with the furies, and the question posed by Yeats at the end of "No Second Troy," is far more apt for her today:

> *Why, what could she have done being what she is?*
> *Was there another Troy for her to burn?*

***

The Second Troy

The only other guy I ever dated seriously was named Troy. I'd like to say this fact had nothing to do with my obsession with the song of the same name, but who knows? Perhaps there was something subliminal at work here. If so, my melodramatic impulse was utterly misplaced because this Troy never burned, or even smoldered. I was still a teenager when we met, but at nineteen, was already straining mightily toward adulthood; the idea of dating a twenty-five-year-old had its appeal. Besides, the mulleted, unicycle-riding, high school boyfriend I'd loved so much had moved across the country for college, and I'd decided it was "unrealistic" to keep up a long-distance relationship. So now I shuttled back and forth between Troy's dim Somerville apartment and mine, pretending to like mellow indie music. I stopped singing during the year I dated Troy. He didn't like my singing, and consequently, I stopped liking it, too.

I spent that year telling myself the reason things felt so different dating Troy was because back in high school, I didn't know what real love was. *That* kind of love was just a passing fever; *this* was the grown-up Real Thing, where you saved your receipts and always drank a glass of wine at the same time each night. I told myself that right up until the morning I woke up and thought, "I can't stand any more of this."

Then I picked up the phone. And came to Jesus.

All That I Can Say

Charlotte Druckman

It won't be easy,
you'll think it's strange,
when I try to explain how I feel

"**I**s that you or the tape?" my father asks. I am seven years old. We are in the hunter green Buick. My three-year-old brother is sitting next to me in the backseat. Dad is at the wheel and has popped the cassette-of-the-moment into the slot. He and Mom have seen the US debut of the Andrew Lloyd Webber musical *Evita* on Broadway, and as much as they initially appreciated Patti LuPone's interpretation of the title role, my father has discovered the original London cast recording and prefers Julie Covington's Eva Perón. He has declared her the better singer, and denounced Ms. LuPone's vocals as histrionic and overwrought. I've listened to both recordings a lot—first, the Broadway version, on the record player, and then, this tape. And I must have been singing along to myself. At some point, it seems I'd learned every word and note.

"Me," I answer. I don't think I realized I was singing out loud, or that anyone could hear me, or that the tape hadn't started yet.

"That was you?!" my father asks with what sounds like an exciting mix of incredulity and wonder.

"Jimmy," Mom says to Dad, as if I'm not there in the car, "maybe we should get Charlotte voice lessons."

I feel a prickly surge of electric heat, and the urge to hug myself. It is one of my earliest memories of feeling proud, and just a little bit special. And I liked it. "Yes, please!" I perk up.

But then nothing happens. There are no voice lessons. There are piano tutorials with an exacting, lightly mustachioed older woman named Mrs. Whitman, who is kind but stern. There are Mozart minuets, Beethoven sonatas, Chopin preludes, and Schubert impromptus. But there is no singing to be done.

The following year, I get cast as Annie in my day camp's production of that orphan-centric musical, and my parents don't seem particularly surprised (although they did when I had a bit of fun and told them, with mock distress, that I'd been chosen to play Daddy Warbucks and hoped they wouldn't be disappointed). But I was surprised. And I was more surprised when my fellow campers would make me sing, on demand, while we were sitting in a circle playing Duck, Duck, Goose.

"Do it again! Sing 'I Think I'm Gonna Like it Here.'" And again came that rush—not so much for the attention, exactly; more like reveling in the pleasure of knowing you had a little something you could call your own.

Or in my case, a little big something—I could belt.

And I knew what I'd do with my life.

I was going to Broadway.

I toed the line, kept up the piano charade. But, in fifth grade, I also asked for guitar lessons, which, as long as I continued to practice the sonatas with Ms. Whitman, were sanctioned. And so I started strumming my pain, or Carly Simon's, and Suzanne Vega's—James Taylor's and George Michael's, too. I crooned of having faith, and leaving on jet planes; of an abused kid named Luka who lived on the second floor and bridges over troubled water.

A few months later, high school started, and from then on, my desire to take the stage was slowly replaced by an even stronger desire to flee it. There are many reasons for the shift from stuff-strutting ham to mousey milquetoast, and Peggy Orenstein has covered most of them in her writings about the crises of confidence so many teenage girls endure. Surely, navigating the rarified prep-school world of New York City and attending an elitist all-girls school on the Upper East Side compounded the issue. But, no matter the perfect storm of ego-crushing factors, the fact remains, stage fright set in. Simultaneously, my goals changed. I now wanted to be a journalist or a magazine editor.

Something else changed, too.

My love of music remained; the voracious devouring of tapes, followed by compact discs, carried on; the insatiable quest for voices, rhythms, and melodies that were new to me—it all continued. The more I retreated inward, the more music I absorbed. A constant soundtrack began playing through my head; years later, it has yet to stop. They come faster, freer flowing, and more unexpected in their randomness and variety. They arrive in the form of rapidly changing, seemingly bizarre cravings. Sometimes, if I can't play one immediately, I become obsessed, distractedly so, like a junkie itching for a fix. If I'm in public, I have to withdraw to some place of shelter where headphones can be popped in and a "play" arrow tapped. If I want to sing, it's more difficult. I have to control the impulse and wait until I'm home; it's a little like having to pee really badly and holding it in.

But the biggest change was my unholy spirit.

Julie Covington, Evita, Frances Ruffelle, Eponine—these voices had no effect anymore. If anything, they annoyed me. I had heard The Voice.

Aretha Franklin.

Why wasn't I born Aretha? Why couldn't I sing like that? Dear Lord-I-don't-believe-in, let me open my mouth and have that sound come forth. Please.

I don't know that, if said deity had answered my prayers and graced me with such super powers, I ever would have taken the stage again. It's doubtful. I didn't care if anyone heard me. More accurate, I didn't want anyone to hear me. I just wanted to be able to sing, like that, for myself.

It wasn't "Respect" or "Natural Woman" that moved me. "Dr. Feelgood," "Spanish Harlem," and the Queen of Soul's cover of "Eleanor Rigby;" those were my jams. I could do a mean "Rock Steady," at home, in my room, with the door closed. Or at least, I imagined I could.

It was as though, by killing off Broadway Baby, I had awakened a spectral alter ego—a moody, needy inner diva who hungrily fed on a diet of soul. It turns out, if you have any kind of music in you, the harder you try to mute or contain it, the stronger it will fight to get out.

I rounded out my listening jags and sing-along marathons with the B-52s, Lady Miss Kier, Terence Trent D'Arby, Prince, and Sinéad O'Connor. At the same time, I was dabbling in De La Soul and A Tribe Called Quest, which laid a foundation for an ongoing love of early hip-hop.

That's when I heard that first thrilling trill of an *Oooh,* backed by a piano, that started high and shimmied, tumbling into waves down to a lower register as a beat was dropped, introducing a riff about lovers who had made it through the storm.

God, it was catchy, both the tune and rhythm. But that's not why it hit me so hard. To hear Mary J. Blige sing "Real Love" in 1992 was to hear a completely new sound. This was hip-hop, sung. As much as I loved (still do) the Aretha tracks I'd listened to over and over again, I had instantly recognized something retro in them; that's, in part, why they had appealed. When Mary's debut *What's the 411?* dropped, it signaled a passing of the torch. Here was the heiress to the Queen of Soul's throne, and the new royal was giving that seat a makeover. The sentiment and power carried through, but the dominant influences—rhythm, language, and production style—were pure hip-hop.

There was sand in that voice, like the silty sand you find in fresh clams too hastily shucked. And there was shade; not a Slim Shady kind of shade, but something ominous that the album cover promised with its black-and-white shot of Ms. Blige's face, her eyes obscured by the shadow cast by the brim of a hat. This was in keeping with the prevailing hip-hop and rap throwback gangster-inspired iconography, but it was new for a solo performing female vocalist.

Chaka was one of Mary's inspirations, or targets, depending on how you look at it. Blige's cover of Chaka's "Sweet Thing" is so transformative that if, like me, you listened to the newer version before the original, you might actually find yourself disappointed by the predecessor. It might seem a little bland, or too even-keeled. You might call it "sweet." When Mary digs into those lyrics, she makes a mockery of sweetness.

And that's where Mary gets me every time. She can be singing the peppiest ditty; it may get your toe tapping, your hips swaying, but there will be a streak of something bitter, salty, or baleful in it. Her pitch is perfect, but the delivery of each note is charged in a brilliant, unstable-seeming way.

Appropriately, her first single, "Real Love," displays that

paradoxical contrast and sets the tone for the rest of her repertoire—ballad, prayer, dance-hall track, or otherwise. There you are, bopping along, thinking—based on the upbeat bass and initial lyrics—you're hearing a song about finding deliriously happy, sunshine-and-daffodils love. But if you're listening to the timbre, you can't help but pick up on something being chafed. If you haven't caught on yet, the bridge gets you there.

> *Love so true and oh baby, I thought that your love was true*
> *I thought you were the answer to the questions in my mind*
> *But it seems that I was wrong*
> *If I stay strong maybe I'll find my real love*

For anyone who was paying attention (or heard Mary speaking to her), it was already clear that this search for real love emerged from some grave disappointment. Blige, via this song, is using the lessons learned from being conned by a douchebag to be a wiser seeker of true romance. It's a hopeful attitude, but it requires effort.

There's the perpetual shrugging. And then there's the nodding; specifically, that head-bob Mary made famous in the video for her duet with rapper Method Man. "I'll Be There For You / You're All I Need" borrowed the chorus from an R&B duet written by husband and wife team Ashford and Simpson and made famous by Marvin Gaye and Tammi Terrell (Aretha Franklin covered it, too). Mary sang the sampled bits and Method Man rapped lines like "Cheeba cheeba y'all, and you don't stop / Yeah yeah, cootie in the chair," or "We can make war or make babies / Back when I was nothing / You made a brother feel like he was something / That's why I'm with you to this day boo no frontin' / Even when the skies were gray." She's his sunshine, it would seem, making him happy in his darkest hour.

When Tammi sings "Like sweet morning dew / I took one look at you / And it was plain to see / You were my destiny," that destiny (her co-singer Marvin, presumably) is a rosy one. She sounds as though she has found God. Not Mary. Her rendition comes across as a sigh of resignation. She saw her fate, and knew she was stuck, forever. "With you I'll spend my time / I'll dedicate my life / I'll sacrifice for you." When she sings "sacrifice," it almost sounds like one. And still, there we are, nodding our heads along with her, to the infectious rhythm. We're drawn to the song in the same way she's drawn to Method Man. Can't help ourselves.

Eight years later, Jay-Z and Beyoncé (Hova and B., respectively) revisited this genre that Method and Mary invented with their tune—the "Thug-Love" duet. I admit to having a thing for "'03 Bonnie and Clyde." Still do. But I can also tell you that when B., borrowing liberally from Prince's "If I Was Your Girlfriend," claims "And so I put this on my life / Nobody and nothing will ever come between us / And I promise I'll give my life / My love and my trust if you was my boyfriend," I didn't quite believe it. Still don't. Not the way I was certain that, when Mary says she'll sacrifice herself for her man, she would, and that, surely, it would be her undoing.

The difference is that, while Beyoncé uses the lyrics to tell whatever story she and Jay-Z are spinning, Mary uses her voice. And sometimes, Mary's voice tells its own story—one the lyrics omit, or one that almost clashes with the song itself. She can be bitching about premenstrual syndrome (yes, there is a Mary J. Blige tune titled "PMS" and it touches on everything from "feelin' quite ugly," to lower backache, clothes that don't fit, and the rest of the symptoms associated with that monthly precursor to The Curse), being (giddily) in love, worshipping The Lord, or getting everyone up on the dance floor. It's her voice—its crackles and breaks, its smooth pitch-perfection shifting into a rougher guttural line of enthusiasm or despair, its cooing joy unsettled by some wistful note, its longing and its tenacity—that guides and rewards the listener.

You rarely hear that when you're sitting in the audience of a Broadway musical—the book's plot must be honored. There can be no ambiguity, unless, of course, the narrative arc calls for it.

I didn't hear it again for a while, myself.

And then, the first semester of my sophomore year of college, I walked into Professor Neil Leonard's History of Jazz class. Leonard, who passed away in December of 2012 at eighty-four, introduced me to Louis Armstrong like I'd never heard him before; to Ragtime's Jelly Roll Morton, and stride piano masters Fats Waller and Art Tatum, all of them virtuosos with wonderfully playful dirty minds; to Duke Ellington, that Cotton Club maestro, to Miles Davis, the "Prince of Darkness," who was as modern as we got before the course ended; to New Orleans' brass, Big Band sound; to beret-crowned Dizzy Gillespie's bebop with its dizzyingly speedy, jumping arpeggios and scats; to the "jungle style" of the Harlem Renaissance.

I'd never realized the ease with which I could discern between human singing voices until I was asked to do the same with horn blowers; I was a disaster. And because Professor Leonard's reverence for those trumpeters and saxophonists was fanatical and abiding, my inability to recognize who was playing which song by ear was deeply disappointing—to me, and, in my mind, to him, too. Perhaps that is why, the day he put a Bessie Smith vinyl on the record player, and a rafter-shaking echoing sound exploded out of the shoddy speakers, it startled me out of my somewhat foggy audio state.

Vibrato can be a subtle or an elusive visitor—some singers work hard to cultivate it, to coax, will, or train it out. Others face the opposite challenge and struggle to restrain or control it. Either way, the goal is to be able to use it on command, and at whatever pitch and volume is required. Without it, even when sung right on key, songs can sound simpering and wan. When an unruly teen has a shaking-quaking in her voice, she is a train derailed, blaring, and careening. Which is what you could easily write Bessie off as.

But you'd be wrong. This woman was the incarnation of vibrato. No note of hers lacks a tremor. Somehow, it's not too much. You don't wish she'd pipe the hell down, or sit a few out. Maybe it's because each syllable is so purely struck. Her voice may leave a sorrowful impression in its wake, but it's never imprecise; it's haunting. Even when she breaks into "'Tain't Nobody's Biz-ness If I Do," a generally upbeat, sassy number, she manages to imbue it with a stones-in-your-pocket, foreboding heft. "If I should take a notion / To jump into the ocean / 'Tain't nobody's biz-ness if I do," no longer comes across as playful or bemusedly riled up. Now, we're listening to a song about someone who has given up on living. I've heard this tune countless times by other artists. It's only when I listen to Bessie sing it that I find myself registering the lyrics themselves.

What I thought was Mary J. syndrome is, in fact, Bessie syndrome. Bessie got there first. Her voice transcends the songs. And it has that dual nature—so clear and precise, and also rough. There's a catch in it, a sting—like the burn that whiskey leaves on the back of your throat. Mostly it's anguished, occasionally angry, and sometimes, bawdy.

It's the blues.

Her embodiment of the blues as a performer was so strong that it spilled over into the public perception of her character and life. Lots of people who see her as synonymous with the blues haven't listened to her work much. They didn't have Professor Leonard to start them off with "St. Louis Blues" and lead them into "Backwater Blues," followed by "After You've Gone." They didn't get to relish those rare recorded snippets of guttural, nearly violent pleasure in "Gimme a Pigfoot and a Bottle of Beer," or the sly sexual innuendos of "Kitchen Man:" "His frankfurters are oh so sweet / How I like his sausage meat… Oh how that boy can open clams / No one else can catch my ham."

Bessie Smith is remembered as "Empress of the Blues," and despite the fact that she was the top-selling blues artist of her day, a savvy performer, and enterprising thinker, the royal nickname is associated with hard-and-fast living, depression, alcoholism, and tragedy. When she died in 1937 in a posthumously sensationalized car crash, the forty-three-year-old "has-been" was in the process of staging a comeback. Bessie had peaked in the twenties. Until 1972, when Chris Albertson wrote her biography, *Bessie,* the singer was known mostly for her gin and the rumors that surrounded her death. To be honest, I don't remember what Dr. Leonard told us about her life story because I was rapt in the music. I don't recall much about the personal lives of any of those musicians whose sounds wafted through our classroom. The sound was where I looked for my lessons. In terms of my relationship with music, I've always been something of a formalist. The songs tell me everything I need to know; I'm not interested in looking beyond them—in ascribing an extra layer of analysis based on an assumption or trail of gossip that might bias my interpretation.

Call it naïveté or blind faith, but I don't believe you have to be mired in misery, riled up with rage, or floating in a balloon of elation to communicate those emotions as an artist. And the reason I admire Bessie Smith so much, the reason her voice could command my complete attention as I sat crammed into that wobbly excuse for a desk under the fluorescent lights of Neil Leonard's linoleum-floored lecture room, was that, like a force field, it seemed to take all the hurt in the world and hurdle it out there, like Zeus throwing a lightning bolt, into the presence of anyone who wanted to receive it. Her voice could do that with a song about the most mundane of activities. She sang of having a "Hot Time in the Old

Town Tonight," of blowing horns, keeping your man happy, and going on buggy rides. She sang lyrics written by other people. She sang it all with the same voice, the one she was born with—the one that socks you in the gut with its magnitude of feeling and sonorous boom. That's what the blues sound like. And anyone's got a right to sing them—even a privileged, white, high school girl from the Upper East Side of Manhattan, sitting at the desk in her bedroom, door closed, doing her math homework in her pajamas. For all you know, she's the reigning Queen of Pain, or one of the Shiny Happy People.

But I didn't want to sing the blues like Bessie. I wanted to sing like Mary J. And though it doesn't matter in the slightest, Ms. Blige's life was more hip-hop than Ms. Smith's was blues. Mary is a self-proclaimed "child of the ghetto," and has been candid about her bouts with alcohol and drug addiction, and being physically abused by a former boyfriend. She has discussed recovering from those ordeals and taking control of her life and career. God got her through. These days, the songs she writes often touch on devotion to Him. When she sings of real love, it's with a gospel fervor.

If I were Mary, I'd do more duets. When Mary J. doubles up with another musician, it's a goosebump-inducing production. If you ever wanted to be in the presence of the human divine, you need to hear Wyclef Jean and Mary perform "911." It's a more extreme thug-love harmony, as its title indicates. Mary isn't exactly standing by her man as she was in "There for You;" it's more like she's standing over her man, holding a gun, which, spoiler alert, she has just shot. "Someone please call nine-one-one," begs Wyclef. "The alleged assailant is five-foot-one, and she shot me through my soul. Feel my body getting cold." The vocal back-and-forth is even more intense than the lyrics. Better not to focus too much on the words so you can appreciate the song's operatic qualities as opposed to its soap-operatic ones. Mary acrobatically blazes up and down scales and octaves, building power as she progresses and, at the height of her prowess, sounds more eviscerated than her victim, as though eviscerating her own gut. As the tune expires, both parties are spent; the breath leaves their bodies, their notes dwindle—*so cold, so cold.*

Six years later, in 2006, she left the thug behind and did an unloved harmony with Bono. It was gutsy of him to tamper with a U2 classic like "One," gutsier to do it as a duet, and gutsiest for Mary to rise to the challenge and take the song so far from its former self. She changes the melody, nearly beyond recognition; if Bono wasn't there to be the equivalent of a vocal straight man, sticking to the original—more or less—you would mistake it for an entirely different track. I couldn't be sure how I felt about it on first listen; for one, I couldn't sing along with the tune changing up on me, turning corners, and leading down unfamiliar paths. I felt somewhat protective of the *Achtung Baby* version—I'd always considered it untouchable. Something about the whole remake smelled a little bit like a stunt to me. Bono going hip-hop seemed contrived, an attempt to reach a new audience.

But as I listened, I couldn't help wanting to figure out Mary's note sequence and sing along; I couldn't help being stirred by the ecstasy she finds in the agony of those lyrics. She also brings a fury to it. When Bono first sang it, he sounded melancholy, and he repeats that here. Not Mary; she's fed up. At the very end of the track, after crying out the verses' list of grievances and accusations with an increasing amount of vitriol, she reaches a crescendo. "You ask me to enter, / And then you make me crawl," she spews. When she follows that with, "and I can't keep holding on to what you've got / When all you've got is hurt," you hear the hurt, and the letting go of it, too. It comes so close to being over the top, but the feeling she expresses is too believable to make any histrionics a nuisance; she keeps it real—honest.

Sometimes she does go over the top. It may be impossible not to when you put two divas together on one track; if those two divas are Mary J. Blige and Aretha Franklin, one might argue that there is no such thing as too far. When I found out my alter ego's two role models had recorded a song for Blige's fourth album, *Mary*, I made a note of its release date, and bought it that day, August 17, 1999. Titled "Don't Waste My Time," the duet, which features the older and wiser Aretha giving Mary advice about her love life—"seen it a million times before, you shouldn't take his stuff no more"—is just as you'd imagine. They harmonize over and around each other with all the requisite emotion.

But it's not the best track on that album. That honor goes to my favorite song Mary J. Blige has ever sung. It, too, is a collaboration. Written and produced by Lauryn Hill, "All That I Can Say" has a trippy mellowness to it, a relatively lengthy instrumental finale, and one of the trickiest melodies to master. Over the years, I have tirelessly practiced singing along—usually in the shower—to pin down that tightly composed melody line. The background music wobbles, deliberately, which makes keeping up with the precise notes Mary is hitting all the more challenging. The song is not up-tempo in the way that a dance track is—where the rhythm dictates the good vibes. This is a song about being overcome with delight at having found someone to love. "Loving you is wonderful, something like a miracle," goes the first line. Its worshipful lyrics border on gospel, especially at its climax, which is what I wait for, as both a Mary fan and shower diva. This is Mary J.'s "Dr. Feelgood" moment. Where Aretha sings, "Don't send me no doctor / Filling me up with all those pills / I got me a man named Dr. Feelgood / And oh! Yeah! / That man takes care of all my pains and my ills," Mary gives us, "Genuine seraphim / Sweeter than cinnamon / Heaven-sent gentleman / Synonyms for loving him." The "synonyms" is questionable. Others have written it as "Sent him here for loving him," but I always thought it was, "Sinning is for loving him," and that's how I plan to keep singing it.

In addition to being my ultimate Mary song, "All That I Can Say," ironically, marks the end of my great aspiration to be Ms. Blige. I don't know if it's the found happiness registered in the track, or, more likely, that my taste was changing and I was opening my ears to other voices. I haven't stopped appreciating or listening to Mary and doubt I ever will. But as soon as I heard Stevie Nicks's early Fleetwood Mac work or was clued in to the stories Neko Case tells, I'd found new voices I wished to inhabit. Neko can manage these things, too, with her words—the narratives they form—and her crooning. "I'm so tired," she admits, wearily, "and I wish I was the moon tonight." It sends a shiver, and someone walks on my grave.

This is what I want, the powers of haunting and the howling; the ability to convey the things I brought indoors when I lost the nerve to get up on a stage and sing them. I seek them out—traces of a howl, notes that haunt. And I find them, in diverse voices, in Mary and Bessie's. They express something that words alone can't get to; that's why I listen, and, in part, why I try to sing them myself.

> *I wish I had words to tell*
> *This feeling that I know so well*
> *But I don't. I don't.*
> *All that I can say.*

Pressing On

Jennifer Nix

The plain fact is, I don't remember a time when I was unaware of June Carter Cash. She hovers over my entire forty-odd years of sentience, from earliest memory of happiness to present and tangled heartache. Mapping the seminal moments and parallels into which June figures is to plot what I know of my father's life and death, and to trace how a daughter becomes estranged from the mother she loves—which is to say, maybe by telling my story about June, I am hoping to find a way back to my mother.

The story begins, happily enough, with June's TV appearance on a Saturday night in the summer of 1969 at the dawn of my conscious desire. This involved a sudden longing for a plastic, daisy-decaled guitar, which also happened to be pink because I was not quite three years old. Clearly I'd seen such a wonder among some other child's toys or while tucked at my mother's side as she turned the pages of the giant Sears catalog, but my laser need for that specific guitar bubbled up as I sat cuddled on the couch between mother and father in the paneled basement of our little tract home in Adrian, Michigan.

My young parents' delight charged the air. Sparked by expectation of something really good about to happen and catalyzed by our focused attention, I registered this high-octane togetherness as simply the best feeling. Then from our brand new color TV came a simple greeting: "Hello. I'm Johnny Cash."

It was the premiere of *The Johnny Cash Show* and without June, the black-clad man might have been a little too scary for me—I tended toward fear of strange men on TV and in person, especially Santa Claus because he visited too infrequently. Instead, on that summer night a dual contagion of excitement and connectedness thoroughly infected me. I developed a virtually familial attachment to June over the next year, but what imprinted that night is just how very happy my parents were as they sang along, and the man and his wife on TV were so tickled together, too. All the elation and music, smiles and love conflated into my ideal of how things should be. This fulgent moment became the one against which all others are measured.

ABC launched Cash's weekly show on June 7, 1969, by beaming an hour of communion with Johnny and June, Bob Dylan, and Joni Mitchell into my family room. These artists all occupy pantheon seats for me today, but my fascination then was all about June. (Of course, there is now a YouTube video of the premiere in its fifty-two-minute entirety to provide a handy touchstone.)

"Right now, here's a lovely young lady. My wife, June Carter," says Johnny, and June shimmies out and curtsies to high applause in a sparkling green gown that highlights a remarkable hourglass figure. As I watch the video today, I'm struck by how alike June (despite being fourteen years older) and my mother looked at the time, both five-foot-five, blue-eyed, and amply curved, with their beauty-queen smiles and dark-brown, long bouffant flips, and I realize this similarity must be one of the reasons I took a shine to June. I note the way she sways and swivels her hips, harmonizing with Johnny over his train-beat strumming as the two rock their first hit single, a 1965 cover of Dylan's "It Ain't Me, Babe." I get a little tingle when I see her flirty nose crinkle and the admiration June oozes into, "You say you're looking for someone / who's never weak and always strong / to protect you and defend you / whether you are right or wrong."

June's charms stirred more than just one little girl that night. A *Rolling Stone* critic named Patrick Thomas attended the taping at the Ryman Auditorium, which was then still home to the Grand Ole Opry, and declared June "a woman who absolutely means to entertain or know the reason why. She's got that hash-house flash and she really drives."

I still admire that flash and drive but what moves me now, as a middle-aged woman married fourteen years, is the dewy joy and attraction in June's eyes as she looks at Johnny. This is the roused gaze every happy woman longs to keep holding for her partner as the years go by. June had become Mrs. Cash only the year before, after their famously tumultuous, multiyear struggle with "Ring of Fire" love while still married to others. In that pre-Internet and -TMZ era, I'm certain my parents had no idea June's second husband during those years was a man named Edwin "Rip" Nix (no relation, as far as I know).

Wayne and Sharon Nix celebrated their fifth anniversary that summer of sixty-nine and, like most Americans of the non-judgmental human variety, were smitten with Johnny and June's love story. The most-played record on our hi-fi then was *Carryin' On* with Johnny Cash and June Carter, which includes their Grammy-winning and biggest hit, "Jackson." The album title still emits a whiff of naughty; as even though June was legally free by this August 1967 release and Johnny and Vivian Liberto Cash filed for divorce in 1966, it wasn't finalized until January 1968, just days before his famous Folsom Prison concert. Some of my parents' rapture while watching Johnny and June sing on that first broadcast had to involve at least the unconscious appreciation and titillation of forbidden love made good. I get another little tingle considering the fact that nine months after the premiere, both couples welcomed new babies—a boy for the Cashes and a girl for my parents—thus extending connections to that happy time.

For me, though, it was a guitar.

I don't remember pointing at the television and saying, "I want a 'kitar,'" but this is a stock story from childhood told by my parents and tied to my subsequent obsessions and ambitions. For months after seeing Johnny's guitar, I pestered and pleaded for the pink guitar and finally Santa placed it under the tree, even though I'd tearfully refused again that year to sit on his lap. For the next year and change, I picked and strummed away, showing precisely zero talent for the instrument, and during each episode of Johnny's show I stood a foot away from the TV screen holding my guitar and trying to sing along with June. But I never did learn to play it.

ABC canceled *The Johnny Cash Show* in March of 1971 during the "rural purge," a season in which all three networks responded to the tectonic societal and cultural shifts of the age by swapping out their folksy, heartland-themed shows (think *Green Acres* and *Lassie*) for edgy offerings featuring city dwellers, racial politics, and black humor about war (think *All in the Family* and *M*A*S*H**). The Dow was headed into bear territory for the next decade, Nixon's enemy list was growing, and body bags were coming home from Vietnam. The whole country's mood was polling downward but all I knew was that my June was gone.

A more distinct gloom settled over our family life in the months following the show's cancellation in spite of what should have been exhilarating developments, like my father getting a better-paying teaching job and moving us to my mother's dream home, a 1910 farmhouse in the nearby small town of Tecumseh. There were still good days, but my parents grew increasingly distracted and short-tempered. Bedtime stories stopped, no music played, and most of the time my father looked too tired to stand up. Sometime between age five and six and highly attuned to our domestic climate change, I abandoned the pink guitar in a corner of the creepy cellar and retreated to my room to embark on a quieter obsession: reading.

My relationship today with books and words fits with the findings of Stanford professor Shirley Brice Heath, a linguistic anthropologist and the author of *Words at Work and Play: Three Decades in Families and Communities* (2012). To sustain a lifelong attachment to serious literature, Heath's research shows one of two paths are possible. This first type of serious reader is a person who as a child has parents who lead by example by reading, and who later finds friends with whom to discuss books. The second type is the social isolate, a child who from an early age feels very different from those around her. An important dialogue begins to happen internally between such a child and the authors of the books she reads. I could read by age four because my mother initially spent so much time reading to me, but the social-isolate part delivered a goosefleshy moment of clarity when first reading Heath, because I recognized that when the gloom descended and behaviors changed—without explanation—I began to feel like an outsider in my family and sought connection in books. Heath also says social isolate readers are more likely to become writers, and though I treasure what's been a life dedicated primarily to word-related pursuits in media and activism, I wonder now whether my early and solo retreat into books was the first unconscious wedge between mother and daughter.

At that age, I tied June's disappearance to all the postliminary strife but the reality was my parents were overwhelmed and just beginning to grapple with the terror of my twenty-nine-year-old father's mysteriously declining health. By early 1972, they learned he was in the final stages of kidney failure.

My mind samples only a few soundless images, like animated, looping GIFs, from the year or so following that crushing demarcation. I see smoke rising from the built-in ashtrays of vinyl chairs in a waiting room at the old University of Michigan hospital. I see my saddle shoes walking the many-colored maze of lines painted on the floor, which corresponded to various diseases and led away from the lobby toward treatment rooms down dingy corridors. The lines on a New York City subway map can take me right back there. I see my father, weak from nausea, crawling up our stairs. I see men delivering the dialysis machine to our house along with the first tall stacks of medical-supply boxes, because my parents decided Dad would dialyze at home, with my mother as caregiver, rather than suffer a commute to Ann Arbor and the depressing emotional toll of facing a dialysis unit three days a week, four hours at a time. We never called this contraption by its proper name; it was always just the "kidney machine" and it lived in our "TV room." We ate dinner in there while Dad sat in a La-Z-Boy with his blood pumping through the clear plastic lines. I see my mother pushing butterfly needles into the swollen veins of my father's forearm and I see her dozing on the floor, waiting to clean up the detritus at each run's end. I see Mrs. Osburn, too, standing in her cheery classroom putting an index finger to her lips, gently hushing thirty first-graders in an instant. I loved school and thrived there; that was the part of my day when I didn't have to think about the scary stuff.

There would be a failed transplant attempt in 1975, with Dad near death in a hospital bed for three months, and a four-month period when I was "home-schooled" in our Ford Turtle Top van in a Florida campground because my mother knew he wouldn't make it through that Michigan winter. On a temporary disability check, such accommodation was all they could afford, so they towed a small trailer and set up a mobile dialysis unit right there at the campsite, making us, I was told, the first family to camp with one of the early, stove-sized hemodialysis machines.

At some point my parents got their heads around the idea of my father being on dialysis for what they thought would be the rest of his life, and a new kind of normal contoured around us. In our kitchen appeared a sign stating our adopted family motto: "When life gives you lemons, make lemonade." My father returned to work and got back into his passion for music with a fervor. Elvis, Hank Williams, Bill Haley & the Comets, the Platters, and, of course, Johnny and June were all back in heavy rotation on the turntable housed in our smack-digity Zenith console.

One summer afternoon my father emerged from the cellar with an old reel-to-reel tape machine and asked me to help him set it up on the screened-in porch. As he mined a box full of unmarked tapes for two particular treasures, the speakers projected my father's teenaged deejay-wannabe routines, which involved not only the spinning of records but snappy backstories about the songs or artists and amusing banter with my grandmother when she entered his room with a snack or reminder. Hailing from the birthplace of commercial radio, Pittsburgh, Pennsylvania, Dad's teen years coincided with the emergence of rock and roll and the heyday of two of the nation's most popular disc jockeys, Cleveland's Alan "Moondog" Freed, who actually coined the term "rock and roll," and Pittsburgh's Jay Michaels, one of the first to play what was then called "race music" on mainstream radio. Heavily influenced by the tastes of those two men, my dad's vinyl collection—a small bit of which I have today—included a marvelous trove of rhythm and blues, country and western swing, doo-wop and that early rock and roll, and rockabilly.

Young Wayne time-capsuled live performances from local and national radio broadcasts, too, and as I sat next to him on the glider that day, I learned Pittsburgh's KDKA was not only America's first commercial station, but the first to broadcast live music and the only station east of the Mississippi River to have call letters starting with a K, not W. All of this information, combined with my father's manifest enthusiasm, gave Pittsburgh a singular glamour. I heard about Sam Phillips and Sun Records that day, too, because one of the reels Dad was looking for held a recording of a live radio concert featuring Elvis Presley, Jerry Lee Lewis, Carl Perkins, and Johnny Cash. He also wanted to locate his bedroom recordings of Grand Ole Opry shows he and his mother had spirited from the airwaves because, in the wake of his illness and the sixties folk music revival, my parents took an interest in old-time Appalachian folk and country music. In particular, he was looking for episodes featuring Mother Maybelle and the Carter Sisters, and this is when I remember first hearing June without Johnny.

An audiophile buddy helped Dad transfer these rediscoveries from open-reel to eight-track cartridges for his sweet, electric-yellow, Panasonic portable player, so I heard the old Opry recordings often over the next several years and can testify that June worked what she had and held her own in those early days. She may not have been graced with Maybelle's virtuoso musicianship, or her sister Anita's buttery voice, but as Mark Zwonitzer points out in his rich biography of the Carter family, *Will You Miss Me When I'm Gone?*, Valerie June Carter was the most single-minded and ambitious of the Carters and "an entertainer for life, she was happiest in front of an audience, and she knew she was good." June became a star by determining the ways to make the most of not only her talent and looks, but of her intelligence, charisma, and humor.

The lambent hours on the porch when my father shared his

love and knowledge of music took hold as my best memory of time alone with him. Happiness fused with my introduction to the Sun Records boys and Carter family classics like "Wildwood Flower" and "Keep on the Sunny Side," while two lines first heard that day in the June solo "Sweet Temptation" ("The most delicious peach / Just always out of reach") became part of our father-daughter argot. She got to us both; there was just something so cheerful and game about June. In her Opry incarnations, she was equal parts sassy singer and cornpone comedienne, always mixing it up with the host and other entertainers, and combined with her beauty, I'm not surprised that both Johnny Cash and Wayne Nix professed teenaged crushes on June. After hearing about my father's admiration for June and her success, I took up the feminine calculus for determining where I might place on the looks, smarts, and talent charts, and how I could—like June—make the most of whatever gifts I'd been given. I, too, would call on humor to fill in the gaps.

With the yellow eight-track player Velcroed to the dash and the "kidney machine" lashed in back, my family spent every vacation and a high percentage of weekends in the late seventies hitting the road in our Turtle Top van. I found soothing the rumble and rhythm of tires on the highway and the country whirring by my window. Plus, I had plenty of time to follow my curiosity through all the books I brought along. Paying no heed to Jimmy Carter's energy crisis, we camped in every state east of the Mississippi and laid eyes on Plymouth Rock and the Mayflower replica, Salem's witch dungeon, Philadelphia's Liberty Bell, and just about every historic marker and Revolutionary and Civil War site. We visited founding father manors and their dismal slave quarters, national memorials, quirky tourist traps, and stunning natural wonders. I also have a photo of my little self, taken with the real Maria von Trapp (yes, *Sound of Music*) outside her lodge in Vermont, and I went to Graceland before Elvis died in his bathroom.

The old recordings of Johnny and June, the Carters, and Elvis provided the soundtrack, along with new additions like John Denver, Kris Kristofferson, the Statler Brothers, and the Oak Ridge Boys. My parents' love of country, gospel, and old-time mountain music inspired repeat trips to the Blue Ridge and Smoky Mountains and remote hollows all over central Appalachia. On one trip, a Carter Family rendition of "Cumberland Gap" even led us, like madly hopeful pioneers headed west, along the Native American trail Daniel Boone developed into the Wilderness Road, and to take turns standing on the exact triangulated spot where Kentucky, Tennessee, and Virginia converge in Cumberland Gap National Historic Park.

June grew up an hour east of there, in Maces Springs, Virginia, which also happens to be where her uncle Alvin Pleasant "A. P." Carter started the original Carter family trio, with his wife Sara and June's mother Maybelle. A. P. is known today as "the father of country music" even though the group disbanded in 1943 and, according to Zwonitzer's book, he died in 1960 feeling his music might be forgotten. Dad drove our Turtle Top down A. P. Carter Highway on the way from Maces Spring to Bristol, the town straddling Virginia and Tennessee's border where in 1927 the Carters (and a few other performers, like Jimmie Rodgers) made the very first recordings of old-time mountain folk songs for the Victor Talking Machine Company, and then spread across the country along with Orthophonic Victrolas.

The Bristol sessions are known as the "big bang of modern country music," but Nashville became ground zero, so on we charged in the Turtle Top to Opryland USA. The theme park opened in the early seventies to house the new Grand Ole Opry House when the Ryman got too small for the millions of mostly southern and midwestern fans making pilgrimages to Nashville. I remember riding the Wabash Cannonball and Rock-n-Roller coasters, but my parents never got tickets to an Opry show. Money was always tight, though a Johnny Cash poster bought on that trip did hang in the basement of the small ranch-style house we moved to after my mother's dream home turned out to be too exhausting and costly to fix up. In my online wanderings I found an old Hatch Show Print like what I remember; it's an advertisement for a 1967 Minneapolis show featuring Johnny and June, the Tennessee Three, Mother Maybelle, the Statler Brothers, and Carl Perkins. It has that whiff-of-naughty, *Carryin' On*-year vibe, so I had to buy it.

Rushing headlong out into the country gave our family an endorphin boost in those first few of the seventeen years Dad would endure dialysis, and my parents' joint passion for country music and its history (with June so integral a part) set a true purpose and course for our rambling. I see this passion as part of a romantic rural ideal my parents held, after choosing to leave the big cities of Pittsburgh and Detroit to create a life together in a small town— though they had little in common with that era's hippie back-to-the-landers, and nothing at all with today's hinterland right-wing preppers. The amalgam of these rural and musical elements provided my parents with what the poet Donald Hall calls a "third thing," and describes as being "essential to marriages, objects, or practices or habits or arts or institutions or games or human beings that provide a site of joint rapture or contentment. Each member of a couple is separate; the two come together in double attention."

In our case, this third thing was essential for the whole family, and it took root for me in June. Her voice underlays the montage of buoyant moments from my childhood, whether we were on the road or just cleaning the house together on a Saturday morning. For a stretch of years, Dad's trick to wind up my mother for a night of dancing at the Golden Nugget Saloon was putting "Jackson" on the stereo and channeling Johnny, and all was right in our world when my mother belted out June's rejoinder: "Go on, you big talkin' man…goodbye, that's all she wrote!" June's spirited and sometimes slightly off-key voice offered reprieve from the otherwise monotonous dirge of physical, emotional, and financial burdens faced by a young family living with a dialysis machine in their home.

The mutability of memory keeps me from locating an exact end point, but our June-infused third thing began to fade away with the onset of my teenage years, Reagan's voodoo economics, and the migration from eight-track to cassette. Our family life wasn't all bad, to be clear, but it became significantly less good as the trips and communal participation in our music ritual dwindled. Dad tossed the old Zenith console and yellow eight-track player in favor of a glass-doored tower stereo system, but he never warmed as much to cassettes, never transferred any of the old-time mountain and gospel recordings to the new format, and I never saw the open reels holding June and the others again. Something essential got lost.

Other factors contributed to my family's foreclosed togetherness, like the hamster-wheel of complications with my father's illness, the drudgery of dialysis every other day, year after year, and the increasing frequency of fatigue and temper trumping Dad's humor—at home, anyway. He saved his strength and positivity then for his students and football players, which resulted in Teacher of the Year honors and an induction into the Michigan High School Football Coaches Hall of Fame. By contrast, there was no public kudos for my mother, and her depression deepened over a rerouted life of medical caretaking, having fewer children than she'd wanted, and money pressures shoving her into the workplace as a teacher, too. She'd wanted the life of a stay-at-home mother and only worked because there were bills to pay, not because it fulfilled her or some dream drove her. She also told me several times in subsequent years that she believed not being home factored into my sister's later struggles with addiction. My mother gained, lost, and gained weight in the eighties, and fell asleep on the floor in the living room while watching TV, whether it was a dialysis night or not, rarely making it to their bedroom. I imagine it wasn't all about my father's chronic disease, that there may have been some of the common despair and needling regrets of any couples' mid-life marital years, and perhaps even what the character Walter, in Jonathan Franzen's *Freedom,* laments as "the deep loneliness of the truly married."

My conviction to live a life radically different from my mother's grew each year, despite loving her and feeling closer to her than to my father during my teen years. June's plucky, creative example had embedded itself early on and I looked for other lives to emulate in the books I read. New York seemed the place where such lives were lived. As a young woman, June was drawn to New York as well, studying at the Actors Studio in the fifties with Elia Kazan and Robert Duvall, and dating James Dean. Any life was possible in New York, and I meant to get there. Though my mother encouraged me, in the midst of feeling so desperate about her own life, it must have been a stab of repudiation each time I talked about leaving and all of my grand expectations.

The dark mood continued and corresponds to the lack of June and other music played in our living room then. I picked up the music ritual in the dens of the homes of my best girlfriend and boys I dated, discovering New Wave, ska, and punk, and other post-fifties rock, particularly the first and second waves of the British invasion. My new tastes engendered outsized disappointment for all kinds of unarticulated reasons (though my father did give voice to an irrational hatred of The Beatles for booting Elvis and Johnny from popularity in the mid-sixties) and my parents couldn't stand to hear my vinyl purchases from Schoolkids Records on the stereo. It gathered dust while the television droned on, and to this day, a house without music, in which a television flickers all day and night, makes me sad and agitated. I didn't help matters by getting into some typical teenaged scrapes, shoving country music aside (even my June) and snottily rejecting my parents' entire rural, small-town ideal. I started developing stomachaches whenever my father was on dialysis and just read in my room. All my ambition focused on escape from Tecumseh and from a life dominated by disease.

Our period of familial dissolve also coincides with June's exit from the spotlight and a spate of rough years in the house of Cash. There were still joint appearances, but new duets with Johnny stopped and, as their only son John Carter Cash writes in *Anchored in Love*, June's career took a backseat to Johnny's work and his repeat flare-ups of addiction and infidelity. It would be two decades before a return to the national stage and her first-ever solo Grammy.

On YouTube one night, I linked my way to an achingly awkward clip of June promoting her memoir, *Among My Klediments*, on *The Merv Griffin Show* on August 22, 1980 (my parents' sixteenth anniversary, incidentally). I experienced an unexpected cringe of remorse, like I'd turned against an old friend in need back then. I got a little hot with defensiveness on her behalf watching fellow guest Shelley Winters goad June about women's liberation, saying condescendingly, "This is the first time I've ever seen you without Johnny… You're getting liberated." A flustered, fifty-one-year-old June tries to encapsulate her early years of solo accomplishments and explains that now she tries to follow "God's order from the old Bible" of putting God first, her husband second, then her children, and "in being liberated, Johnny Cash lets me be a part of everything he does and he let me come on out here and I'm glad of that." Sitting there with just her autoharp she looks a little lost on the set, and far out of step with the times.

There was talk of divorce at the time in both houses. To heal addiction and their marriage, evangelism served as a third thing for the Cashes, but as they started frequenting Billy Graham crusades in the eighties, church became a fraught subject in the Nix home. My mother's converted-to-Catholic habit remained strong but my dad stopped attending church. I never knew whether this was due to fatigue, anger, or just the excruciatingly tiresome priest at St. Elizabeth's. I do know it worried my mother that despite all the years of homilies and CCD classes, I never found a lasting in-road to the soul through organized religion. I think she'd hoped faith in her God would be something the two of us could share, but this was just another disappointment. Simply pretending to have that kind of deep, inveterate faith June and my mother held so dear seemed to me a profound act of dishonesty. Both women claimed to have received a calling—as children—to religious faith; I wonder for how many people the deal is that real.

I find meaning, hope, and spiritual communion in the voice of certain poets and songwriters, and in the pages of serious literature (other than monotheistic texts)—which, by the way, also jibes with Shirley Brice Heath's social-isolate research. But all these years later, I do channel a peculiar yen for devotional ritual whenever I hear June's renditions of gospel folk songs like "Church in the Wildwood" and "That Lonesome Valley." What I yearn for, however, is not the myth or rules surrounding any ancient prophet, but my father's Panasonic on the dash, my mother's pretty voice harmonizing with June's, and the family closeness of our Turtle Top days.

Rather than the whitewashed myth that June married Johnny and everyone lived happily ever after, I also find far more radical inspiration in the reality of both the Cash and Nix thirty-five-year unions. Now, deep into my own midlife marital years, I admire the grit it takes for any two committed people to wade through all manner of pain and despair—and the accompanying insanities— to discover new joys on farside banks.

"Buddhists speak of seeing your life as part of a pattern," wrote the poet Louis Simpson, "but I do not have to practice Buddhism in order to do this—it happens when I write." This rings true as certain patterns crystallized for the first time through this writing. The early hitching of happiness to travel triggered a nomadic spirit and led to shoestring sojourns around Europe and the Middle East in my twenties. Ambition to escape my small town and Dad's disease landed me first in Pittsburgh (remember, it once seemed glamorous) and then New York in early 1992. For the rest of that decade, as I circuitously and somewhat unconsciously authored myself into a bizarrely close adaptation of my father's dream to work in radio (first as news director for a country music station owned by an old UPI man, then as producer for a National Public Radio show), I had seven different addresses and a period of couch surfing before fleeing a wildly ill-suited job as a reporter for the "showbiz bible" and the riotous debris of an epic romantic fail. Four months later, while recovering away from New York, I got engaged after eight days to a fellow gypsy-soul, married him in the fall of 1999 and lived in two Italian and six other American cities before dragging him back to New York in our thirteenth year. For both good reasons and bad, I see a pattern of flight.

In late 1991, just before my move to New York, my parents and I shared another road trip after Dad got the call for his second transplant. They were visiting me in Pittsburgh, and back in Ann Arbor a wife had donated the organs of her husband just killed in a motorcycle accident. I grabbed a mix tape for that drive across Pennsylvania and Ohio as by then our music troubles were history. We barely spoke for those four hours. My mother drove her Celica and Dad reclined in the passenger seat. I leaned up close from the back and rubbed a certain protruding vein at the base of his neck— an act that always soothed him. When "If I Were a Carpenter" came on, I watched my father's hand find my mother's as Johnny and June sang the lines "Save your love through loneliness / Save your love through sorrow / I gave you my loneliness / Give me your tomorrow."

This time, the kidney took, and on track with the economic boom of the Clinton years, Nix health and wealth trended pretty gloriously upward. My parents bought a lakefront lot on remote Beaver Island and built a small vacation home that provided a new third thing for their marriage and our family. On my first visit, Dad picked me up at the delightfully puny airport shack in his Ford Bronco (he'd traded in the Turtle Top) and euphoric relief dizzied me when I saw the cottage profiled against the almost Caribbean-blue of Lake Michigan. That vision offered a meditative happy place whenever things got too crazy in New York. Dad joined my mother at the little white church in town, and even I could enjoy a liberal priest who quoted from novels and poetry, and joked that his true religion was fly-fishing. My sister was waitressing and showing talent for the guitar and songwriting, and in 1995 delivered baby Anna Rose, sending our family planet orbiting around a new sun. On our summer and Christmas visits at the cottage, CDs were always spinning.

Shortly after my engagement, June burst back onto the country music scene in the spring of 1999 with her solo album, *Press On*, and I picked up a copy on my way to Washington, DC, to watch my father testify before Congress. After the transplant, he retired from teaching and became a nationally-recognized activist. I helped him write proposals and secure initial funding for what became a National Kidney Foundation program to help kidney patients get back to school and work. My father said he felt a debt because he was among the first kidney patients to benefit in 1973 when Congress passed the law to include everyone diagnosed with end-stage renal disease under Medicare insurance. By *benefit*, I mean live. Had that bill not passed, he'd have died within two years of his diagnosis, because no private health insurers covered dialysis or transplants, and only the rich could afford treatment. Corporate dialysis centers found ways each year to squeeze ever-greater profits from Medicare at the expense of patient health, and my father was in DC to tell a Congressional committee about that profiteering.

In our hotel room that night, I broke out *Press On* and we took turns listening to songs on my Discman. Johnny and June's duet "The Far Side Banks of Jordan" visibly stirred my dad, and at song's end he said, "I wonder which one will go first. The other won't last long after that." A room service tray holding two plates relieved of pecan pie sat on the bed between us—I remember that detail because it was the last time I was alone with him. Three months after he walked me down the little white church's aisle, and just three days short of a new millennium, my fifty-seven-year-old father collapsed by the Christmas tree in our cottage and died of congestive heart failure.

I didn't get to say goodbye. I'd left the day before with my new husband to visit his family in Ohio, and when we arrived at the funeral home my mother looked like a lost little girl waiting by the window in a seafoam-green chair. Next to her was a blue Rubbermaid container holding everything she deemed necessary for the trip to bury her husband: a photograph of him taken at my wedding, a change of clothes for herself and two burial options for him, make-up, two six-packs of Coke, and *Press On*.

June won her Grammy for Best Traditional Folk Album two months later, but I couldn't listen to *Press On* again for a long time. The old adage that no two people grieve alike did not prepare me for how grief can decimate a family. Despite the gloomy periods and my escape, it was only after my father's death that I understood how tightly-wound the four of us were by shared worry, relief, courage, and even a sense of exceptionalism. I imagine we were like soldiers who go through combat together, and with my father's gravitational force suddenly removed, my mother, sister, and I each spun out with our own unique and mighty torque. The pathetic details of that narrative contribute to the estrangement with my mother, but sharing them would serve no universal purpose here and would read like a made-for-*Dateline* story complete with a convicted criminal who preys on widows, addiction-fueled misunderstandings, paranoias and betrayals, and desperate acting out by all three of us. The lesson is that we did not mourn well, together or apart. Multiple periods of resentment and silence between mother and daughters and between sisters ensued during the Bush forty-three years, but as I moved about with my husband, my sister got stuck at a dead-end and had two grandchildren for my mother to worry about and support.

A lifetime of wedges—disease, my retreat into books, my rejection of her faith, marital disappointments and resentments, perceived repudiation and abandonment, my sister's battles, and our inability to deal with my father's death—cracked up the good between us and it was easier for all of us to attach during this period to people with whom we did not share such complex and sordid history, so nothing got worked through. Denial, my mother used to say, got my father and her through a lot. I suppose that was our true family motto, and we three still tried to act like a family even after my mother's second marriage to a Beaver Islander with nine adult children who brought additional perspectives, drama, and wedges into the mix. The final break only came when history repeated itself.

The summer before the country elected Barack Obama, I was coming off several years of political book publishing and progressive activism projects, and utterly bone-weary. I found it hard to concentrate and felt depressed, but after eight years of George W. Bush, I knew a lot of people who felt that way. My back hurt and I was forty-two, so male doctors kept telling me to try yoga. Very sensitive to sound, I couldn't bear to listen to music most of the time. On Beaver Island (my husband and I also bought a summer house there, in part so I could work on my relationship with my mother), everyone remarked about how thin I looked. It seemed normal to lie in bed all day counting the logs in the wall and to only have the energy to eat once a day, usually at my mother's cottage where we'd developed a habit of watching Keith Olbermann and Rachel Maddow together. One night I bolted upright in bed after dreaming I heard my father's voice, for the first time since his death, calling "Jenny." The day after the election a doctor told me I was in kidney failure.

Being told my worst nightmare was my new reality literally warped past and present in my mind, left me hopeless about any future, and set a helter-skelter host of time bombs that exploded over the next weeks, months, and years. As my husband drove us down an island road in our seventy-two Land Cruiser that week, I could only think about the vehicle veering into a tree and then just started wailing. It was all just too much to bear, a childhood and adulthood plagued by this damn disease, and I didn't want to turn my husband into my caretaker. I pushed him away. I acted out. I wanted to just end it all. My mother and sister tried to rally around me, but I felt suffocated by all the pain between us, like we were all stuck in some circle of hell, sentenced to playing parts in a devastatingly cruel play for eternity—and that metaphor was actually the reality. I just couldn't look at them anymore, so I returned to our rented cottage in Sausalito, California, and registered for a transplant at the University of California, San Francisco.

Gradually, I got a spiritual grip by reading poetry and listening to a lot of Leonard Cohen. I also placed a photograph of June nestled against Johnny's chest on my bookshelf for some marital inspiration, and I could once again listen to *Press On*. My father had been dead nine years, but when I listened to June I could feel his presence. I don't mean in some woo-woo way, but five years after her own death, June's voice could still stir all the good memories from when I was a kid, and even more importantly, from our time working together on Dad's National Kidney Foundation program, so I could access all the seeds of advice and facts he'd planted, and little tricks he had for coping, which helped me tend to my care and my own mind.

Thousands of miles left room for more miscommunication and hurt feelings with my family and though we never spoke about it, I'm certain having to face another fight with kidney disease seemed grotesquely unbearable on their end, too. But along with my husband and a friend, my sister and her then-boyfriend (and father of her second child), Jimmy, got tested as potential donors for a transplant. Jimmy was a match and incredibly and generously stepped up to be my donor, so my journey with kidney disease would be only a blip compared to my father's. Five months after my diagnosis Jimmy's gift freed me from a life tethered to a dialysis machine—and *then* the bottom dropped out.

The full details here are again clouded by addiction-fueled paranoias and betrayals, but as Jimmy and I lay recovering from our surgeries, my sister broke up with him and decided to make accusations of child abuse in a misguided attempt to get sole custody of their son. One day my mother was thanking Jimmy for saving my life and the next she was caught up in my sister's scheme, and when I tried to convince her to not go along, she told me she would not risk being separated from her grandchildren—and "if you had children, you would understand that." That last bit was particularly cutting, because not only am I *her* child, but I had just learned I never got pregnant in my thirties because of the disease I'd inherited. Even though I would again be fertile, given my age and knowing I had a fifty-fifty chance of passing on the disease, there would be no children. Shortly after this, Jimmy asked my husband and me to testify on his behalf in a custody hearing. We did, and the judge ruled in favor of his petition for joint custody. My mother, sister, and I have not spoken since.

This is our Gordian knot of heartache.

Until deciding to map how June figures into my life, all of these twisted details had me so lost in my anger and hurt I could find no compassion for my mother and sister. I first set out to write a tidy piece about my love for June's voice because it is equated with some of my greatest happiness, and with pretty much the whole world I shared in celebrating the popular myth about the love between Johnny and June. After digging into the reality of that love and life, I am boundlessly inspired by the real woman's story and my heart is open wider. *Anchored in Love* showed me June not only had to deal with Johnny's continual addictions, but she saw her son and two daughters, Carlene Carter (from her first marriage to Carl Smith) and Rosie Nix Adams, struggle with alcohol and drugs, which also led to various estrangements. That they found roads to rapprochement before her death gives me hope and some courage to try to find a way back to my mother. I am a writer, and after five years of impasse, this is how it had to start for me.

Not all endings can be happy, I know. Some people stay lost. Carlene and John Carter got hold of their addictions, but just months after June and Johnny each passed, Rosie was found dead of carbon monoxide poisoning in an old bus littered with the remains of alcohol and drug use. And, as I alluded to earlier, I don't know if I'm in any way related to Rosie or her father Edwin Nix, because my dad was estranged from his parents and only sister for most of my life. I wish I had those old recordings of my dad and his mother from the fifties. He never told me what caused that final break, but what kept them apart for thirty years had to be Gordian as well, and I'm certain now that his leaving home for

Michigan and the pressures caused by disease both came into play. History repeats. "The past is never dead," William Faulkner wrote in *Requiem for a Nun*. "It's not even past."

My hope is that this story with my mother will end like an old folk song, that our circle will be unbroken, by and by. I'm grateful for how all this messy and true Cash and Nix love helped me divine my compassion and memories of my mother's loveliness and strength again, all because one night long ago a woman in a sparkling green dress captured a little girl's fancy. And what I love most about June's example at this stage of my life is how she just kept pressing on through those twenty years of marital and family turmoil, and through all her doubts about her talent when she was out of fashion and lost in Johnny's shadow. My favorite song on *Press On* is the wistful "I Used to Be Somebody" written at a moment when she felt like her best days were behind her. Instead, June won that first solo Grammy at age seventy, kept working right up to the end and then won two more Grammys posthumously for "Wildwood Flower." I'm listening to it now…on my computer. Message received, June!

I picked up the ukulele recently. My husband is playing the guitar again after a long while. We want to learn some old Carter songs and all the Johnny and June duets, and have some fun playing together.

We decided it's essential.

Jesus Freaks, Woo Woo Girls, Faeries, and Björk

Margaret Wappler

Yasmin and I surrounded Arlen in the elevator at the University of Missouri, where we were all freshmen. Before she even opened her mouth, her chin trembled.

"Let's see it," I said.

Slowly Arlen stuck out her tongue: in the middle, a silver spike punctuated by a ball, like an exclamation point stabbed upside down through the muscle that disappeared down her throat. Her tastebuds were a shocked pale pink.

"You did it!" We cheered. "Piercing club!"

"Did it hurt?" I asked, having recently gotten a hot needle driven through my left nostril.

"No," she said, clearly in so much pain she couldn't say much more. A weak smile fluttered across her lips. Yasmin and I tried to be happy for her but her eyes were just so sad and spooked. She'd attempted to do something wild and rebellious but it had scared the shit out of her.

From that point forward, Arlen was a ghostly figure around the dorms. She shuffled back and forth to class but not much else. Pretty soon, Yasmin told me that Arlen had left school to return to her small Missouri town. Nothing too unusual about a freshman fleeing for home but more unusual were the details: she had suddenly gone hardcore Christian. As in evangelical, practically flinging holy water on anyone she saw, and she wanted nothing to do with us heathens.

As the daughter of an Episcopalian minister, nothing fascinates me more than when people "like me" turn full-tilt believer. This isn't to say that I don't have some degree of belief in some kind of higher power; I *think* that I do (long story, obviously) but embracing Jesus—rabidly and feverishly, without shades or doubt—has always struck me as akin to turning into a zombie. I understand what it means to have a constructive, nuanced relationship with what or whom some call Christ because I saw my Dad have that—but I will never understand the kind of belief that hijacks a personality.

In figuring out her transformation, I kept returning to the grandest evidence of Arlen's passions: Like me, she adored Björk Guðmundsdóttir, the Icelandic singer/songwriter whose music existed somewhere in the hinterlands between electronica, surrealism, and the feral animal kingdom. Pictures of the singer in fuzzy mohair and twisty mini-buns adorned Arlen's dorm room. Every time I'd ever been in there, the leonine growls and dive-bombing Nordic vocals of Björk had filled the space like there was one extra girl in there, an especially unhinged and untamed one. But what did this fascination really tell me about Arlen? It's not like all Björk fans become religious fanatics.

I still don't really know, twenty years later. But Arlen, in her own way, gave me permission to escape, too. Shortly after she left, I high-tailed it back to Chicago, my hometown that promised all the things that Missouri did not: a chance to be an artist, specifically a writer who wanted to draw inspiration from the city. After I left Missouri, I lost touch with ninety-five percent of the people I went to school with and never heard about Arlen again.

Sometimes when I hear Björk, Arlen comes back to me as that same girl, surely a temporary incarnation of herself. I think about the identities we try on in a life, only to shrug them off a few months later. Identity, I think, might be a lunar beast that waxes and wanes, or a rain lily that blooms from the right, specific circumstances. Lucky are the people who figure out the correct soil for themselves.

With her 2011 multimedia collection, *Biophilia*, Björk finally became the conceptual artist she'd been heading toward for years, creating songs in conjunction with iPad apps and installations, all informed by her theories on nature. To be honest, *Biophilia*, the album, isn't my favorite collection of songs, but the ambition of the project excited me. Björk is always a reminder to be true to ourselves no matter how weird, savage, or abstract anyone else might find it.

***

"THERE'S DEFINITELY, DEFINITELY, DEFINITELY no logic to human behavior," Björk sings on the opening track to her 1993 album, *Debut*. She simultaneously crashes together and enunciates each syllable of the word "definitely" in a way that perfectly encapsulates our human capacity for specificity and madness in the same breath. Björk's vocal performance in "Human Behavior" is particularly outstanding, though not by far her most Olympian. But it's a playbook of all the Björk tricks: throaty roars, belted high notes, breathy conversational singing in the alto range.

A lot of descriptors are associated with Björk, which, the older she gets, the more she throws off and simultaneously deepens; nymph, pixie, faerie. The fact that she came from Iceland, a popular child singer turned Reykjavík punk with the Sugarcubes (the band she shared with her then-husband Thor Eldon), played to Americans as fetchingly exotic. Surely Björk was some kind of otherworldly creature birthed from the sparkly ashes of one of Iceland's many tremendous and multi-syllabic volcanoes.

But what exactly does it mean to call someone a pixie, besides small, cute, and potentially dismissible? Like slut, cunt, or fag, maybe it's time to reclaim the word; in this case, by examining the powerful nucleus at its center.

In Brian Froud's book, *Good Faeries/Bad Faeries*, he writes that faeries, pixies, et al, have been here "before the Age of Reason and they are all still here among us now. It is wise to remember that we deny the existence of faeries at our peril—for they have a disconcerting habit of breaking into our closed worldview, demanding our full attention in subversive and startling ways." Froud, by the way, was the costume and conceptual designer for *Labyrinth,* Jim Henson's 1986 cult fantasia, so you know this man doesn't come to the idea of faeries lightly. He credits them with corresponding to "both mythic patterns and to human thought," to existing "in both the outer world of nature and the inner world of the mind." Is it possible then to call Björk a faerie and not have it be a dismissive tag, but an acknowledgment of her ability to demand our attention in subversive and startling ways?

Throughout his book, Froud goes on to describe a whole host of faeries, most taken from ancient European mythology but also some new ones to reflect the times—the credit card faerie, for instance, hides out in the swipe machine to tinker with your charges. And though he separates the book between "good" and "bad," Froud's quick to point out that good ones can wreak turmoil and the bad ones can ultimately steer you to the better path. "Faeries," he writes, "lead us astray to show us the way."

Arlen used to sit cross-legged on her bed, her fists in balls as Björk's voice would rattle through the room. Her eyes would flash open and she'd say with maniacal fixation: "Isn't she great? I fucking love her!" After Arlen left, I really wanted to know: Did Believer Arlen still love Björk, or had she cast her aside to follow Christ? Which faerie—Jesus or Björk—had led her astray?

***

IF FAERIES ARE INDEED badass merrymakers and monkey wrenches to the machine, then that's what I wanted to be, even if I would've shuddered at the term faerie at age eighteen. Arlen wanted the same magic for her life, and together we explored weed, fashion, and music, hoping they'd be mirrors reflecting back our true selves. But the image that bounced back always seemed hopelessly contrived, even if neither of us ever said so aloud.

Once, in her room, I caught a glimpse of her future self when the topic of mega-churches came up.

"Those places freak me out," I said while slouching against her bed. "Just thousands and thousands of dumb sheep bleating the same prayers without even listening to the words out of their mouths."

She was uncharacteristically quiet—not offering her staccato laugh that, when loud enough, ricocheted off the concrete walls. Per usual, Björk's *Debut* played in the background.

"How can you say that?" she asked. "Wasn't your Dad a minister?"

"Yeah, but not *that* kind."

"I've been to those churches before," she said. "They're powerful."

"Powerfully crazy," I said.

"Don't you ever pray?"

I didn't know how to answer that. Did silently begging some

foggy notion of a deity for a big, cool, wild life while staring at my dorm room ceiling count as prayer?

We were simultaneously trying to shame each other and pin each other close. To define your friend is to define yourself. If Arlen was cynical about religion like I was, then I was correct in my harsh judgment. If I was open-minded like Arlen wanted me to be, then she'd be validated in her secret interest. At the moment, neither of us was giving the other what she wanted.

Tension hardened around us. Until "There's More to Life Than This" came to the rescue. We'd talked about this song before—I caught Arlen's eye and smiled.

Recorded in the ladies room at London's Milk Bar, Björk sounds more like a prankster than ever. At one point, when she seems to head into some other quieter part of the club, she leans in and whisper-squeak-sings some squirrelly little bit about stealing a boat and sneaking off to an island. A moment later, Björk's in the thick of the party again, the door closing behind her, an irrepressible house beat fusing with laughter. The whole song sounds like a secret she's telling you while the inanities of life rage on.

***

BJÖRK HAS ALWAYS EMBODIED a particularly tonic blend of feral and enlightened, vulnerable and fierce, violent, and demure. Seemingly, those qualities are all at odds, but Björk creates with the bone-deep knowledge that these qualities are all characteristics on the same human continuum. To be enlightened is to value the wild in our nature; fierceness is often an expression of vulnerability, and violence erupts from a lifetime of being demure.

Another way to think about her, from Froud: "Faeries are resistant to all definitions." Björk zooms around on the continuum, radiating out in polarities, unconcerned about seeming contradictions because she knows that's all we really are. Identity is an endless sine wave of contradictions.

One of Björk's prime modes of communication is rupture. Björk erupts not only in her music—her cover of the forties show tune "It's Oh So Quiet" is bipolar theatrics that capture the rushes and panic of love—but she's erupted in real life, too. Most infamously in 1996 at a Thailand airport, where Björk bashed at a British journalist, Julie Kaufman, who greeted her and her nine-year-old son Sindri with the incendiary words, "Welcome to Bangkok." The whole clash, available on YouTube (of course), lasts about ten seconds. Kaufman suffers Björk's swipes with the politely aghast cries of "ouch" and "oh my god," until Björk's lighting designer, Paul Normandale, pulls her off.

A similar incident occurred in 2008 when Glenn Jeffrey, a New Zealand photographer, snapped some photos of Björk's arrival at the Auckland airport, only to find the back of his shirt clawed off a few minutes later by his furious subject.

In both cases, Björk was quick to apologize and neither journalist pressed charges.

I don't mention these temperamental episodes to paint Björk as a raging imp (as some headlines joyously did). In fact, just the opposite. Sometimes the only sane response to fame is for those on display behind the glass to occasionally snap and scratch at our protuberant noses. Another way to say this: Björk may be crazy but she gives as good as she gets.

Flashes of anger are all over Björk's music, though we know from her performance in Lars Von Trier's *Dancer in the Dark* that she can also play downtrodden and passive. Although rage surely factored into that performance, too: the Icelandic untrained actress and the Danish director fought bitterly throughout the shoot, with Björk accusing him of psychological annihilation. That dead swan dress that she wore to the Oscars in 2001 might've represented her slain self. Fortunately, she rose again to claim the Best Actress Award at Cannes that year, though she swore off acting forever. The dress, meanwhile, was granted eternal life by appearing on the cover of her album *Vespertine*.

In perhaps her most testy warning call on record, she opens *Post* with the crashing tectonics of "Army of Me," her voice sounding simultaneously thrashed and menacing. "Army of Me" and the rest of *Post* was a chance, Björk told *Q Magazine,* to cast aside the niceties of *Debut* and show the audience her true ferocity.

One of Björk's most deft skills is to capture not only the marquee emotions of rage or "big-time sensuality," but the allure of the nebulous middle range as well. "Possibly Maybe" is a flower opening in the dark, reveling in the potentials of love while acknowledging that life could veer any which way: "Who knows what's going to happen?" Björk belts. "Lottery, or car crash, or you join a cult." In the video, shot by her ex-boyfriend Stéphane Sednaoui, she appears as a goddess, floating out from a numinous light-streaked background. Clearly she could steer your life any which way, for good or for bad, and it might be hard to tell which one at first. "I'll heal you," she sings in "All Neon Like," "with a razor-blade."

***

ONCE WHEN I WAS still at Missouri, and hadn't made up my mind to leave yet, I crashed in my bed for three days straight, crying and only getting up to use the bathroom and eat the littlest amount that would keep me from passing out. (So much for the "freshman fifteen;" I turned scary thin that semester.) The only person who witnessed this breakdown was my roommate Belinda, an unabashed fantasy nerd. On the corkboard above her bed: a series of drawings of fairies flitting about wet rocks and foamy sea. All over her desk: geodes, crystals, and Wicca texts. Sometimes we played Magic: The Gathering on the cheap rug in our room but for the most part, we didn't really hang out.

But on those few miserable days, when I couldn't pretend anymore that I was having a good time, when I was enraged by so many things, like my mother barely ever calling to check in, Belinda was actively worried about me. "Can I get you anything?" she asked, as I huddled under a blanket, facing my own corkboard of photos with friends and drawings I'd done in high school. I finally agreed to a cafeteria sandwich or some other such protein loaf. As I ate it, Belinda said, "I think the fan is haunted."

I broke into sobs all over again.

"Don't worry," she said. "We'll do a spell on it. It's just possessed by something—maybe the same thing that's making you so upset."

I didn't have the wherewithal to tell her that the fan wasn't haunted; wind just blew through it from time to time and so the propellers spun, even when it wasn't plugged in. Instead, I quietly listened as Belinda read off some healing prayer for the fan. I let it comfort me, this ridiculous chant. At least somebody around me believed in something. At least somebody around me was being totally herself, Middle Earth psalms and all. Had I embraced anything even remotely so authentic in the last four months? The answer was clear. It was time to go home.

***

MY TIME AT MISSOURI can reemerge at the oddest moments, like when I'm surrounded by huge crowds at a music festival. Fatigued from the heat and the overwhelming scene at Coachella, which I was covering for the *Los Angeles Times* in 2007, I was primed for some kind of rapturous experience.

Guided by the clatter of *Volta's* "Earth Intruders," which Björk wrote after a dream where a "tsunami" of "poverty-stricken people" wiped out the White House, I moved toward her stage from the farthest point away on the acres-deep grassy field. I was a sweat-stained, dust-cloaked pilgrim, exhausted and wired, stepping over crushed water bottles and beached bodies to get closer, all of us finally reprieved from the punishing desert sun that ruled the days. In the dark, we were a mass of familiar and unknown, strangers united by one common preference in an infinite range of them.

Once I got close enough, the full regalia of Björk's headlining presentation was revealed: picture *Game of Thrones* meets some sort of advanced futuristic matriarchal society—tribal flags, an all-female choir, and Björk in a skeleton dress with rainbow tatters. I was home.

Even after years of listening to Björk, especially submerging myself into *Homogenic* so much that now when I play it, I anticipate every song with a near-primordial certainty, I'd never seen her live. I wasn't fully prepared for the emotion that closed over my scalp, for the electric wire that flared through me when I recognized some essence of myself on the stage. Some dark, brilliant jewel had been struck with light. I saw something I could relate to, and aspire to, in this person who tirelessly explores the hidden places—in her psyche and in the natural world. She revels in those discoveries no matter what the consequences. No matter who approves or gets it.

As I stood in the night desert, I thought about Arlen. She could've been there—rabid believer or not. If she still did believe, I hoped for her sake that she was flexible enough to allow this old obsession. The crowd seemed like such a flowing multiplicity that anyone could've been there: my old roommate Belinda in a witchy velvet cape; my former self who went by the nickname Maggie exclusively for that semester, despite having never done that before. Had I really fled that person, or even meant to? Had I become the person I wanted to be when I left? Possibly, maybe.

I looked around at the crowd—a collection of whites of the eyes, day-glo bracelets, hands reaching toward the sky at a chorus they liked, and then stroking back down again by their side. On stage, Björk shape-shifted into several people I knew—the calculated "Hunter," the sensualist in "Pagan Poetry," the morbid dreamer in "Hyperballad."

The other parts of Björk were there, too: animal, musicologist, faerie, scientist, deity, tech fetishist, and whacked-out mysterion. The thrill of the show was in knowing that any one of these identities could come out to play—or scare us.

Why Do Fools Fall In Love?

Kim Morgan

"*Baby do you know what you did today? Baby do you know what you took away? You took the blue out of the sky. My whole life changed when you said goodbye. And I keep cryin'…cryin'… I wish I never saw the sunshine. I wish I never saw the sunshine. 'Cause if I never saw the sunshine baby. Then maybe…I wouldn't mind the rain.*"

A summer night. The door was open. Not my house. I didn't care. I walked in. You were asleep. You looked so stupidly handsome. Did you ever not? I'll take care of that. I woke you up with a two-by-four to the head. In my one moment of homicidal rage, I missed. Blessedly. I was nuts. But at that moment, you were lucky, you lousy, cheating son of a bitch. I can handle the one. I can take the two, the three. But the countless others…those girls? I wasn't mad at *them*. I was mad at *you*. Oh, was I mad. And heartbroken.

You ran down the stairs. You called me crazy. "Get that bitch out of here," you yelled to the frightened girlfriend of your new roommate. (I didn't blame you for saying that, even at that moment.)

I broke your records. *I broke your records.* I would never break a record. I ran out of the door.

I drove home, screaming…screaming and crying. Tears not just running down my cheeks, but ridiculous Niagara Falls tears. The Horseshoe and the American Falls all at once, drenching my tank top on a hot summer night, a night when I should feel pretty and happy and young and in love. Driving MY CAR, ASSHOLE. MY CAR. You don't get this car. I bought this car. This beautiful black car that you loved driving around. I don't care if you put a CD player in this beautiful black car for my birthday, complete with a ribbon and some CDs—T-Rex and Jackie Wilson, I believe. (God, I loved you so much back then. Oh, I could listen to whatever I wanted. You were such a great boyfriend then.) Now, this oppressive, wounding, maddeningly hot night I hit play and then…

Bah-bah-Bah-BUMP, Bah-bah-Bah-BUMP…

Oh god, *No.* Not Ronnie. Not The Ronettes. Not now. Not the song that reminds me of the first time I saw you. When I knew it. When I knew I was in love. Instantly.

But of course, Ronnie. Ronnie is perfect. She knows how this feels. She can't possibly sing like that without knowing how this feels. I somehow think she knew how I felt before I was even born and met this man and all of this shit happened. She just knew. The tears blinded my eyes and I had to pull the car over before I crashed into a streetlamp. Goddammit, Ronnie Spector. I *need* and *don't* need you right now. And Phil. I don't need Phil. Or perhaps I do… He's a reminder. Run! Keep driving. Far, far away. Don't drive back. You should have run away sooner before the crazy set in like a shrunken baby in formaldehyde. Get the fuck out of this crazy.

Crazy. I met him and he was already taken. I wasn't really sure. I couldn't have him. I knew he liked me; I could see it. But

I met him for a full day—then, poof! He was gone. I didn't even remember his name. I hoped to bump into him. The city wasn't that large. I thought I saw him buying beer at the 7-Eleven but it was some other guy. I drove past his apartment a few times, feeling a little creepy, hoping he might just happen to walk out. No other man was on my mind. He didn't know it then. And, smitten me, I didn't know he was feeling the same thing. "Oh, since the day I met you. I have been waiting for you. I will adore you, for eternity…" And then, there he was.

You came into the store where I worked. We turned around, you intended to meet me again, me swerving to shelve a title, and our eyes locked. THERE. INSTANT. No questions. You strode down the aisle all cool and handsome and who the hell IS this guy? You asked me out on a date. No email. No social media. No phone call. In person. I'll never forget you walking toward me. That serious face I didn't know was actually nervous, that determined and well-postured gait, looking exactly like Ray Liotta in *Goodfellas* before he beats the shit out of that guy hassling Karen. Who the hell looks like that? You did.

Of course I said yes instantly. We exchanged numbers. We'd go to a movie. Tomorrow night. Dear god, tomorrow night. How romantic. I don't even know this guy. I drove home in that exalted state of stupid bliss. What song was I listening to on that happy drive home? Jesus Christ, Ronnie Spector…what were you doing to me? I was listening to "Be My Baby." How mystical it sounded then. Wrapped in this magical wonder of thrill and fear. My mind running and rushing and I was already falling hard and fast and tumbling down that dark well of beautiful insanity. I'd never fallen in love at first sight—I got it. "The night we met I knew I needed you so…"

It made me happy. It made me terrified. It made me cry. But it also made me think, deep down *something is not right*. And *this will never last.* And to be fair to him, *this will be my fault, too.* And *he will feel terrible about a few things.* And *I'm no angel in this story.*

It lasted. Too long. And then it was over.

Don't worry, Ronnie…it happened again with another, that whole "When I Saw You" business. For the last time. I hope to god for the last fucking time.

(But that's *my* fault. It's not fair dragging you into all of this, Ronnie.)

It's not your fault you were born with that pleading, sassy, sexy voice. A strong yet vulnerable voice of such immense vibrato that men fell in love with you even before realizing that you were (and are) gorgeous. Gorgeous, and real, and sexy in that *And God Created Woman* way. You even look a bit like Brigitte Bardot with those heavy-lidded, lined eyes and sensuous lips. You said yourself that you wanted to be the "Marilyn Monroe of East Harlem." You got it, Ronnie. I think of John Lennon taking a look at you, the American exotic, those perfectly arched eyes and mini dresses and piled up hair and lush maw, the product of a Cherokee Indian/African American mother and a white father. What was he thinking? His mind and libido exploding: "Who moves and sounds and looks like that?" Ronnie did. You were not a Supreme, you were not a Crystal, you were the tough girl from East Harlem who was setting the style. But you weren't so tough. No one is.

That "Whoa, oh, whoa! Oh, oh, oh, oh, oh…" It could have been a gimmick. It wasn't. It was your heart, and perhaps, your mixture of wisdom and naïveté. Your fun-loving, flirtatious stage persona commingling with all that family sadness and future torment and all that you had witnessed in your life already. So when you sing with your sister, Estelle, and your cousin, Nedra, and with Phil's symphonic fortress, rooted in his brilliance and psychosis of sound and sadness—a pain planted in the past. Not just "Be My Baby," but the entire Ronettes output feels mythic and lost in a mysterious reverie, even as Ronnie often sings of her dreams, her dreams for a loving future. (It's not a surprise that many of the tracks were recorded and unreleased after Phil sealed these little symphonies in a vault for years.)

The songs are swooningly romantic and hopeful, they're lonely and full of young heartbreak, but they are dysfunctional (aren't all love songs?) and beyond that, they move past the term timeless. It's *Mean Streets:* Harvey Keitel laying his head on the pillow before those super-eight images flicker through his mind to…"Be My Baby." Memories. An unknown future. A song from the past, permanently etched in his brain. Keitel's *Mean Streets* is 1973. Ronnie's career was already a collection of images by then, as she drank and watched Bette Davis movies and walked around the mansion, wondering if she'd ever sing again.

I wasn't there, so I can't be sure. But listening today, your songs seem to feel like a remembrance. Like life speeding up so fast, you have to listen to the song over and over again before it is gone…to keep it in your current. But you never forget it. Ever.

Perhaps I should thank your ex-husband. That beautiful lunatic and convicted murderer. "To Know Him is to Love Him?" What a lovely sentiment—and song. The number-one hit written by Phil Spector for his one and only group, The Teddy Bears, in 1958. A song named for the words on his father's gravestone after Phil's dad committed suicide when Phil was just nine years old. There are murder ballads, but Spector, ever the innovator, created a suicide ballad. (Where's Nick Cave on this potential cover?) Love equals death. But love must live on. He found it with The Crystals, with Darlene Love, with The Righteous Brothers, but to me, he captured it most powerfully with Ronnie's voice. That innocent but knowing voice must have harkened back to something buried deeply within that traumatized kid. I imagine Ronnie's voice was something he'd dreamt about as a boy, drowning out his strange overbearing mother and his mentally ill sister. Life! And sex. Look at all that sex. To hear Ronnie was to feel alive and in the moment and sexy and time waits for no one…so one must hold on to that life. Preserve that voice forever. Phil would take that life, enclose it in that famed Wall of Sound, narrowing in on his Rapunzel, soon to be trapped in that castle. It began as it ended. William Faulkner put it best: "The past is never dead. It's not even past."

Bah-bah-bah-BUMP…

But that's not the song Ronnie (then, twenty-year-old Veronica Bennett) sang that stopped Phil Spector's heart. This was (sing along):

> *Why do birds sing so gay? And lovers await the break of day?*
> *Why do they fall in love?*

After un-impressing him with "When The Red, Red Robin Comes Bob, Bob, Bobbin' Along," Ronnie and the Ronettes belted out the song that inspired her most. Frankie Lymon's ode to the stupidity of love. Little Frankie Lymon. So wise singing a song that's often all so true. And embracing the recklessness. You're never too old or too young for that.

At that very moment, for Phil, this was the girl. This was the voice. This was the look. He knew. Tom Wolfe, who called Spector the "bona-fide Genius of Teen," who exalted the producer as a "flowering genius," comparing him to Emperor Commodus, Benvenuto Cellini, the Earl of Chesterfield, Dante Gabriel Rossetti, and, for god's sake, Thomas Jefferson. That eccentric, tortured virtuoso had found his next muse. And wife.

> *Why do fools fall in love?*

Good question, Frankie Lymon. So let's go back, for Ronnie fans should thank not Phil Spector, but Frankie Lymon for the creation of The Ronettes. As Ronnie wrote in her memoir, "A lot of entertainers can't, or won't, tell you where they got their style from. But I know exactly where I got my voice. Frankie Lymon. If he hadn't made a record called 'Why Do Fools Falls in Love?,' I wouldn't be sitting here writing this today." Ronnie was just twelve years old and she'd swoon over Frankie Lymon: "With his innocent voice and perfect diction—my hands got all sweaty, my toes curled up, and I climbed right under that old box radio, trying to get as close to that sound as I could. I pressed my head into the speaker until I got Frankie going right through my brain."

What a glorious, insane sensation. Wanting to feel a singer go right through your brain. What a vision of little Ronnie. And what dreams she harbored of that innocent diction-perfect voice. But her dream image of little Frankie, only thirteen when he sang that song—*Thirteen!* How does a thirteen-year-old sing with any knowledge about such things?—collided abruptly with reality when she finally met him. He dropped by the young teenager's house. Ronnie was just thirteen and excited to meet her idol. Frankie Lymon! She was aghast. She couldn't believe he was only fourteen years old. He was liquored up. Full of himself. Sleazy. When he told her she was beautiful and leaned in for a kiss she smelled alcohol on his breath, which, as she wrote, "reminded me of my father." Ronnie yearned for him to leave but, as a confused thirteen-year old, wasn't sure just how to get him out of there. So she locked herself in the bathroom for a full hour until he left. A portent of her wedding night with Phil, when she slept on the bathroom floor with her mother. To repeat for emphasis: *Ronnie slept on the bathroom floor with her mother on her wedding night.* Phil screaming and hollering outside the locked door, calling her a bitch only interested in his money. "Why?" wailed Ronnie. "Why did you marry me?" "Because I'm a romantic! A hopeless fucking romantic," Phil screamed.

In the case of Ronnie, Frankie was right. Love is a losing game. But he was a cocky little kid, a sad casualty with a heavenly voice. He died of a heroin overdose at age twenty-five. As we all know, Phil's still very much alive.

I hear the joyous "Why Don't They Let Us Fall in Love?" and I think of Ronnie, Nedra, and Estelle, the hottest teenagers in East Harlem, hearing it, too, all their dreams of dancing at the Peppermint Lounge coming so true that they must have felt such pride. And they should have. Yes, the production is inspired. But those young women…and Ronnie! Your voice makes my heart swell so much I almost feel hopeless. Hopelessly in love with the one I love, hopelessly in love with you, hopelessly in love with love. I believe John Lennon fell in love with you. Bruce Springsteen fell in love with you. Joey Ramone fell in love with you. Billy Joel, Steven Van Zandt, The Raveonettes…it wasn't just Phil.

But Phil got your voice. He captured it. And he pressed his butterfly in his shuttered up mansion, making you drive a car with an inflatable Phil in the passenger seat (so no one would think you were without him). He ruled. Take Phil and your last real single, "You Came, You Saw, You Conquered," released a month later under *The Ronettes Featuring the Voice of Veronica*. What a ridiculously perfect title. And lyrics: "My enemy was warm desire. You shot me down with lips of fire. I ran for cover straight into your arms. Oh baby. Footloose and fancy-free, nobody could get a hold of me. Then you kissed me tenderly and baby. Ooo you came, you saw, you conquered all the love in me."

"A hopeless fucking romantic!" Phil screaming. Screaming. Maybe crying? Maybe Phil was and is. That's not a popular sentiment to anyone who knows the history of the man, his relationship with Ronnie, whose career was shut away in that demented fortress, or his troubled working relationship with The Ramones or Lennon or Leonard Cohen or Dion with his brilliant dirge "Born to Be With

You" (and Phil was right on that album—it's exquisite—just as he was right about Tina Turner's "River Deep Mountain High" one of the most exalted, God-like odes of love ever recorded). And then, of course, all that went down with tragic Lana Clarkson.

If any of those signs were present in the beginning, how could Ronnie marry that guy? Hopeless fucking romantics. I don't believe Ronnie was simply careerist. I think she fell in love with that man. We fall in love with the wrong people. I have, to my chagrin, had frequent shame- and rage-filled, tear-soaked drives away from those who conquer and catch with those "sweet ties of love that bind."

Bruce Springsteen howled it out to everyone in his Spector-inspired hit, "Hungry Heart," a song he wrote for Joey Ramone but realized it was too good to give away. He should have written it for Ronnie. It's not just his "Ho-ho-ungary-heart" phrasing that sounds like Ronnie; the entire song reminds me of Ronnie. Ronnie relating to the world. Or Ronnie *trying* to relate to the world. Not Ronnie locking herself in the bathroom, or getting locked in closets, or drinking herself into a stupor before sullenly watching Phil's obsessive viewing of *Citizen Kane* for the millionth fucking time. No. Ronnie trying to climb into that radio to press Frankie Lymon into her brain. Little Ronnie practicing routines in the living room with her sister and cousin. Ronnie first signing with Colpix as a teenager in 1961. Ronnie running around with The Beatles and the Rolling Stones. Ronnie putting her eye makeup on and girl-talking with Cher in Spector's studio. Ronnie wanting to be loved.

I sometimes fantasize that Bruce is that prince in the story, never mind the time frame doesn't match up—singing "Hungry Heart" outside the princess's castle, saving her from the evil witch, and riding her off into the healthy, democratic pain of love. But who am I kidding? That's a fairy tale. And an unhealthy one. But love ain't healthy. Not the kind Ronnie sings about. Not the kind Phil produced.

Perhaps that's both hopelessly romantic and cynical to believe. In Mick Brown's *Tearing Down the Wall of Sound,* Atlantic Records producer Jerry Wexler, who respected Spector's hits, said he hated Phil's sound. He called it a "muted roar." Oh, but that's why I love it so. That muted roar. That's love, and anger, and madness, and that *feels so damn good* sometimes. Ronnie's voice both cut through, and merged, and awakened that muted roar.

Ronnie survived Phil. She's still singing. She's still beautiful. She's still Ronnie. She still inspires. She's probably brutally real and a little delusional. She's lived through hell and loved through hell. Love songs are delusional. Not all, but most. And most of love is, too. One way or another, everything is going to end. Love, friendships, life. But the music, the memories remain. Like my stupid self, charging into that house when I knew damn well it was ending anyway. Like Ronnie escaping Phil in her bare feet. Like Harvey Keitel resting his head on that pillow. It all becomes a visual story. For some, like me, the pain fades and it all starts to make sense and everything and everyone is humanized. Ronnie's relationship with Phil was too inexplicably agonizing to compare to most love-gone-wrong stories. But it all becomes mythic. Ronnie helped create one of the greatest pop songs of all time, "Be My Baby," out of all that madness. And remember, it started with love.

To me, it's okay to love the delusion. We know that delusion and darkness are always creeping around the corner. And if we feel it in music, we can't stop listening to it. We turn into "Be My Baby"-obsessive Brian Wilson, who said the song "was like having your mind revamped." Like falling hard for someone, it's mysterious, and wonderful, and even a little twisted. We should pay attention to those feelings; we should heed the warning of the men at the soundboard, and then choose to ignore them. Otherwise, what's the damn point? Even when we *just know.* Like when we pray to God. We know it's not *really* gonna work. As Martin Scorsese speaks for Harvey Keitel in *Mean Streets,* "You don't make up for your sins in the church, you do it in the streets. You do it at home. The rest is bullshit and you know it." It is. But even Scorsese knew this, and so did Ronnie: What do we go to sleep to at night? What thrills us in our happiest highs, what connects us to our past joy and present melancholy and haunts our dreams? "The night we met I knew I needed you so. And if I ever had the chance I'd never let you go."

Strange Angel

Isabella Alimonti

"**G**ood evening. This is your captain."
We are about to hear Laurie Anderson. "O Superman." Please lie down in a comfortable position. Close your eyes. Listen.

I WANTED YOU. AND I WAS LOOKING FOR YOU.

As a music listener, my method is a little mad. When I fall in love with a song, I have to hear it on repeat. The same song, over, and over, and over. For hours. For days. It's only when the obsession calms that I can begin to listen to it like the moderate person I will never be. For this reason, each of my favorite songs is bound in my mind to a specific period of life, though most follow me through others. Cat Power's "The Moon" means summer nights driving alone around my no-longer-home hometown; Slow Club's "Two Cousins" means delirious study breaks, autumn 2011, with my friend Stevie; Edward Sharpe and the Magnetic Zeros' "40 Day Dream" means high school.

"O Superman" occupied my second, and second-to-last,

semester of college at the University of Southern California. I feel I have to admit how I first heard it—in a movie trailer for an eccentric French drama about a young couple coping with cancer in their infant son. I have found some of my favorite music through accidents like this, though I'm embarrassed to say so—there must be a cooler way. The movie trailer opened with this intoxicating *hah hah hah hah hah hah* that made me want to hear more of it. Because I didn't (and still don't) know how to spell *hah hah hah hah hah* properly, in letters that truly capture the essence of the sound, I replayed that trailer several times to listen for bits of lyric, buried in French dialogue, to fill my Google search. Then I found it, and there was YouTube, there was *hah hah hah hah hah* over an image of a full moon, then there was Laurie in an all-black suit, singing and making shadow puppets in the spotlight I had mistaken for the moon, precise and alluring in her motion and sound.

I had already spent a good deal of time that year lying down with my eyes closed, in the deep fatigue of a depression exacerbated by my immediate realization, as I began life on campus, that I'd chosen the wrong place. So it happened that on the third or fourth push of the play button, I plunged back into my standard position—legs still crossed as I'd been sitting pretzel-style, shoulders tucked beneath me in hopes of easing the pain in my back and neck—to experience "O Superman" as I would always hence instruct my friends to do so. I felt the song's full impact, all its intricacies and layers of sound, like standing before some massive painting or landscape so overwhelming that all you can do is breathe, *Whoa.* I let it wash over me, over and over and over.

BEISPIELE PARANORMALER TONBANDSTIMMEN.

Hah hah hah hah hah hah hah hah. This sound astounds me. It starts out as a human voice and for eight minutes and twenty-five seconds never ceases, never changes, though by the end of the song it seems mechanical. Like children repeating an ordinary word again and again until it sounds like nonsense: table, table, table, table, table, table, table, table.

With *hah* Laurie throws down the first element of a masterful collage. The best word I can come up with to describe how she builds this world in voice, instruments, and electronics is mastery— ignorant as I am of the technology, I know all the more when I am witnessing the work of an expert. She piles sounds upon each other and then whittles them down for a trajectory that's like the topography of a mountainous region. When I call it a song I use the term loosely; "O Superman" waxes and wanes with the magnetic force I've more often experienced being engulfed in a film or a piece of performance art. And this makes sense—I can't even read about the breadth of Laurie Anderson's accomplishments across media without feeling that I'm as close as I can get to the mythical figure called "Artist." Only a fragment of the song's effect depends upon an intelligible lyric, but, as with all the best stories, you lose yourself in it. You don't even notice as Mother's voice on the answering machine gradually becomes more synthetic, seamlessly transforming into the voice of "the hand that takes."

In the final ten seconds of "O Superman," Laurie brings us back to the beginning, to the singular simplicity of *hah hah hah hah hah*. If I turn the volume up loud enough here, its pulse almost drowns out the beat of my heart.

THIS IS THE TIME. AND THIS IS THE RECORD OF THE TIME.

I couldn't have known then that I was in what would be my only year of the real college experience, oscillating from dorm room to dining hall and squeaking with every shower-shoe-clad step upon that speckled industrial carpeting designed to hide filth. I think that, overall, I made decent use of this interlude. During my first week there, an ill-timed shower and a fire alarm forced me out onto the quad wearing nothing but a towel (I made some new acquaintances that day). I went to portions of two football games, which equaled one football game more than zero. I tore my leggings jumping a fence to escape a party invaded by campus cops. (As it turned out, this was unnecessary—those security officers wouldn't do anything but tell you to go home. But vodka and the spirit of rebellion made it seem necessary, and so it was done).

But there were many dark and lonely moments also, and in those I suffered like only a heartbroken teenager can. When I sent out my college applications at age seventeen, with the definite intention of getting as far from home as possible, I didn't anticipate the difficulties of relocating to the opposite side of the country. When most people move to LA they picture an endless sunset on Venice Beach; once there, I wound up much further from water than any place I've lived in New York. I was out of my element, and I felt it acutely. The morning light in LA has this harshness to it, which I suspect is some effect of the sun's rays bouncing around in the smog. Southern California natives would tease me for hating sunshine, immune to what, for me, made stepping outside every day hurt like a hangover. I closed my eyes and listened to "O Superman." It helped.

When Laurie says, "This is the time. And this is the record of the time," in the first song on *Big Science*, "From the Air," she might be talking about 1982, the year the album came out. She might mean the present, too, and the future, but she certainly does not refer to my odd compulsion to listen to one song in a loop until it forever defines that phase of my life. To me it's nonetheless true. "O Superman" is the record of my winter and spring, age eighteen, in Los Angeles, California. Several people suggested to me during this bout of depression that I try meditation, and each time I resolved to take their advice. I bought how-to books that I hardly opened and felt guilty for my lack of drive. Now I recognize that "O Superman" was, and is, my meditation. It is my foolproof route to calm; I forget and rediscover this endlessly. Lyrically the song is the opposite of comforting, from the eeriness, post-9/11, of "Here come the planes / They're American planes," to the warped vision of "So hold me, Mom, in your long arms / Your petrochemical arms / Your military arms / In your electronic arms." Yet there's something in her voice, in her architecture of words and sounds that, strange and beautiful, soothes me like nothing else.

AND I SAID: THIS MUST BE THE PLACE.

I found my way back east, transferring to Barnard College after remarkably little deliberation for someone who screwed up the first time around. My mom made a gentle suggestion mid-summer, which I embraced easily. I filled out the Barnard application and no others. When the acceptance letter came to my California mailbox, I heaved a deep sigh of relief. The next few months proved a familiar ordeal in hyper-speed: heightened expectations rattled by the awkwardness of orientation week, several momentary resurgences of enthusiasm, and an ultimate landing on mind-numbing stress. But New York was the impulse, here was New York, and that was enough for me. One day I stumbled upon a bookcase in the Barnard library displaying the work of alumnae and stopped to peruse. Jhumpa Lahiri, I knew, Zora Neale Hurston, and a few others—I'd seen their names in the pamphlets sent to prospective students as encouragement to choose Barnard. Then my eyes flitted across the little letters on one spine that spelled out LAURIE ANDERSON, a name I hadn't spotted in the advertisements. I breathed, *Whoa*, and pulled the book from the shelf.

The One

Marisa Silver

This was late seventies New York City—the subways were dirty, the garbage was everywhere, muggings were commonplace, and 42nd street was not a theme park. I was a well-defended kid and knew how to steel my gaze to make it through a dicey neighborhood, how to clear a wide circle around a girl gang, how to walk unscathed through a minefield of dog shit. But while friends were losing themselves in music that seemed made for those dangerous times, the satisfyingly obliterating nihilism of the Ramones and the Clash, I was still dedicated to the singer/songwriters of the earlier part of the decade whose music seemed to speak more to the truth of my wobbly, vulnerable teenage heart. This was the music that felt dangerous to me, the communiqués of singers laying out the raw materials of their fragile emotions for everyone to see. I was working overtime to hide all my inchoate longing and self-loathing, all the confusion about what the hell I was supposed to be doing and who the hell would ever love me, and here were a bunch of musicians who seemed determined to expose me. There was no thrash and clamor to hide behind, nothing to bang my head into to help me avoid myself. Listening to these songs felt like walking across a ravine on a rickety wooden bridge. I was either going to make it to the other side, my weakness safely disguised by my tough boots and my heavy eyeliner, or I was going to fall into the river and drown. The attraction of both possibilities was undeniable.

These were private songs and listening to them was a private affair. Me in the den with the door closed, the LP on the stereo, the empty sleeve balanced on my chest as I pored through lyrics or studied the names of musicians and recording studios in a mysterious Los Angeles and an even more mysterious San Fernando Valley, people and places that seemed to me to be oracular sources of truth. Sometimes I'd hover on the skin of an album, surfing the tracks, drawn to the songs but not drawn *into* them. But every so often, I hit on a song that made it impossible to avoid falling off that bridge, one that reached into me, threading its way right into the center of my emotional confusion and lodging there. Listening, I knew something big was happening to me, but I didn't know what it was. And so I would lift up the needle to play the song again. And again. And again. It happened with Laura Nyro's "Eli's Coming" and Joni Mitchell's "Cold Blue Steel and Sweet Fire." It happened with the Kossoy Sisters' eerie rendition of the murder ballad "In the Pines." The impact of these songs was cellular; I heard them and something inside me said: *Right. Exactly. Yes!* and then: *Wait. What's happening?* Ten times, twenty times, a hundred times I'd listen to these songs, their words becoming quickly less important than the modulations that carried within them some coded message that went beyond the lyrics, that seemed to suggest that my sense of myself was horribly limited and that there was more of me, more of the world, more of me in the world if I could just understand what these songs were doing to me.

There was always one phrase, one perfect musical turn that was just *ecstatic*, that made me realize that there was *this* to reach for in life, this kind of heart-stopping, visionary, essential instance of beauty. It was a moment that was both blessed and frightening, an offering of the possible and a sure knowledge that the possible was unattainable. Each time I played the song, I would anticipate this moment, knowing exactly when it would come and what damage it would do to me, knowing that I would be dazzled and finally bereft. Because each time that moment ended was an abandonment. This was addiction and it came complete with the accompanying harrowing sense that this moment of perfect feeling was like water. It could be touched but never grasped. It would always slip away.

I came to the music of Judee Sill as an adult, when I'd supposedly laid on enough body armor to guard against being kidnapped by obsession and untoward feeling, when I supposedly knew myself well enough not to be looking for answers to what ailed me in a pop song. At first, my interest in Sill was an intellectual one. Always fascinated by ephemera, I was curious about people who were lost to our collective consciousness, the victims of the culture's unrelenting amnesia. Who was this obscure singer who had lit such an instant, bright fire only to see it just as quickly put out? I wanted to know why this young woman in the granny glasses and the stick-straight, center-parted hair of her day had missed out being one of those other center-parted, singer/songwriter superstars like Joni or Carole or Carly.

It's hard not to conflate a singer/songwriter's life story with her musical output, hard not to try to parse the confessions for clues and gossip. Judee Sill's life was about as rock and roll ready as they come. A father who died when she was a young girl, a mother who was an alcoholic and remarried a hard drinker. Acting out. Reform school. A bad heroin addiction accompanied by bad boyfriends. Robbing banks and turning tricks to feed her habit. Next, a kind of spiritual transformation fueled in equal parts by Kazantzakis,

Rosecruscianism, and the psychedelic philosophies of the day. And then, the discovery story: David Geffen signed her to be the first act on his Asylum label. Great reviews, the respect of her peers, piss-poor sales, and Geffen moved his attention to The Eagles and Jackson Browne. Flameout. The story ended as badly as it began. Sill died from an overdose well after she was forgotten as a musician, having reentered the world of drugs to treat chronic pain, the result of multiple car accidents. What was left for the ephemera bin: two albums, a third not quite finished.

We fall in love with musicians as much for their personas as for the music they create. Joni wore her heart on her sleeve, but she was funny and dead clever and you always had the feeling that as much as she got turned around and upside-down by love, she would be redeemed by her ability to perceive what had gone on with shocking emotional clarity. Carole was an earth mother who we never had to worry about; she was going to take care of us. Carly was sexy and urbane. She let herself be the object, hated being the object, and wrestled with how to control being the object, all the while smiling at us with those Jagger lips.

So who was Judee Sill? A weird, gangly, intense girl with a fixation on Jesus Christ who she saw not as a spiritual leader but as a sexy heartthrob. Not hard to see why she didn't catch on.

But when I started listening to her music, it took about a nanosecond for my intellectual preoccupations to fall away. Time collapsed and there I was again, sixteen or seventeen years old, ready to let down my guard and open myself to someone's intimate excavations, hoping that their insides looked a little bit like mine. Sill's voice, an impossibly clear alto, felt like it was whispering in my ear. Her melodies were often sweeter than the words that accompanied them, a dualism that made me itchy, uncomfortable, compelled. The nearly baroque beauty of her orchestrations filled with the strains of fugue and gospel riff and cowboy music supported a pitch-perfect voice that was singing songs that could be mistaken for secular love ballads but were filled with overt religious imagery. This woman loved, and lost, and yearned—for Jesus, for redemption, for a connection to some ineffable higher something, her voice reaching into an inchoate James Turrell landscape of light and space in an attempt to touch the impossible. Most of the songs I liked. Some I liked a whole lot.

And then came The One. It's called "The Kiss," and I was stunned, unnerved, carried away. Like many of Sill's songs, "The Kiss" treads the line between romantic love and religious yearning. The song is nominally about the power of a single kiss, and it sounds like it's about sex and intimacy with a man, except that Sill uses words like "communion" and "crystal choir" and "hosts" so there can be no mistaking that she is conflating her twin obsessions. She's looking for her man. And she's looking for Jesus. And sometimes, uncomfortably, those two guys are the same. "The Kiss" might not be Sill's most adventurous song, either sonically or lyrically. That award might go to "The Donor," a song that could be regarded as the apotheosis of her entire project, and into which she writes a classical Kyrie Eleison, drawing the romantic confessional into the territory of an oratorical Mass. But the relative simplicity of "The Kiss" makes it the one I can't shake. Each stanza ends with a gorgeous descending triad, the commonplace beauty of which is offset by the danger of the expressed sentiment. She's reaching for a "Sweet communion of a kiss" or to learn "How to give my heart away," and I start worrying that this perfect union she longs for will be accompanied by a kind of self-obliteration. And then I worry that this is what she wants, and that it's what I want, too. Don't I? Do I? The notes fall, and fall, and fall, and they take her and me right down with them.

She nabbed me with that song. Listen to her voice. That clear, clarion, vibratoless instrument that seems nearly celestial in its purity. Listen to those arrangements that are lush, layered, and, in combination with her sometimes florid, dreamy imagery, even a bit purple at times. But that voice. That strong, uninflected instrument that speaks of yearning as if it were like breathing, a basic condition of existence. Desiring, reaching—however you dress those feelings up, even if they end up looking a little bit like JC—these emotions just are, and without them, we just aren't. I don't relate to Sill's religious obsession, and I look for transcendence elsewhere, maybe in art, maybe in small unguarded moments when a laugh or a gesture or a revelation reveals some heart-piercingly pure kind of beauty, but I know exactly what Judee's searching for. Call it spiritual, call it sexual, call it drug-induced—it's all the same stuff—the desire to crack open the known and see into something and someplace beyond. The One was always about yearning for me and it still is. Because yearning doesn't end with growing up. It doesn't even end with getting things you want. It's something else altogether, the unending sense that if you reach a little further, a little higher, you might just nearly touch something as beautiful, as sad, as *right* as the way that song makes you feel each time you listen to it.

So I listen to "The Kiss." And I listen to it again. And just as I locate some perfect moment of untrammeled beauty that seems to encompass everything I feel, that knits all the wayward parts of me into something that is nearly tangible, it escapes me. And so I play the song once more.

NOT A ROCK N ROLL NIGGER

Dael Orlandersmith

'm Black/female and love rock and roll. I love all kinds of music but I am *specifically* moved—defined—by rock and roll.

As a young child in the sixties growing up in Central and Spanish Harlem and later the South Bronx, the music that played in the house and on the streets was R&B, Salsa, Calypso, and Reggae. Eddie Floyd's "Knock on Wood," Joe Cuba's "Bang, Bang," Desmond Dekker's "Israelites," were blasted in our living room on Saturday nights and on summer nights. Record players were put in windowsills so people could dance in the streets. There was blue-eyed soul like The Righteous Brothers' "You've Lost That Lovin' Feelin'" and the sexy, smoky voice of Dusty Springfield stroking, jiving, whispering "Son of a Preacher Man." Those two songs were the precursor for the *last* song—*the* song of all songs—"Dock of the Bay." When the couples, and the people who wanted to be coupled, held each other doing the slow drag, and after doing that slow drag they looked at each other, kissed, and headed quickly for home.

My cousin Johnny would yell out, "Now the Righteous Bros

and Dusty, *them* white folks can sing, man, and they lead up real good to Otis Redding, man."

I LOVED that music and I danced the Tighten Up Boogaloo Temptation step just like everyone else. But I also liked other music—namely rock and roll.

On Saturdays and Sundays, as I watched *American Bandstand* and *Ed Sullivan,* I would sing and dance along to sixties bubble gum and garage rock like The Cyrkle's "Red Rubber Ball," "96 Tears" by Question Mark and The Mysterians, The Vogues' "Five O'Clock World," Sir Douglas Quintet's "She's About a Mover". I'd air-play the organ and yell, "Well, you know I love you, baby / Woo, yeah, what'd I say, hey, hey."

I sang "Satisfaction" with the Stones before Jagger became the Luciferian midnight rambler figure. I was teased for liking white boy music by relatives and people in my neighborhood. My liking rock and roll (particularly in the sixties, when racial tension was at its height) made me a target and I was made to feel that I was a traitor for liking music other than Black and Latin music. People would say to me "How could you listen to THEM after what they did TO US?"

The late sixties and early seventies anthems ripped through the ghetto streets. People stopped what they were doing when "Say it Loud—I'm Black and I'm Proud" came on and shouted along with Mister James Brown. "We're a Winner" turned many a bell-bottomed, huge-Afroed brother or sister around to raise a fist with Curtis Mayfield. "Oye Como Va" floated down el barrio salsa streets.

I understood the anger. I watched white policemen stop Black and Latin boys for no reason and proceed to laugh at their fear. I, too, became enraged when white kids would drive by our houses and roll down the windows yelling "Nigger!"

I was aware when I took the train at Lexington 1-2-5 (that famous/infamous "Waiting for the Man" stop) that one stop on the 4 or 5 train—roughly a five minute ride—to 86th Street and Lexington put me in a different world.

I was aware of the doormen and cleanliness of the street.

Even though I was a child, I, too, received the dirty looks from white people downtown and saw the old ladies clutch their bags as I walked passed them. A child of color born in a ghetto must learn fast and hard. A female child of color born in a ghetto must learn extra fast and extra hard. So, yes, I, too, was angry.

BUT

For me, being a Black rock fan and being angry were not mutually exclusive and I had the anger—even as a child—that the adults around me had, but there was something else that lurked within me that went beyond race and everything around me. There was always a sense of more. Why, suddenly, did I feel alone, when a few minutes before I was laughing? Why am I angry at this moment? Are there other people that feel the same way? Who are they? Where are they?

The first time I heard "Light My Fire" it was sung by Puerto Rican folk singer José Feliciano and he crooned with his Latin beat and we all sang along and I assumed it was his song and left it at that.

Then I heard the original.

I was ten years old in 1969. By this time, I had discovered DJ Cousin Brucie who was at the time on WCBS-AM and played the original "Light My Fire" by The Doors.

I was sweeping the living room floor for my mother's weekly Saturday night party. I was looking over at Mount Morris Park (now Marcus Garvey Park) and dropped the broom. Jim Morrison's voice, Robbie Krieger's guitar, John Densmore's drums, and Ray Manzarek's keyboards haunted me, lulled me, and disturbed me. By listening to them, I felt their angst, and knew their angst *was* my angst.

I knew "Light My Fire," the feel beyond a love song, the sound of longing, which I couldn't define as such because I was a child, but I felt things, things I couldn't define, and the sound of The

Doors summed it up for me with guitar, drums, keyboards, and voice. I no longer felt alone. I looked over at the rocks in Mount Morris Park, thinking, *The Doors know what I feel, so there must be people that feel like I do. I have to find those people.*

That Saturday night, the adults came and drank, and danced, and sweated, and demanded that I dance with them as usual, but I didn't want to. I wanted to listen to The Doors.

I went into my mother's room and turned on the radio and listened to Cousin Brucie and sure enough, I heard "Light My Fire" again. That night, I was frantic to hear rock and roll but I wanted to hear grown up rock and roll and I knew nothing about FM radio. I went back to the Black station—WWRL—that everyone listened to. The DJ was Frankie Crocker (later, from the early to late seventies he became known as Frankie "Hollywood" Crocker on WBLS-FM, playing the true devil's music—disco), who often played all kinds of music and particularly late at night. By the time I was ten (besides the parties in our house), I was finally allowed to stay up late on Saturday night.

So, that special Saturday night—the same Saturday I heard The Doors, lying on my mother's bed staring at the ceiling, Frankie Crocker said, "Here's a brother I feel that is changing the face of music, period. I know a lot of you feel that he's not a brother, but he is. Here's Jimi Hendrix doing 'Hey Joe.'"

That Saturday my life was altered. After hearing The Doors AND Hendrix—things would never be the same. I actually felt a shift of consciousness.

After that, I would channel surf specifically to hear rock and roll. I discovered Steppenwolf, Creedence Clearwater Revival, and I wondered if there were any girl rockers. Not just singers, but women who played guitar and drums, just like the guys. I wondered if there were other Black people that played rock and roll like Hendrix, that played it dangerously like he did.

I knew Chuck Berry and Little Richard but they didn't convey any longing or angst in their music. They are, without a shadow of a doubt, the godfathers of rock and roll, but their music is good time music, and I was searching for something deep and different.

In terms of Black women and music, there was Aretha, and Gladys Knight, and when my mother and her friends would get together to mourn for and rage against the latest boyfriend, the latest man who broke their hearts, they would gather in the living room with their arsenal of Scotch, playing Billie Holiday and Dinah Washington.

The Black female singers that spoke to me were Etta James and Tina Turner. I loved that neither one of them had a pretty sound, that they weren't afraid to sweat and stomp like James Brown or Wilson Pickett or Jackie Wilson.

BUT

I wondered if there were women—Black or white—that wrote like Jim Morrison of The Doors?

Were there women who didn't just sing what I called back then "my man" songs? Were there women who QUESTIONED authority, who wanted to kick society's ass just like the guys, screaming down a microphone like Morrison. Were there women throwing one arm around wildly with a sneer like Pete Townshend or setting a guitar on fire like Hendrix? What woman was breaking on through to the other side?

That question was answered in my second year of high school. I was fifteen in the tenth grade. I went to Washington Irving High School in 1974 when it was an all-girls school. I specifically wanted to go there because it was close to the Village.

I dated very little during my teens and the boys I dated found me weird. At that time, I had only dated Black and Latin guys. I found myself attracted physically to them but we had nothing in common. Their tastes in music—disco being huge at the time—

separated me from those boys. The double whammy for me, within the Harlem community, was that I was not Black enough or female enough. I got called "white girl," "butch," and "weird."

I knew no one in the Village at that point and that created a greater sense of loneliness. And when I went to the Village and came across another Black or Latin rocker, particularly if they were female, I'd stare—I'd be anxious and hungry to talk to them because they must have known the isolation I felt. I wanted to run to them and scream, "How do you handle your own people not getting you? How do you handle getting called 'butch' or 'dyke' just 'cause you don't dress in high heels? What do YOU DO?

That year—age fifteen I was sitting in English class, humming "Rebel Rebel" (I had bought *Diamond Dogs* and was obsessed with Bowie and his androgyny, as was everyone else in the Village, it seemed), and Paula Rossi—Italian from Little Italy—heard me and said, "You like Bowie."

And I said, "Yeah."

And she said "Do you know who Roxy Music is?"

And I said, "No."

Then she said, "Do you know who the New York Dolls are? Actually, now they're The Heartbreakers—you should come with me to Max's Kansas City."

That weekend I went with Paula and her friends, Dee Dee, Michael Ann, Fern, and a Puerto Rican girl named Sandy— gorgeous, a Bianca Jagger-type who was heavily into Led Zeppelin. Sandy and I kept looking at each other and smiling because we were rock and roll girls of color who found each other. That night in Max's we saw a band called Television and they were hypnotic. Tom Verlaine (real name Tom Miller) sang a song called "Little Johnny Jewel," and I couldn't quite wrap around this sound. I'd never heard any rock and roll quite like it.

After Tom Verlaine sang, he invited a friend on stage to sing

"Gloria." Tom stuttered, mumbling, "Well, here's a friend to help us with a song. Here we go—Patti Smith."

The crowd went wild.

I saw a tall woman who looked a lot like Keith Richards, dressed in a white shirt and black pants, make her way on stage and launch into "Gloria." I looked at her and then back at the audience, and as she sang and then rapped 'G-L-O-R-I-A,' she began to chant poetry and I looked at her and thought *YESSSSSS. This is it. She is it.*

The men in the audience also adored her, and I heard one guy say, "She's a fuckin' female Jim Morrison, man," and another guy yell out, "PATTI, I WANNA FUCK YOU!"

I kept looking at her.

I couldn't take my eyes off of her and I looked at her thinking *I can do this.* I can be female and do this, too. I can *do* this.

After that, I began to go to Max's Kansas City, CBGB, Great Gildersleeves. I got heavily into punk rock. I now went to places like Bleecker Bob's or St. Mark's Records to buy forty-fives like Blondie's "X Offender," "Slash" by the Tuff Darts, "Love Comes in Spurts" by Richard Hell and the Voidoids, and last but not least "Piss Factory" by Patti Smith, with a cover of "Hey Joe" on the flip side.

I played "Piss Factory" and "Hey Joe" to death. I would go into St. Mark's Bookstore and read Patti's poetry book, *Witt,* over and over again until I could finally afford to buy it. I bought baggy clothes like Patti Smith. I thought of myself as a mix of a Black Patti Smith and a female Jim Morrison. I began to jot down my thoughts in specially bought notebooks, the same ones Morrison and Patti used.

Punk validated me. Patti Smith validated me. But within punk there was racism. The love and peace generation in the sixties and the Me Generation of the seventies were worlds apart. Disco was at its height. Gloria Gaynor, Tavares, KC and the Sunshine Band, the

Village People, and the queen of disco Donna Summer dominated the airwaves, and rockers hated it.

Disco, of course, is a form of Black music, and because of that I was met with racial violence. Until people got to know me at the rock clubs, the first thing a doorman would say to me would be "We don't play disco here." That doorman would not look at my clothing and see that I was dressed like a rocker. He did not see my DISCO SUCKS button or my Patti Smith or Velvet Underground button. All that doorman saw was BLACK. I then would say, "I know where I am and I know who I'm seeing."

Once inside of the club, there would always be yet another person or group of people seeing only my Blackness saying, "Oh shit—she thinks it's a disco! She doesn't know where she is." Then, as I sang along with the Ramones, the Talking Heads, Television, I became cool. I was no longer "one of them," I was cool. Some people would venture so far to say, "You know you're not a NIGGER, you're a BLACK person." Or, "You're not like the rest of them."

Certain white boys would say, "Wow, Black chick into rock and roll. I never made it with a Black chick. Come home with me." Paula, Dee Dee, Michael Ann, and Fern would look at me and turn away. Even Sandy's eyes would drift.

Different bands attracted different crowds and punk rock subdivided. The Talking Heads and Television were art rock bands, Blondie, Tuff Darts, and The Shirts were power pop bands with fifties greaser, sixties garage, bubblegum, girl group influences. Bands like The Heartbreakers were hardcore and attracted hardcore junkies as well. Lead singer and junkie Johnny Thunders openly sang about his need/love for junk in the song "Chinese Rocks." He also used the word nigger.

In his case, the way he used it was supposed to be hot, daring. One particular night in CBGB, before closing his set, he slurred, "Yeah it's hotter in here than a nigga's dick." All my friends at the table looked nervously at me, but smiles played at the corner of their mouths. Dee Dee said, "Oh come on, it's rock and roll bad boy shit. He didn't *really* mean it like *that*." I looked at another Black girl on the scene named Felice (who is a great bass player and has a band called Faith) and she and I gave each other the Power sign.

Her friends didn't support her, either.

Afterward, standing outside, a very angry, semi-wasted white boy looked over at me and sneered, "NIGGERS SUCK! NIGGERS CAN'T Rock and ROLL."

I looked at his shirt. He was wearing a Chuck Berry T-shirt. I couldn't believe he was wearing a Chuck Berry T-shirt as he said this. I grabbed him by his Chuck Berry shirt and proceeded to beat his ass, and again my "friends" did nothing.

By this time, there were other people on the scene that knew me, and one guy came over and pulled me off of me of him and called the guy an asshole, and I thought, *Uptown they hate me, call me 'white girl' 'cause I like rock and roll and I have to fight. Downtown I get called 'nigger' and have to fight.*

After trying to hail a cab for ten minutes, one finally stopped, and as soon as got home I put on Patti Smith. I thought, *She's an outsider, too. She may not be black, but she's an outsider.* I played "Piss Factory" and "Hey Joe" three times and went to sleep.

The following week, Patti Smith was playing the Schaeffer Music Festival in Central Park. It was 1975 and *Horses* had just come out, and the night before, Scott Muni on WNEW-FM played the entire album.

Patti came on stage, grabbed the mic, leaned in à la Jim Morrison and leered/chanted, "Jesus died for somebody's sins, but not mine." We all screamed and chanted "G-L-O-R-I-A." She followed up with "Piss Factory" and "Hey Joe," and again I'm over the moon. I'm dancing, jumping, cruising, signifying feeling like I'm channeling Morrison and Hendrix with her.

THEN

She rears her head back and yells, "Outside of society, that's where I want to be…Jimi Hendrix is a nigger / Rimbaud is a nigger / I'm a nigger / Rock and roll nigger…"

I stop dead in my tracks. I can't quite believe what I'm hearing. I can't quite believe what I'm hearing from her.

The mostly white audience sings, repeats, "I'm a nigger / Rock and roll nigger"

In that moment, one doesn't know what to say. You're used to being called "nigger" by cops and by the kids that cruise by in cars yelling out of windows, but to hear it in that moment from someone who has defined you, who has spoken to you heart to heart, to hear it said from people that you're friendly, maybe even friends, with, you're left speechless.

I make eye contact with a Black girl I know from the scene. She and I lock eyes. I signal her to come over and she does. I ask her, "What do you think, man?"

And she says, "I don't know. I mean, I can tell she doesn't mean it that way, but still, I don't like it. And look at all of them singing it, yelling it."

We looked at the sea of white faces chanting, calling themselves nigger with Patti leading them. By now, a young Black guy dressed in punk gear stood next to us, and he looked back then to the crowd and said, "This shit is fucked up. Totally fucked up."

The three of us stand together. We stand together.

In that moment, we needed to stand together and we didn't talk. We didn't need to talk.

The concert ended. We embraced each other. We didn't know each other that well but we knew each other. We needed to embrace each other.

That night I did not go to CBGB, nor did I go the following week. I went two weeks later, and still loving and needing rock and roll, I made a point to connect or try to connect with other people of color on the scene. I made a point to see the few bands that had people of color in them, like Ivan Julian, who played with Richard Hell and the Voidoids. I went to Mink ("Willy") Deville concerts and purposely made eye contact with the Immortals. Neon Leon was a fantastic guitarist and did a great version of "Heart of Stone" and wrote a great song called "Waiting for the Bus to Japan." A few years later, I saw Bad Brains at CBGB and loved them.

Although I was attracted to white guys, I became wary when they would approach me; it always seemed to be about trying a Black girl to see what it's like but not wanting to have a relationship. In some cases with friends, I was cool enough to hang out with in the clubs but was not good enough to take home to meet their families.

I debated whether to throw away my Patti Smith records. I wrestled with this for a while and decided not to. I came to realize she was racially naïve, as opposed to being racist.

There was a part of her that must have known that the word would bring attention. There was that part that wanted controversy and notoriety, but I don't think she fully understood the breadth of that attention.

I read a quote of hers about Edie Sedgwick in the biography by George Plimpton and Jean Stein saying how, "Edie danced funny, just like a white girl. She didn't have that nigger grace."

Having read that and having seen Patti Smith dance—she, too, dances like a white girl—I get angry. Does she think because she's an outsider, because she was raised around a lot of Black people, that by doing her rock and roll bad girl bit, she can use that word so freely? Does she really think she can reduce the word nigger to suit her romantic ideas about the artist as outsider?

Her poetic savior and aesthetic spiritual husband, Arthur Rimbaud, ran guns and slaves in North Africa. Did she read that?

She has a love for Jimi Hendrix…I doubt very seriously he would accept her explanation. Hendrix knew hardcore racism internally and from whites.

There is romance in using the word. She is an outsider, both by nature and by choice. She can use that word and create controversy and stop using it by choice and say it was a phase.

Over the years, I've heard her talk about the horrors of racism. I've heard her talk about the death of Martin Luther King Jr. and how it affected her. I've passed her in the street and she smiled at me and I smiled back.

It is easy to be antiracism and have your own ideas about what that means while not having friends of color or dealing with people of color.

Every New Year's Day, there's a poetry marathon at St. Mark's Church and almost every year I read and Patti Smith reads. I have, over the years, written poems in response to "Rock N Roll Nigger"—some funny, others not. One year, I wrote an angry poem in response to "Rock N Roll Nigger" right before Patti Smith read her poem. After I read, people clapped uncomfortably. When Patti got up to read right after, the applause was defiant. What was said in that applause was, *You will not kill my love for her.*

That was not my intention, as I am anticensorship and she has the right to use whatever language she chooses. I also have the right to respond.

After I read the poem, her guitarist, Lenny Kaye, moved quickly past me.

The following week, at a concert, someone who was at the reading said she did "Rock N Roll Nigger," but before she performed it, she prefaced it by saying it was not a pro-racist song. The song is about how we all suffer and spend time on the low-end things…or something to that effect.

Has she ever talked to a person of color about this?

A few years ago on Houston and 6th Avenue, I saw her on the street and I said, "I like your work." She said, "Thanks," and before she could walk away, I then said "But I have problems with the song 'Rock N Roll Nigger.'"

She stopped and looked over at me, stuttering. "You don't know what it means. You misunderstood. I was only twenty-two when I wrote it." The look on her face was pure horror—fear. Clearly, she had not spoken with anyone of color about this. I didn't bother to answer her. I just said, "Have a good day." She walked on but looked back at me a few times.

I look back on that day and realize that I used my power against her. I could see within that moment that she wanted to know about my experiences as a Black person/woman. She stood before me in that moment wanting to connect as human beings and I would not give that to her. In that moment, as I watched her watch me—it dawned on me that we had not. And that day, as I stood before her, dressed in all black—Black in black—the true rock and roll nigger, as it were—she was rendered speechless.

I write this wanting to connect because there is a consciousness in her. I want to explain what nigger means to me and the hurt it has created. I want to thank her for being the one to break on through. I would also like to know if she ever listened to the Black women that paved the way for her, like Memphis Minnie, The Duchess, Jessie Mae Hemphill, and Barbara Lynn, among others. I want to say to her and others that Black women like Nona Hendryx—rock funkster of LaBelle, who also backed the Talking Heads; Gail Ann Dorsey—bassist with Bowie; Grace Jones, who defies all categories; the delightful Brittany Howard of the Alabama Shakes are not NIGGERS. They are, and I am, rock and roll Black women and women who happen to be Black and into rock and roll. I want to thank them for being on the planet, and Patti Smith—I also thank you.

Hail, hail rock and roll.

Nina, Goddam!

Katell Keineg

Nina Simone doesn't have the most beautiful of voices, but whenever I hear her magnificent contralto with its slight trill and its miracle of phrasing, I start to cry. This is sometimes inconvenient. I might be in a bar, attempting to carry on a conversation, as the flow of my speech becomes strange, or in a shop trying to pretend that all is well and that I have something huge in my eye. Sometimes, as when I first saw her play, in 1999, it's okay. On that occasion, in Dublin, I arrived at the enormous venue with my friend Ashley, excited beyond belief. We sat down far at the back of the shed and settled ourselves in silence. Nina appeared, the first bars sounded, and out came the voice.

It's a weird thing when you've spent years hearing someone whom you've never seen. You stare: *that person is attached to that voice.* (It happened later with Mercedes Sosa in London, when she was playing one of her last concerts. I was there with my brother and I couldn't connect the body to the sound.)

I don't remember what Nina Simone sang first in 1999, I just remember what happened. I started crying. Not a sob, just tears rolling and rolling without end. After several songs, I turned to Ashley and saw that her face was as red and wet as mine. She looked at me and before we knew it, we were laughing hysterically, silently heaving to the annoyance of those around us. Then we went back to crying. It was the beauty of it all, the fluidity, the agility, the depth.

I'm not a music critic; I don't blog and I don't tweet. I've never written prose beyond school essays and the odd paragraph for a newspaper at album release time. I never think about what I think about music. But why is it that the sound of Nina Simone shatters me like that? Creating a sort of trouncing—a peak experience.

When I heard her for the first time, it was around 1992 in Dublin and I was having my hair cut at someone's house. A friend of my boyfriend at the time was snipping away and she put on a cassette, probably taped from vinyl. I had heard the Hothouse Flowers play "SeeLine Woman" a few years before and someone had told me that it was a Nina Simone song but I had never sought out the original.

The music got rolling and I immediately thought, *What is this? This is incredible!* I heard the gospel doubletime and the walking bass. The jagged, syncopated groove and the otherworldly piano. The men's chorus in counterpoint, clapping, call-and-response, tambourine, filigree guitar winding over the rest. In the middle of it was her voice, laying waste to everything around her. I have a distinct memory of sitting in the chair with the scissors at my head. All had stopped.

Soon after, when I moved to New York, my own tapes came with me, copied from here, there, and everywhere. They were very portable for the multiple moves from sublet to house-sit to someone's couch. Apart from my boyfriend, my guitar, and a bag with a few of my things in it, the tapes I owned were the only constant in the strange, dangerous world in which I found myself. I stayed on Christopher Street for two weeks whilst my boyfriend slept in a bathtub in Hell's Kitchen in an apartment that housed a freeroaming python. Later we found a sublet in Alphabet City, way down between Avenues C and D, next door to a crack dealer. The walls were thin, and he constantly coughed up mucus; we called him "Mr. Gob." One night I dreamt that beyond D there was a wooden fence with a stile over it and beyond that, the caribou.

My Nina tapes were all of her live recordings, always my favorites. Many were recorded in New York City in the late fifties and early sixties; The Village Gate in sixty-one, Carnegie Hall in sixty-three. You hear the audience, the sound quality is astounding, it bounces with life. The recording comes into the room you're listening in; their room is now your room. Time disappears and you're together, Nina, the audience, the mindboggling musicians, you. Together witnessing genius. What's not to cry about?

I started to play in New York venues myself. There was The Bitter End, Fez, the Bang On Club at Tramps. Sin-é on St Mark's Place was my regular gig; I played most Sundays, sometimes on a Thursday, too. It was a tiny place; a front room of sorts where people were directly in front of you when you sang and where there were no lights to protect you from the whites of their eyes.

Now that I have access to Nina Simone film footage, I'm flabbergasted by how entirely real and present she seems. She has utter conviction in her own powers and a complete absence of self-consciousness. I wouldn't have been able to see that, then, but I felt it in her voice and I strived for that, too, fighting shyness, wanting the music to do unto me what I would like it to do unto others. I found my voice; I learned to sing entirely exposed, with no persona muddying things up, no shield from the beautiful, receptive Rolling Rock and cappuccino drinkers.

The Sin-é regulars were musicians, writers, and artists, or

transplants to New York from other parts of the United States on their first job, living the cheap life. Some were downtown natives in rent-controlled apartments showing the rest of us the ropes. They were also the Irish young, armed with their Morrison visas—Bruce Morrison was a senator who had managed to pass an amendment giving 48,000 green cards to an island of five million. The French allocation was about 1,500!

Many who hung out in Sin-é loved Nina. She was amongst a group of musicians who were greatly appreciated by us whilst either being forgotten, largely ignored, or considered deeply unfashionable by the world outside. Leonard Cohen, whose *Various Positions* album containing "Hallelujah" was initially passed on in the US by his Columbia label. Karen Dalton, whose albums were out of print but whom we heard because Nicholas Hill of WFMU made us tape copies. He was later instrumental in getting her music rereleased on CD. Tim Buckley, whose son Jeff played at Sin-é every Monday, singing the songs of Dalton, Cohen, and Simone, among others. Very few people knew Tim's music at that time. Even Iggy Pop, who lived down the road on Avenue B, was in-between cool obscurity and his later rediscovery as an icon.

Some of this loose Sin-é band went uptown to Symphony Space and concerts organized by the World Music Institute. I first saw Abida Parveen and Nusrat Fateh Ali Khan there; those were my first experiences with Sufi devotional music. I didn't know whether the androgynous Parveen was a man or a woman, not even whilst I was watching her.

It was the same with Nina Simone: I knew nothing about her. I wouldn't have been able to tell you how old she was, where she was from, or where she lived. I had seen photos of her, but never footage. She never seemed to do concerts, and I remember wondering about that. (Remember, this was the numinous world before the Internet search.)

Years later, I did read her autobiography—a big mistake, don't do it! At one point in the book she writes about a video showing the execution of the son of her ex-lover, an African politician who had broken up with her. She says she watches it when she's feeling blue, so that the memories of her ex-lover are more real. I'm horrified!

Then again, she writes about how her ambitions to be a concert pianist were thwarted by her color. She writes about mistreatment, the Civil Rights movement, living in Paris, blackness. (Okay, read it! It makes me think: I was bathed in a kitchen sink as a baby for want of a bathroom, and it's really, really fucking hard to be a woman in the singing world, let alone to try and make something entirely of your own; but nothing, it seems to me, is harder than being black in America.)

In 1993, Nicholas Hill put out a vinyl single of mine on his S.O.L. label. I gave a copy to Iggy Pop and he gave it to Elektra. I already had offers from other labels but I decided to sign with them. Elektra had been Tim Buckley's label. But I didn't even know that Elektra had just put out *A Single Woman*, a studio album of Nina's. I found it later in the Elektra CD cupboard, in which I was allowed to roam freely.

As I went deeper into the musical-industrial complex, I clung to the Nina albums I loved. They were played in the van and on the tour bus while I circumnavigated the highways of North America and Europe.

Marietta, Georgia, "He Was Too Good To Me," Copenhagen, "Wild Is The Wind," Portland, Oregon…rolling, rolling, feeling lonely and elated, Nina was my friend, my road pal. The Sony Discman made its appearance to replace cassettes, it jumped and wasn't much good for walking but it filled the hotel lull after the gig, drunk and having lost my bearings. "If He Changed My Name," Milan, West Virginia, the Amtrak from Chicago to Seattle and on to Vancouver, "Don't Let Me Be Misunderstood," Nina ripping it up with her band.

I had left a communal life—one in some ways forced upon me by poverty and the immigrant experience—for the anomie and the weird glamour of rock and roll travel. I had a manager who was my friend, an A&R person whom I miraculously liked a lot, and later on I even traveled with other musicians, but I was essentially living a deeply solitary existence. My relationship broke up. I fell in love with a friend whom I rarely saw. Nina became the moon, visible from everywhere.

I admired her fierceness. In the environment where I now found myself, her lack of compromise made it easier for me to say, "this is what I'm doing and how I'm going to do it." That's still not easy in the pop/rock world where the female "auteur" is in a tiny minority and where most male producers, male musicians, and male just about everything else will always be seeking your acquiescence.

Simone was more a sublime interpreter of songs than a great writer. With a few notable exceptions (such as "Four Women," "Young, Gifted And Black," and "Mississippi Goddam"), she sang songs written by others, but she so transformed them that it became hard to listen to versions sung by anyone else. Even in her studio recordings, she often wavered away from the pitch, but she never fell off the note completely, and this created a tension and discomfort in her singing that added to its power. More and more, this stands out in an age of perfect recording, AutoTuning, and comped vocals where a singer sings a part many times and the best words or even syllables are cobbled together to make a smooth, characterless whole. A friend recently introduced me to the term "efforty." It's not a compliment: it means that you're trying, and effort isn't cool. This is the indie rock view, probably a reaction to the sea of ersatz feeling unleashed on us by the music industry. So now there's fake feeling and there's no feeling at all. You're entirely free to choose.

The only good thing about music, as far as I can see, is its ability to crumple you. You might cave in to the dance, shaking it, jumping around the hall or your bedroom, exhilarated and in a sweat. Or you might be vividly alone, the top of your head becoming light and open, your body hair aroused, your eyesight at once dimming and becoming extremely focused. I think they call it a vertical relationship. For the religious, it's a relationship with a god or a mystical being. For me, it's the music entering my ears and blowing through the top of my head, making me weep.

The last time I saw Nina Simone play was at Carnegie Hall, about a year before her death in 2003. I went with a New York friend and we sat near the front. Simone had lost her ability to play or sing with greatness, she was on stage for a very short time; she probably wasn't well by then. The band would play, she'd join in for half a song and then she would walk to the front of the stage and just stand there, lifting an African fan at the audience in greeting. Everybody went crazy; we stood up, we roared, we stomped our appreciation. We knew it was the end and we wanted her to know. Maybe she wanted us to know. Gone were the *froideur* and the severity. She smiled, and waved, and played very little, and it didn't matter.

You hear Nina Simone everywhere now, on adverts, on film soundtracks. I can't imagine that she would have wanted to promote half of those things, given her political beliefs, but her music belongs to others now, and in fact much of it already did in her lifetime. I'm not sure that she had any control over the inclusion of "My Baby Just Cares For Me" in a Chanel ad in 1987. She reputedly hated the song.

I still don't know much about her life. I bought another copy of her autobiography before writing this so I could check that I wasn't making it up when I wrote about the video and the African politician. While I was ordering it (from Amazon—apologies bookshops!), I quickly read the synopsis of a biography of hers that was also on sale; I saw something about undiagnosed bipolar disorder. The posthumous diagnosis of mental illness by nonmedical professionals is quite the rage these days.

I don't really want to know. I want to go back to the days when I didn't know much. I've never wanted others to know much about me, either. That's why I don't blog and I don't tweet but here I am, writing an autobiography of sorts, saying far more than I intended. Wanting to entertain.

Better Than Clearasil: How X-ray Spex Allowed Me to See Past a Germ-filled Adolescence

Daniel Waters

When someone asks me, "What's your favorite album?" my answer is immediate and a little *Manchurian Candidate*-y: *Germfree Adolescents* by X-ray Spex. My favorite film requires no explanation; I'm a man born before 1970—it's *The Godfather*. But how a screeching, British-Somalian punk-pixie in braces who called herself Poly Styrene became the soulmate, muse, and idol of a gangly, pimply, teenage Hoosier boy—well, that takes a while longer to unpack.

In "Plastic Bag," Poly wailed from across the Atlantic, "Nineteen seventy-seven and we are going mad!"…but I wasn't listening yet in 1977. That was the year of *Star Wars*, *The Spy Who Loved Me*, and Notre Dame winning another national football championship. For a lad growing up in South Bend, Indiana, life was awesome. And it was still fresh and original to refer to stuff as "awesome" back then.

Musically, throughout most of the late seventies, I was content to lie in an FM radio-hammock of Bob Seger, Van Halen, pre-Run-D.M.C. Aerosmith, and REO Speedwagon. "Roll With The Changes" was our prom theme. Mosquitoes of curiosity occasionally roused me from my relaxed position: novelizations of R-rated movies I couldn't get into...Pauline Kael raves for foreign films that would never come to a theater near me...and what's this punk rock thing that *Saturday Night Live* likes to makes fun of?

Like a farmer in the eighteen hundreds, reading by candlelight about the invention of the light bulb, I experienced punk through words long before I heard any of the songs—"shocking" snippets on ABC's *20/20* notwithstanding. I devoured as many not-just-*Rolling-Stone* articles I could get my hands on, with monthly pilgrimages to the downtown library for special *Village Voice* sessions. I could tell you the letter grade that Robert Christgau had given to an album, but I couldn't tell you what it actually sounded like. Boy, could I bluff, though.

I read and I read, but I did not hear. There was no live streaming of Wire's *Pink Flag*. No iTunes ninety-second preview and no Amazon thirty-second preview of "God Save the Queen." No downloading of the first single off *Young Loud and Snotty* from The Dead Boys' website. Beyond the "kids today have it easy" of all this, the simpler truth is that South Bend, Indiana, did not have that Cool Record Store or that Cool Radio Station. Or at least I never found them.

It is unsettling to recall just how much of my pre-income days were spent imagining what music sounded like. I had no doubt that Gang of Four's *Entertainment* was "a silky reinvention of the raw punk ethic and a sly attack on the politics of exploitation," but I had to build it in my mind first.

I've come to realize that Joy Division's "Love Will Tear Us Apart" and Laurie Anderson's "O Superman" are indeed two of the greatest songs ever, but in my broke, lonely college days, all I had were the rhapsodies waxed by Pazz & Jop voters in the *Voice*. No song could live up to such nuanced praise, nor to my subsequent aural daydreams.

I had even more such experiences with film, to increased traumatic effect. A *South Bend Tribune* editorial asserted that the vicious Charlton Heston Western *The Last Hard Men* should be rated X for violence; this spurred visions in me of naked cowboys having their genitalia shot off.

As Dan Savage now promises all teens, it did get better. My participation in a locally produced, *Zoom*-meets-*SCTV* television program gave me friends with a higher level of taste (The Clash, Elvis Costello, Talking Heads, The Specials) and actual albums (or eight-track tapes). A paper route gave me meager funds to get into the music-buying game myself, and a divorce gave me a sister city, Montreal (Dad got a professor gig at McGill University), a magical place that *did* have the mind-expanding radio stations and record stores I had always fantasized about. It was there, north of the border, that I first came upon Poly Styrene and X-ray Spex.

Sometimes the wrong note heard at the right time changes everything.

From Cool Radio Station came the wildly warbled "Some people think little girls should be seen and not heard. But I think, oh bondage, up yours!" It was a banshee blast of wit, wonder, saxophone, and actual melody, something that my expertly daydreaming brain could never have concocted on its own.

I tracked the group to Cool Record Store. The album cover immediately mesmerized me with its image of the band trapped in test tubes, especially the girl in the middle tube. Wait, was that the singer? That skin, that hair, that outfit, that attitude—there wasn't a

Poly Styrene to be found in Indiana. Teenage boys generally don't have much use for females they can't instantly masturbate to, but I had a feeling about us. When the purchased album hit my father's turntable, my fear and confusion turned into worship. Poly Styrene went from succubus to goddess.

It was love at first listen. I didn't even notice right away that the song I so needed to harness, "Oh Bondage, Up Yours!," wasn't even on that vinyl pressing, because it was just all so intoxicating and perversely accessible.

By now I had experienced my first taste of punk, yet there was only so much I could relate to in its growls of drinking, drugging, fucking, and anarchy-ing. Trenchant anticonsumerist satire on the other hand, oh hells yes! The true punk of my teenage self was found in my grandmother's lacerating Tom Lehrer albums and in Wacky Packages, Art Spiegelman's renowned cavalcade of product-subverting stickers. The truly surprising glory of X-ray Spex was not just its sound and style, but its content:

> *I know I'm artificial, but don't put the blame on me.*
> *I was reared with appliances in a consumer society.*
> *When I put on my makeup, the pretty little mask's not me.*
> *That's the way a girl should be in a consumer society.*

I got it. I loved it. Ah, the sweet, sad joy of remembering anticonsumerism as an artistic concept, or even as a concept concept. It can't help but make one feel the faded glamour of an old revolutionary musing about the good old days before the tanks rolled in. I mean, even Christmas-has-become-too-commercialized editorials still had some juice in the late seventies.

Whew, talk about a war that was lost. You don't need me or *Adbusters* magazine to tell you that satire is no longer used as an attack on anticonsumerism but as a clever prop to sell more stuff.

To complain about product placement in film, or product shout-outs in songs, is to be a party pooper (at the time of this writing, six of the top ten songs in the country are unironically name-checking Patrón).

The beyond-parody outrage of Spex and the blistering presentation of Poly Styrene were a wacky package that gave me goosebumps that I couldn't categorize—not nervous, amorous, or chilly, but closer to awe. An important life lesson was learned: a shrieking woman gets your attention, but a woman shrieking brilliance unnerves you forever.

It's a lesson not every man wants to learn, not even my father. Despite the whole divorce thing, I had one of those "Great Dads," which is certainly better than a "Bad Dad" (violent, drunk, absent); but as those who have been there know, having a father who checks in constantly to see how you are feeling, compassionately monitoring if you are depressed, gay, or on drugs, can be its own kind of burden.

I wasn't even aware of having any rebellion in me, but when Dad rushed into the room where he kept his stereo, helplessly roaring "What the hell is *that*?"—how could I not feel a sense of achievement?

My scorching alchemy was further inflamed by my reading material of the moment: *The Bacchae*, Euripides's not-so-tragic tragedy of bacchanaling, cow-killing, men-shredding women…the perfect emotional libretto for the outrageous opera I was playing over and over that Christmas vacation.

X-ray Spex had only one album. One was all they needed. Poly Styrene can be found in the last paragraph of every punk article and in the last five minutes of every punk-rock doc (in the obligatory "girls did it, too" section) as well as in the first paragraph/five minutes of every Riot Grrrl article/documentary.

Unaware of any ultimate historical contextualization, I

triumphantly returned to the States with the album as if it were a fabled Canadian girlfriend. I'm not sure anyone was as blown away by *Germfree Adolescents* as I was, but that only enhanced my feelings of superiority. (Back then I don't think I adequately appreciated what a Holy Grail the album was, as apparently it never even got an official US release until 1991.)

My X-ray Spex success caused me to develop a case of First Kid On My Block-ness. It pushed me out the door to the Musicland at the mall literally next door (I could hear people being paged at Montgomery Ward from my bedroom window) to force them to order at least one or two of the multitude of albums they were not carrying. My mightiest victory, still talked about in the Bend, was when I corralled an unheard-of album on the basis of this refreshingly accurate *Rolling Stone* gush:

> "I Will Follow," the kickoff cut from the debut album by Irish whiz kids U2, is a beguiling, challenging, perfect single. With its racing-pulse beat, tinkling percussion, and mantra-simple chorus of dogged affection…

While the U2 discovery went over big with my pals, there was a slight stigma for a guy in Indiana to listen to music by a girl, even though no one could dare accuse my X-ray Spex album of being girly. Poly Styrene's warped siren's call led me to other goddesses whom I unapologetically threw myself at the feet of: Patti Smith, Debbie Harry, Chrissie Hynde, and most daringly, Joni Mitchell. This Poly-led brigade led me into yet another arena: feminism.

Yes, feminism. Let's just say my Jaclyn Smith poster didn't make the trip to college. I took women's studies courses. (The Production of Desire in Literature and Film continues to be a source of inspiration.) I took note that Marguerite Duras had written, "No man has ever finished Virginia Woolf's *A Room of*

One's Own" so I finished Virginia Woolf's *A Room of One's Own*. I referred to *Flashdance* as "pornography" in conversation. I treated Simone de Beauvoir's *The Second Sex* as good science fiction; it would later be one of the roommate-wearying pull quotes I would over-use during my press tour for *Heathers*.

Such a lovely, innocent time, but alas, like all good and pure male excursions in feminism, it was crushed by the clumsy, oafish behavior inherent in men when they start actually having relationships with real women. Reality has a way of ruining everything, especially when it involves boys, girls, and sexuality, no matter how much Virginia Woolf has been imbibed.

While I feel bad that I couldn't keep it up (my enlightenment, that is), how dreary it would be if the only gift Poly Styrene gave me was feminist understanding. My love for Poly always had less to do with a noble worship of the X chromosome than with all-out admiration for what she created: art that was not just cheap parody or even just brilliant satire. *Germfree Adolescents* was both art that was *about* something and art that *was* something. Malevolently incisive and delightfully delivered: the most exhilarating of combinations…

> *Identity is the crisis you can't see*
> *When you look in the mirror, do you see yourself*
> *Do you see yourself on the TV screen*
> *Do you see yourself in the magazine*
> *When you see yourself, does it make you scream?*

Strange as it may seem, the whole content thing has gotten a bad rap over the years. People are insanely quick to label anything that goes beyond stylish and gratifying as "pretentious." Unpretentious has oddly become the new pretentious, in that the most arrogant, insufferable, and sanctimonious artists are the ones who haughtily brag that their work is intended to be nothing more than "a good ride."

Luckily, I was naive to all this when I made the jump from watching, reading, and listening to creating. It would turn out that my secret weapon, as a would-be writer, was my special, off-kilter, Poly-induced brand of feminism, which thankfully never went away. It just became a little more mercenary. Between Shakespeare and David Mamet, men had been done to death. Everything is more original when a woman does it, so I had a woman do it.

Most of my poor, Styrene-less, male-writer brethren make the mistake of thinking of a strong female character as someone who can throw and take a punch like a man, usually while delivering tired "but I *am* a lawyer/doctor/spy/the sheriff!" dialogue. I never forgot the lesson that there is nothing more destabilizing than a woman with her own particular swagger and sense of humor.

That lesson was key in the creation of my first finished work, the screenplay for the apocalyptically humored megabitchfest, *Heathers.* Poly and X-ray Spex had taught me to go ahead, tackle something important: it can't be pretentious if you are dancing, which I transformed to "laughing." (Perhaps, like X-ray Spex, I should have stopped at one, as well!)

When I let myself be devoured by big-studio writing work, I managed (in *Batman Returns*) to transform Catwoman into something much more outrageous and complex than the femme-fatale jewel thief of the comic books. Even the character I created for Sandra Bullock in the macho sci-fi universe of *Demolition Man* upheaved everything around her with subversive estrogen.

I definitely would not have gotten to where I needed to go as an artist without my cultural blind-spot daydream upbringing. I like to play a chilling parlor game with myself, imagining *what if* I had use of the Internet when I was that pimply teenage Hoosier, watching endless Desireé Cousteau clips, reviewing Ms. Pac-Man, blogging about *The Night Stalker*… I would never have picked up a pen, I would never have left Indiana, I would never have left my bedroom. Kids today have it hard.

As Poly sang, back in the day in a way that would make Nostradamus blush:

> *My mind is like a switchboard with crossed and tangled lines.*
> *Contented with confusion that is plugged into my head.*
> *I don't know what's going on. It's the operator's job, not mine, I*
> *said.*

I never met my anti-doppelganger soulmate, Marianne Joan Elliot-Said (Poly's real name) and I never saw her play live, nor did I really keep up with her life. I know there was a bipolar Hare Krishna period in there somewhere, but I did take delight in the adorable solo album she released soon before her death to cancer in 2011. Songs like "Virtual Boyfriend" and "I Luv Ur Sneakers" had a Zeitgeist-tweaking twang without the in-your-face-ness of Spex. Poly Styrene seemed happy at the end, but then she seemed happy in the during. It was Poly Styrene's secret exuberance, more than her punk-assumed rage, that allowed me to dare to bond with her.

So that's why X-ray Spex's *Germfree Adolescents* is my favorite album. Now why *Banacek* is my favorite TV show, I have no fucking idea.

Beautiful Child

Susan Choi

'm about twelve. Certainly no older than thirteen. I haven't yet begun my driving lessons, and in Texas this process starts early. The man I'm with is older, I don't know by how much. In my twelve-year-old eyes he's a man; he might be as young as nineteen or as old as forty. His name is Jack. I remember most clearly his pocked skin, and his coarse black hair, almost clown-like in its uneasy relationship with his skull. He must have accepted his homeliness. He never touches me, never so much as implies that he might. Ours is an affinity of a higher order. We are fellow initiates. Mystics.

The apartment is squalid. Unfurnished, in my memory, except for stained wall-to-wall carpet. And some plastic kid stuff; or perhaps the presence of a child is indicated to me by noise and crying coming from the next room. I don't consider myself remotely like this unseen child. I am one of the adults, whoever they are. Friends of Jack's, with whom he forms a mystics' circle, into which I have now been admitted. A metal chalice of some kind is filled with some kind of dried herb. Matches are struck, fires ignite. Words are chanted, bewitchments in some unknown tongue.

How have I come to be there, in that room, with those people? The chains of causality often confound us, but not in this case. Stevie Nicks is the reason.

The Chain

Somewhere between childhood and the so-called "teen years" FM radio saved me. It's a familiar story. I was an only child, brainy, awkward, fashion-challenged, clad in braces that shredded the insides of my lips, and clothes that were ordered from Sears. My parents had split up, my mother was ill, we had moved across the country to an unfamiliar and hostile environment, and we were suddenly much poorer than we'd seemed to be before. Once we'd owned a house; now we rented. Once we'd owned a car; now a lanky Iranian student who'd answered an ad drove my mother and me, once a week, to the grocery store. I won the spelling bee and hated myself. One afternoon, lying on the living room floor with the radio on, my heart seemed to suddenly lurch as if shocked by electrical currents. Hairs stood up on the back of my neck. Pure listening, that rare condition that involves every pore, overtook me. A guitar riff of such desolated yearning, and yet such grim resolve, played and repeated with a slight variation. A martial mustering of rhythm, and a keening voice, issuing and obeying a summons in the same utterance. This has happened to me only twice in my listening life: a shocked recognition of the wholly unfamiliar and at the same time profoundly expected, as if some lost part of myself had returned. The second time was in 1991, driving down a country highway outside Nashville, when I heard "Smells Like Teen Spirit" for the first time. I had to pull over. I don't know what it says about the state of the radio, or of me, that it has not happened since. This first time I hear it, "The Chain" has been a radio staple for years, but I've been a radio listener just a short time. When the song is done playing, I call up the station—this was when you could do that, and the DJ would actually answer. "What was that?" I say breathlessly.

It feels important to affirm that the music got me first, that I would have fallen in love with her blind.

Sisters of the Moon

It was a good time to fall for Stevie, a propitious time, vaulting onto the broomstick as it took the sharp turn for a solo flight path. This was the summer *Bella Donna* was released, so that, appropriately, my remedial education in all things Fleetwood Mac was from the start in the service of Stevie. But it would have been thus even if she had not just gone solo. Although my appreciation of Fleetwood Mac developed, over time, from its origins as the by-product of a hysterical girl-crush into an authentically ardent listenership, it'll always remain the setting for the stone, or, perhaps more appropriately, the setting plus the velvet-lined box plus the floppy lace bow. With Stevie included, the band is her equal; without her, the band stops making sense. Even pre-*Buckingham Nicks* Fleetwood Mac, Peter Green's Fleetwood Mac, for me is infused with her imminence, with the transformative arrival we now know was on the horizon. At the same time, Fleetwood Mac turned out to be just as integral to Stevie as she was to it; *Buckingham Nicks,* her and Lindsey Buckingham's only album in their pre-Fleetwood form and the reason they received the invitation to join, itches the scratch of all those Lindsey/Stevie fan-fiction freaks (see: the Internet) with its throat-closing nude cover photo, but the songs—all good, none great—have a phantom limb quality. Real life, with its deliciously distressing complications, has not yet begun. The two of them are merely young, beautiful, talented, and in love. It's not yet enough to make rock history.

My copies of *Fleetwood Mac* (1975: "Rhiannon," "Crystal," "Landslide"), *Rumours* (1977: "Dreams;" "I Don't Want to Know;" "Gold Dust Woman") and *Tusk* (1979: "Sara;" "Storms;" "Sisters of the Moon;" "Angel;" "Beautiful Child"), were all quadrillionth pressings likely acquired through the Columbia House Record Club, which might account for the stutter flaw at the end of "Gold Dust Woman" that required me to hover over the record as it played to nudge it forward at precisely the right moment, and that to me will forever seem part of the song, a literal manifestation of the inner brokenness belied by Stevie's strident, take-no-prisoners delivery, so that to hear the song play normally always feels abnormal. My copy of *Bella Donna*, by contrast, was purchased hot off the presses, at Cactus Records and Tapes, where Jack of the herb-burning coven could sometimes be found at the register. I was a real fan now, a role with which I have never become comfortable, and which Stevie seemed peculiarly designed to make even harder for me. I was and remain not just self-conscious on my own part, but on the part of others, and unself-conscious flamboyant displays such as Stevie excelled in scared me.

Back then, at least, fandom was simpler. There was not yet the Internet's inexhaustible supply of esoterica, the mastery of which, at that age, would have been my final social ruin. It was sufficient to live with one's idol in a private world concealed in one's mind, decorated with the scraps a preteen, on her own time, might scavenge. My primary text was Timothy White's September 1981 *Rolling Stone* cover story, "Out There With Stevie Nicks," better known to me as the article that went with the picture of Stevie holding the big white bird; for years I had that photo taped above my bed, and now, reexamining it (thank you, Internet), its least details dilate like rooms in a memory palace, and I remember how many hours I spent in unsettled contemplation of, for example, the length of Stevie's nails and the apparent double-jointedness of her middle finger. From that article I learned things about Stevie that didn't just emblazon themselves upon my memory (I've gone back and checked, and been amazed by my flawless recall of information acquired more than thirty years ago, when much of what I learned three years ago and even three days ago is now lost to me) but that radically influenced, for many if not all the years since, the sort of person I thought I should be.

Stevie adored fairy tales, welcomed spectral visitations, was besotted with Cocteau's *Beauty and the Beast*. Most strikingly for me, she regretted wearing corrective lenses because, as she put it, "for most of my life, every light blurred and became a star. I had this incredible light show going on because of the way I saw. Maybe that contributed to my magical outlook on life. I don't look at anything but in a romantic way." Dutifully, I read fairy tales, watched Cocteau's film, dabbled in tarot, and wore the crescent-moon-and-star pendant around my neck that had led Jack the record store clerk to invite me to hang with his coven. I became fond of velvet, gathered crystals for a New Age-y shrine, and made friends with a cousin who was practicing the meditative spinning of the Whirling Dervishes. None of this was a good fit for me, as even then I could intuit. By the time I was out of high school, the beret was shoved deep in a drawer and all the crescent-moon pendants abjured. But the fundamental lesson never left me: that the unlovely aspects of life might be draped in a length of chiffon, the same way one hides a cheap lamp. She was my first romantic poet.

Storms

Put on a mental blindfold, close your eyes to the scarves and the boots and the spinning, to the doves and crystal balls, the beret and top hat. Try, as I've tried for years, to forget about the video for "Gypsy." Forget, even, the beautiful unadorned face, the downturned corners of her mouth, the sad eyes, the cataract of blonde hair. Whether you loved it or loathed it, that unending feast she served up for the eyes, try to wipe it all out of your mind. Only listen.

She was great.

Okay, not always. Not so much recently. And not so much, paradoxically, in her solo career, although her songs with the band stand out in such relief from the Fleetwood Mac oeuvre as to seem like solo tracks, insistently unto themselves—yet this is precisely because they're tied down within the structure of the band, fully realized through the limits placed on Stevie by her bandmates' stupendous musicianship. Left to her own devices, even banging around with people like Tom Petty, the results aren't as good. "Edge of Seventeen" is great, as great as anything she's ever done. But by the time of Fleetwood Mac's *Mirage*, which spawned "Gypsy," the following year, 1982; and then Stevie's second solo album, *The Wild Heart,* the year after that, I was already living in the past. It's the body of work she made in her first three albums with Fleetwood Mac, and particularly the relatively lesser-known tracks from *Tusk,* that are lodged like a handful of nails in my heart; that articulate my inarticulate moments of tenderness, or loneliness, or pain; that I most want to listen to when I get drunk.

When I first listened to these songs, as a musically ignorant, socially incompetent preteen, recording favorite lyrics in a spiral-bound notebook in my painstaking handwriting, decorating the notebook covers with, god help me, images of multicolored melancholy mimes, or of equally wistful monochrome teddy bears, the fit between me—an inexperienced child-woman, inchoate with longing, soddenly sentimental, wholly willing to wear the beret— and the almost unbearable vulnerability of the songs was so snug, it seems inevitable that the songs would turn out to be bad. As a woman I met recently said, listening to Stevie's songs back then was like reading her diary, to which another woman added, "her *quilted* diary." Undeniably true. How remarkable, then, that these songs—"Storms," "Angel," "Beautiful Child"—don't merely hold up, they actually turn out to be great. Perhaps an as-yet-unformed part of me knew. Those songs, more than any others, prepared me for falling in love. They prepared me for pain.

Silver Springs

I wrote the fan fiction, too. Back then, it didn't have a name, or at least, not a name I had heard. I would have been shocked to know it was a "thing." For me it was utterly private, perhaps even shameful. That was my quilted diary, those top-secret tales of romance I wrote down in my spiral-bound notebooks, along with her lyrics. Almost poignantly chaste, these stories tended to feature a San Francisco Bay view at twilight, a Woman, a Man, and Art. They lacked recognizable plot. The real plot—of high-profile love and higher-profile breakup; of accusations and admissions and appeals aired not just in public but on Top 40 radio so that, if you were Stevie and Lindsey, you might enjoy the peculiar solace of your thousands of fans singing all of your breakup songs at you from the stands of a vast sports arena while you and your ex, both on stage, led this chorale of vicarious grief; what the hell was *that* like?—was, then as now, more than enough. To this day, I, too, will spend hours sampling the blogospheric archive of Stevie/

Lindsey High Intensity Moments, which continue to occur with such delicious frequency as the two of them count off the years that you have to wonder if it isn't fan-pandering schtick—but then, as a true fan, you have to refuse to believe this. I did and still do love their love. I appreciate Lindsey Buckingham's undiminished hotness and undisputed status as a guitar deity entirely because it makes him worthy of Stevie; to quote the blogger Hipstercrite, "they were my personal soap opera and I couldn't get enough." For precisely that reason, and to a startling extent, Stevie and Lindsey remain a repository of all my most girlish beliefs, and here, as with that beret, is where problems begin.

To this day, aged forty-six, published author, supposedly self-realized gal, I can't shake my young girl's hot crush on the Lindsey-and-Stevie-train-wreck; I can't shake my gut-deep, retrogressive belief that somehow it's better to be the girl about which songs are written than to be the girl writing the songs. I love Stevie's songs—but for their vulnerability and longing, their ragged edge. It's not the fact that she's torn herself free—it's what she tore herself *from*. By the time I was in college, fumbling toward self-realization via the exceptionally inflexible identity politics of the late eighties, Stevie was setting off my feminist alarm bells. I'd already ditched the beret. Maybe I had to forswear the whole package.

On the other hand, it's this same vulnerability of Stevie's—and the emotional accessibility that comes with it—that makes her so beloved among women. It makes her, if not an exemplary feminist, an exemplary sister. And which would you rather hang out with? In a 2013, post-Thurston Moore interview with Kim Gordon, *New Yorker* writer Alex Halberstadt describes Gordon cooking him dinner at her house in Northampton, forcing him to watch *Friday Night Lights,* and then falling asleep next to him on the couch. The scene is weirdly similar to Jancee Dunn's account of interviewing Stevie in 1997, when after hours of trying on clothes, reading old diaries, and spying on the neighbors together, Stevie and her gaggle of giggling assistants urge Jancee to stay and have a slumber party with them: "They all planned to make a little dinner, play some music, watch *Golden Girls* reruns... I was tempted, but I thought I should maintain a professional boundary." It's as useful a tool as any for the classification of female rock stars: would she invite you to sleep over and watch TV with her, or not? Janis Joplin: for sure. Courtney Love: without a doubt, though you might be afraid to accept. Joni Mitchell: never. Patti Smith:... Could we dare to hope yes? When I think about the female rock stars about whom I can't hazard a guess, I realize I don't care about them.

In the fall of 1982 I saw Fleetwood Mac live at the Summit in Houston, Texas. I was thirteen years old. The Summit then was in its golden age of hosting big rock shows, an age which ended in 2005 when the city of Houston sold the Summit to the Lakeside Church. And Houston has never since had the right kind of venue for the rock shows that I grew up with, the shows that physicalized the centrality of the role FM radio once played in our lives. The Summit, with its 17,000 seats, was exactly the right kind of big. It was intimate-big—no matter where you were seated, you still felt you were close to the artists. At the same time it was monumental—it was the adequate shrine for our gods. In many ways, my transition from childhood to adulthood was measured in ticket stubs torn at the Summit. These were my first forays into the world without an adult chaperone. These were my first opportunities to exercise taste, to spend my own money (I had started with menial jobs almost solely in order to buy concert tickets) on the things that expressed who I was, independent of parents or school. Looking over a list of shows played at the Summit in the brief era, 1981-1983, during which I routinely attended concerts, I'm surprised by how many I saw; it's more a question of which shows I skipped. I saw Rush, and The Police, and David Bowie, and Robert Plant, and Golden

Earring, and Genesis, in some cases (The Police and Rush) multiple times. The wearing of a concert shirt the next morning at school was a declaration, of both independence (from parents) and affiliation (with fans). Leaving the Robert Plant show I was mugged for my just-purchased shirt by a gang of bigger kids who overpowered me and my friend. I fought back, with all the savagery of one for whom a concert, on a given date, in a given place, with a given band, was a singular historical phenomenon, never to be repeated, never to be approximated, and the concert shirt the only possible documentation. There was no deathless life of all performances on YouTube. There was no archive of the set list to Google, there were no thumbnails of those precious ticket stubs I enshrined on my bulletin board. Things happened and were finished and lost and you had to go looking for more. I risked stabbing to hang on to that T-shirt and was rescued by Guardian Angels, and I wore the shirt proudly the next day along with my bruises.

By my second year of high school I'd lost the knack of unself-conscious fandom for marquee rock stars. Sexual awakening, heightened self-doubt, and a growing awareness of countercultural ideas had formed a perfect storm and ruined Stevie Nicks, and much else, for me, even while enabling much that was good. But for years afterward I would remain unable to reconcile, say, *Horses* with *Rumours*; it seemed I had to choose. Off came the beret, replaced by misgivings about Stevie that remain to this day—that she's too mainstream and perhaps just too silly. I made it to that concert in 1982 through the narrowest window of overlapped freedom and fan innocence; the previous year I had not been allowed to see rock shows at all, and less than two years later I would declare myself too cool for them. I'm glad that I enjoyed them while I could. I didn't know that enjoyment's worst enemy, the hyperactive judgments of the self, lay just a handful of months down the road. My best friend, Suzan Seggerman, and I had obtained lousy seats, as far off stage right as it was possible to go without watching the show from the rear. Felicitously, Stevie's microphone was off to stage right, in front of a huge speaker stack that blocked Suzan's and my view of much of the rest of the band. We didn't care. Stevie was who we had come for. We thrilled to her singing, and stamping, and spinning, and at one point, to her repairing behind the big pile of speakers to brush out her hair. She was hidden from the view of all but our poorly-seated two percent of the crowd, and in that relative privacy, the privacy of a woman who is momentarily performing not for fifteen thousand people but a mere several hundred, she brushed and brushed her hair as if under conditions of unlimited time and serene solitude. For a while she brushed bending forward, her whole head obscured, attacking the torrent of hair back-to-front. Then she flipped the hair over her head in a gesture that could have left lash marks, and started again front-to-back. Who knows how the rest of the band occupied itself during her absence. I have no recollection if they were playing or not. Stevie was all that I saw; she was that luminous blur that she'd taught me was preferable to plain life. She was the star, here with a fresh lesson that to this day I still haven't learned: *Always* perform. And, perform as if no one is there.

Sister

Elissa Schappell

In my dream I am standing alone in the California desert. Then, suddenly, a red Rambler fishtails up in front of me in a cloud of dust. The driver, a cool blonde in black shades leans over and opens the door. It's Kim Gordon. "Get in," she says.

I get in.

At which point I wake up, reach for my phone, and before I lose it, type in fast: "Dreaming, I wrote this. Dreaming of how to fix it."

It is this essay.

If you are familiar with the music of Sonic Youth, the seminal post-punk art rock band that Kim Gordon cofounded with Thurston Moore and Lee Ranaldo, you might see how this line echoes a line from "Tunic (Song for Karen):" "Dreaming, dreaming how it's supposed to be."

The song, which Kim wrote and sings in the voice of the tragic seventies pop star is, at its center, about the desperate need many women feel to be perfect. In the case of Karen Carpenter, who died at thirty-two of heart failure resulting from chronic anorexia, it killed her.

Being unable to articulate how Kim Gordon has, over the last twenty years, influenced me personally and artistically wasn't killing me exactly, but it had me in a twist. I couldn't find my groove, couldn't find the right voice, the distance, the structure. The piece was, at its best, the rambling mash note of a fangirl, reports from an accidental stalker, an overly earnest feminist treatise. It was far from perfect.

The next morning when I reached for my phone, I heard a line that Kim channels from the lowest register of Carpenter's consciousness in my head—"I ain't never going anywhere... I ain't never going anywhere..." That soul-crippling, ego-annihilating loop of self-loathing had been on repeat in my head for days. I was sick of it.

Fuck it, I thought. I know exactly why I got in the car with her. I stared at the screen. I'm just not sure where we're going.

The first time I saw Kim was at CBGB. It was the late eighties. I was out of college and living in NYC with my new boyfriend who was a big Sonic Youth fan. I didn't know that much about the band; I liked their stuff, especially the new song "Sister," although my boyfriend called it "pop-y." I'd heard about the show, (a benefit for a record store that had flooded), through *Spy*, the magazine where I was working.

When we arrived, the band was gathered in the shadows just off stage, waiting to go on. Ten feet away, the crowd was in full thrash and there was Kim leaning there against the amp looking slightly bored but focused. Even from the back of the club I recognized her. Recognized her type. Kim was that cool older girl, aloof and mysterious, who everybody was in awe of. She was the one who strides across the parking lot of the 7-Eleven pausing to flick her cigarette at the dudes in muscle cars catcalling her. Yeah, I'm a girl. Unintimidated in cut-offs and boots, a band tee, hair bleached blonde, unaffected by the macho posturing. Sure, take it all in. She was that girl who stares down the assholes in the parking lot and says, "I got no time for your nonsense." We—and she meant the rest of us girls—we've got no time for your nonsense.

And when she strapped on her bass and took her place in the front of stage, it was clear she had no time for nonsense. And I had no time for nonsense.

Seconds later the stage is electric, a wrecking yard of sound and dissonant fury. Thurston is screaming into the mic and jamming a drumstick into his fret as Lee bleeds distortion out of his electric guitar with a screwdriver; in the back Steve Shelley is unmercifully pummeling his kit, while Kim in the middle working over her bass, head bobbing, hair in her face, is holding it all down. This is a revelation. That's a girl standing up there in front of this mass of people, unself-consciously ripping apart her bass and singing; playing like we're not even here, like she's alone in her basement, only she's not alone, and she's hooked into our energy and you can tell when she lifts her bass, screaming feedback up to the amp like an offering to the gods of noise and holds it there, and holds it there, and holds it there, howling, calling forth this transcendent distortion, the music is her gift to us. She's not like other people.

Kim is remarkable. In an industry that is all about marketing female performers as virginal girl-next-door cutie pies or ticking sex bombs, Kim is feminine but not girly, sexual but not for sale. In the dawning age of alternative rock and grunge, a universe overpopulated by dudes, Kim is a unicorn. A female up front, trading vocals, seemingly as comfortable hanging out with the lads as she is with the ladies…

Not long after that first show I discovered that Kim and Thurston were a couple. No, Kim and Thurston were married.

Which shouldn't have surprised me; onstage they were so clearly riding the dissonant soundwave they created together, but they'd exchanged no moony-eyed we're-*so-in-love* gazes. There was no bullshit psycho-sexual tension. They were equal, separate, and together.

At the time this equal, separate but together thing mattered to me. I was freaking out about being in love and thinking about getting married. Since I'd begun working at *Spy*, a fount of snark and irreverence, the amount of irony pounding in my veins had tripled. The world was one big joke.

So I winced when friends teased me about getting "hitched," which sounded like a lifetime consigned to pulling a plow. The word "wed" was softer and more poetic, if uncomfortably close to "web." And yet, and yet, there were Kim and Thurston, the ultimate hipster couple, hitched, wed, married.

I couldn't know what Kim and Thurston's personal life was really like, only that in public they appeared easy with each other, simpatico, the vibe very much like what they gave off onstage. I'm just stepping in and taking my place, which is right up here in front, beside you. It confirmed my belief that my boyfriend, who was also a writer, and I could do this thing. There was something un-ironic, and brave, about declaring your love for someone. No joke. It felt akin to rebellion.

In addition to working at *Spy*, I was also working as a freelance journalist. Being a small female with a dyed-blonde pixie cut and a pearl stud in my nose, I was used to not being taken seriously. It pissed me off. What I wanted was to be as self-possessed—in possession of my self—and powerful as Kim appeared to be. I also wanted to be able to wear a mod leather mini skirt, white go-go boots, and a shaggy faux-fur coat.

At that time it would never have occurred to me that Kim might encounter the same sexist bullshit I did. But there it was, in *SPIN*,

Kim interviewing future Grammy host, then rising rap sensation LL Cool J, who was promoting *Walking With a Panther*. I expected what she might have expected—that with her indie hardcore cred, and her general badassitude, she and LL would, if not click, at least have a substantive dialogue.

Kim vs. Cool J is a classic in the pantheon of awkward interviews. High on his new stardom, LL can scarcely be bothered to offer more than monosyllabic answers to Kim's questions. He does get it up for his fellow friend of the workingman, corporate rock deity, Bon Jovi: "Bon Jovi I can relate to." It's clear that not only can't he relate to Kim but when he declares, "a guy has to have control over his woman" he doesn't respect her. Surely, this bleached-blonde indie chick is so zonked on his testosterone-jacked man musk she wouldn't write this down, or even if she did, she wouldn't call him out on being a witless misogynistic prick. And she doesn't.

She doesn't do that until a year later when Sonic Youth's new album *Goo* drops, and it becomes clear that the ill-fated interview is the inspiration for "Kool Thing," which will become the band's first major-minor hit. The songs on the album written and sung by Kim have an unabashedly subversive feminist message. Despite the fact I've always been a feminist, only now, in the early nineties, am I calling myself one, and out loud. In my mind, growing up in the seventies and eighties, there is only one kind of feminist. She is a mirthless, furry-pitted, bra-burning man hater who melts down other women's lipstick to make war paint. A strident, sign-waving screamer in comfortable shoes, who screams herself hoarse trying to reach an audience that, instead of listening, plugs their ears.

Yet, here is Kim. Darkly funny, killer chic, and smart as hell, the Kim-style approach to revolution is more stealth. You can't get inside people's heads if you can't get them to listen. The best way to blow up the machine, especially if you're female, is from the inside.

Goo is the most accessible of Sonic Youth's albums. Kim's songs are the most obvious representation of her fascination with our country's celebrity obsession and the effect it has on women—the cost of taking a ride in the dream machine.

Rap savvy readers will pick up on the humorous references in "Kool Thing"—the lines, "walking like a panther…let me play with your radio…," the repetition of the lyrics, "I don't think so." Even the video, directed by a young Tamra Davis—in which the "panther" is played by a black house cat that Kim cuddles—recalls LL's video for "Going Back to Cali." At the time what I was struck by most was the way that Kim was able to take the disastrous interview and elegantly turn it into something much larger than its parts. Working at *Spy* I was used to putting myself into the path of trouble and when it found me, I took notes. Kim had taken notes—there they were in *SPIN*—and then transformed the experience into a witty social critique of gender, race, and power that you could dance to. "Kool Thing" is more than Kim's assault on LL Cool J's ego, but a dig at her own liberal politics. The sarcasm in her voice when she addresses "Kool Thing" (played by Public Enemy's Chuck D) in the breakdown is self-mocking—the female voice inflated by privilege and naïveté. "I just wanna know, what are you gonna do for me? I mean, are you going to liberate us girls from white male corporate oppression?"

Yes, it's a joke at her expense, sure, or so it would seem until she gives us that line, like a kiss with a razor blade under her tongue, "I just want you to know that we can still be friends…" At first listen, it seems like such a throwaway line, a joke, but it's not. It's code. The aggression in that line resonates with me. Because that's what girls like me, from the time we're small, have been conditioned to say when really what we want to say is, "Fuck you." Kim is saying what women mean but can't or won't say. And she means it.

Two years later, Sonic Youth's album *Dirty* presents "Swimsuit Issue," which is inspired by Kim's discovery that a Geffen executive was being sued for sexual harassment. The narrative is much straighter. Dialed back and dead serious. She says what women who are being abused by powerful men, again want to say, but often can't. "Don't touch my breast / I'm just working at my desk / Don't put me to the test / I'm just doing my best". The coup de grace, Kim ends the song by reciting the names of all of the models in the March 1992 issue of *Sports Illustrated*'s Swimsuit Issue.

For years Kim had been an inspiration, but now she was beginning to insinuate herself into my conscience. What I saw was that, not only can a woman make serious art that reflects her reality, she should. When I give away my power, I am giving away women's power. Why not make art that was political and angry and funny? Why not stick my finger in the chest of all those that say, "Be a good girl now?" There was no reason.

The songs Kim was writing are the kind of stories I want to write. Stories that unapologetically reflect the experiences we share, but because we're afraid or ashamed, or simply can't articulate our feelings, we don't talk about.

It isn't until I tune into the feminist message Kim is putting out there on *Goo*, that I realize it was there two years ago in the song "Kissability," which is on Sonic Youth's masterwork, the epic *Daydream Nation*. I just hadn't really thought about it, although even without intellectually keying in, I'd had a visceral reaction to it.

In "Kissability," Kim turns the dirty casting couch on its end. This time, writing from the point of view of the male, a predatory director she sings in the flat voice of commerce, "Look into my eyes, don't you trust me / Yr so soft you make me hard / I'll put you in a movie, don't you wanna / You could be a star, you could go far." His heavy breathing building with the song, until he's panting, and you can almost hear the sound of the teeth in his zipper parting. "Yr driving me crazy, I feel so sick / Yr driving me crazy, give us a kiss."

I can't help smirking every time I listen to that song. What a relief, for once, not to be the victim. There is something radical in the way Kim inhabits the character of this pervy creeper. How, instead of punishing him herself, she gives him license to talk, allowing him to become a victim of his own ridiculousness. It's like she's taken his hand off our ass and twisted it behind his back.

That feels good.

***

THE MORE I THINK about my dream the more I realize it's no accident that Kim appears driving a big red car. Cars are a stand-in for male power and sexuality. She's taken the wheel.

It's a fact that men help men. Women, despite the extraordinarily high premium placed on female friendships, are often less willing than men to help each other. You know, there are only so many spaces at the big man's table, thus we have to fight over them. Rarely is the amount of power one has commensurate with one's willingness to share it. Even though, as the saying goes, "There is a special place in Hell for women who don't help women."

What women who help women discover is that, instead of their power being diminished, it grows, and they reap the benefits.

Kim inspired Kathleen Hanna and legions of Riot Grrrls to take back the mic and claim the stage for themselves. To unapologetically raise their voices, get loud, and get busy. She was coproducer of Hole's first album, *Pretty On The Inside,* and an early supporter of Tamra Davis, who directed the "Kool Thing" and "Dirty Boots" videos.

She's been good to the boys, too. She gave a fledgling Spike

Jonze the opportunity to direct the video of "100%," featured her old LA pal Mike Kelly's art on the cover of *Dirty*, and was a mentor and friend to Kurt Cobain.

Being part of a thriving arts community is a big deal. The year my daughter turned one, my husband and I had an opportunity to be cofounders of a literary magazine called *Tin House*. It was an exciting prospect, but also perilous. Not only did starting a magazine require tons of work, it would mean working together more than we already did. That seemed crazy.

Then again, Kim and Thurston were married and they worked together, right? I mean, there they were onstage, tidal waves of sound crashing around them, smashing guitars, yet in this sonic vortex they were solid. Maybe we could do it, too.

***

I DON'T REMEMBER IF in my dream there was a child's car seat in the back of Kim's red Rambler, but there might have been.

In 1994, Kim and Thurston had a daughter, and named her Coco. I will confess it was something of a relief. In the same way that I believed that to marry was to lose a part of your self, I believed that, by having a baby before I published a book, I was forfeiting my ambition. I believed the lie that women have to choose, that if a woman is serious about her work there can be nothing but the work. (Outside of fucking, drugs, and travel.) Family trumped art. Male artists could have children because no one expected them to raise them, that was the job of the art wife. Daddy keeps rocking, while Mommy rocks the cradle.

Apparently Kim didn't get that memo, or maybe she trashed it. As with everything else, Kim was taking on motherhood on her own terms. Not only did she keep making music with Sonic Youth; there were her side bands like Free Kitten and Ciccone Youth, and when she wasn't making music she was making art and curating shows, and, oh yeah, launching a clothing company called X-Girl, and a limited edition fashion line, Mirror/Dash, "clothes for cool moms." Who better? Kim was *the* cool mom. Hell, she was the coolest. The rebel swagger that attracted me to her before—the noise, the rad feminist lyrics, refusing to be pinned down to one art form, being major but not mainstream—had since exploded tenfold. If Kim could do it I thought I could at least try.

Not only that. On and off stage, Kim, in vintage minidresses, tight-patterned trousers, and stacked heels, is still a style ninja, only it's a baby strapped to her chest instead of a bass. Maybe I couldn't pull off the black slip dress six months after my daughter was born, and I'd never have Kim's killer gams, but still.

If anything, Kim's art and music seemed to be getting smarter and deeper, and I had to wonder, maybe if I had a kid there might be the chance that my own work would do the same. It seemed that as she was getting older she was becoming less afraid, more willing to take risks and trust herself. She was able to make herself more vulnerable, and there is strength and real power in that.

Years later, when I had my own daughter, I understood the importance of Kim demonstrating that power and strength. Because I believe, as Anaïs Nin says, "Life expands or shrinks in proportion to one's courage." Kim embodied that statement. Not that she was perfect or held herself up as a model mom. Sure, you don't have to give up anything to be a mother and an artist. You just have to accept that sometimes you're not going to do everything well, and that's okay.

You also have to accept that sometimes you have got to make a change. While I wasn't about to give up my Brooklyn digs, I admired the decision Kim and Thurston made to leave Manhattan for Northampton, Mass. so they could raise their daughter in the most normal way possible for two high-profile indie rock stars.

Their move gave scores of new families (I am hardly alone in the "If Kim and Thurston can do it" camp) the permission—or cover—to leave city life for small town living.

I reached a point while writing my last book, *Blueprints for Building Better Girls,* a collection of linked stories about a cast of archetypal female characters—the slut, the party girl, the perfect mom—where I wanted to write a story about a grown woman— not a young woman—with anorexia. There is no way to write about the dark side of women's lives without addressing the fraught relationship many women have with food. Even so, I was squeamish. The critic in my head was merciless on the subject: *How trite, how tedious, how silly.*

Every book and every story has a soundtrack, and so I found myself listening to "Tunic (Song for Karen)" a lot when I was trying to gin up the courage to write the story. In "Tunic," Kim Gordon sings in the voice of seventies pop songbird, Karen Carpenter, half of the preternaturally sunny brother and sister duo, The Carpenters. Wildly popular in life, her legacy had been overshadowed by her grim death from anorexia. She was a joke. A punch line.

Kim wasn't laughing though. Because she thought Karen Carpenter's story was tragic, and deserved to be told, I found that playing "Tunic" really loud over and over again while I was writing drowned out the voice in my head saying, *This is stupid no one cares about this shit.*

Because fuck them if they didn't care about my story. It just made me take my story—and this story—more seriously. Everybody thought they knew Karen Carpenter, but they didn't know shit.

The more I listened to that song, the more I keyed into the detachment in Kim's voice. That was essential. The fluctuating distance of the POV, the mordant wit and the tonal shifts—that was what my story needed for it to transcend being just another story about a woman starving herself. It was the same thing she did in "Kissability" and "Kool Thing." The woman's power may seem only skin deep—she's a pretty white girl, a sex object, a pop superstar—but that's because that's all our culture values about them. That's why the culture thinks they have the power, but Kim turns it around.

The song opens with Kim as Karen, an angel from above speaking to brother Richard and her parents in her best-girl-in-the-world voice. *Don't be sad,* she says, Heaven is great. *There's Elvis, Dennis, and Janis.* She's in a band and playing the drums again.

I'd forgotten she was a virtuoso drummer. For years I'd thought of Karen Carpenter as little more than the star, in Barbie form, of Todd Haynes' cult biopic *Superstar.*

There is a sick dreaminess in Kim's voice, as she recites Karen's diet: "another green salad, another iced tea." This line hits home. Women know how important it is to our survival not to take up too much space, figuratively as well as metaphorically.

Every time I listen to "Tunic," I anticipate the moment when Kim as Karen's voice darkens and drops into a menacing incantation, "You aren't never going anywhere / I ain't never going anywhere." It's terrifying. Equally scary is how, when addressing her parents, Kim as Karen's voice suddenly shifts, scampering back into the higher register, up into the light, so angelic and bright it hurts.

"Tunic" was for all the girls who felt they had to be perfect, all of us who felt like no matter how we might succeed it would never be enough. When Karen's mother responds to her daring to say, "the band doesn't sound half-bad" with "Honey, don't let it go to your head," some part inside me shrinks. That's not just her mom, that's the culture speaking. This is what we've been hearing our whole lives. *Good girls stay small in every possible way.* Witnessing

Sonic Youth perform "Tunic" live can be an intensely cathartic experience. Watching Kim, hair sticking to her face as she haunts the microphone, while the guys churn up a tsunami of sound behind her; being engulfed in the crowd, jostled and borne toward the lip of the stage, everyone moving back and forth together, some singing with their eyes closed, some swaying and mouthing the words, and some pounding the air, screaming along with the lyrics, reclaiming the power that was stolen from them, you feel a part of something, you feel known.

The stereotypical rock and roll marriage lasts for about as long as a European tour, or until the Cristal runs out. Kim and Thurston, married for twenty-seven years, were destined for the Rock and Roll Matrimony Hall of Fame. The story of the husband who, longing to once again feel the wind in his thinning hair, trades in his old wife for a newer model (barely street-legal) is so tedious and clichéd it's embarrassing. Yet, it's what Thurston does. The announcement in 2011 that Kim and Thurston are splitting is met with howls of disbelief and true sadness. Fans aren't only lamenting the fact that there will be no more music, but also mourning the death of a marriage that had seemed to be proof that you could have it all.

I don't know why I was so surprised, but I was. Naive and ridiculous as it sounds, it's true. It's not that I couldn't imagine Thurston cheating (although, I couldn't have imagined he'd been carrying on for six years), I couldn't imagine why... I wasn't the only one. The Chorus of the Dumbfounded was enormous. Our common refrain, *What was he thinking? How could he leave Kim Gordon?* And then, *Why would she put up with this shit?* Of course no one knows what goes on in other people's marriages, what deals they've made, or sacrifices. We can't begin to know how others fare against their demons. We shouldn't. It's none of our business. People change. Become strangers. And they go their separate ways.

What is true is this: as you get older there are fewer forks in the road, but they are bigger. The decisions you make seem more dramatic, even more so when everyone is watching you. In the case of Thurston and Kim, it has been all eyes on Kim. Since the break up, Kim has had gallery shows in the US and abroad, and she's started a new band with Bill Nace called Body/Head, an experimental, improvisational noise band whose guitar and feedback sound recall the early No Wave days of Sonic Youth, before they became stars. However, the emotion and lyrical content on *Coming Apart* is miles away from those early days. The feminist themes that have been weaving through Kim's lyrics for decades—female identity and male power, the roles women are conscripted to play and those they choose out of duty or desire—are in the forefront now. The work Kim is making now is the most emotional and honest in her career. It's naked. How many sixty-year-old women would let you see them naked?

***

IN MY DREAM KIM and I are on the road. We've been listening to the radio and eating candy and having those kinds of intense conversations you only have on the road. At some point she slows down, pulls over, and gets out of the car. "You drive," she says.

I can do that.

Running Up That Hill

Lisa Catherine Harper

All I ever wanted—to be normal.

In grade school, I had enough friends—a small, tight knot of cool girls and the cute, athletic boys who circled us—to fool myself. They had their satin jackets, their feathered hair, their divorced, key party-throwing parents. I had a satin jacket, too, but I was bookish. My best friend affectionately called me "Poindexter." My parents were together and they took me, my sister, and brother to church, and me to ballet class. They kept me away from the spin the bottle parties, and yet still, I think of those years as a pause, the time before adolescence and those so-called friends hit hard.

Our suburban New Jersey town was settled on a hill, and we lived halfway up, which provides a convenient metaphor. I was constantly walking up that hill—to get to grammar school, to get home from junior high, to get home from the train that carried me to Manhattan—it was a quick, inexpensive, safe trip, and I took it as often as I could. That was the thing about our green, hillside town. It had good schools, a large library, abundant parks, thriving local businesses, a community pool, even a local musical theater for kids. It also had New York. You could have all the ease of suburban life. And, if you were like me, you could not only dream your escape, you could just get on a train and go.

My sister found me hysterical on our front lawn. I remember: a gaggle of dark, feathered heads, circling me in front of the junior high, the same way they'd circled a half-dozen others over the past weeks. I'd seen it happen: the shunning, the insults, the cold, deliberate destruction of a girl. As soon as they started to gather, through some force as invisible and fatal as gravity, I knew. Even before they closed in I knew it was my turn. I stood in front of that innocent pink-bricked school, my books clutched to my chest, and turned my back on them, but there was no getting away. Insults poured down like toxic rain. I knew better than to respond. They swarmed, and eventually, I escaped. I ran straight up that hill, black-eyed with fear and betrayal, all the way home where sister found me. I wept myself into a blackout.

There were new friends, but they evaporated by high school. One lost to drugs, another to a Swiss boarding school, a third to a schedule of classes that would never intersect with my own. There was the long, silent slog of high school, but I excelled. After school, after dance class or gymnastics practice, I'd climb the three flights of stairs to my attic room and read, or write, or study, and generally disappear to the world below. My family felt like distant relatives. I loved them very much, but I didn't feel like I quite belonged.

In 1983, girls had big hair. Even my sister had a perm. They lined their eyes and went to weekend football games and booze-soaked parties. They had sex in their parents' bedrooms, sex in vans, some kind of sex in the more obscure wings of the high school. The girls still traveled in packs, the boys were banded into teams: the lacrosse team, the championship soccer team. There was the football team, and a basketball team I was peripherally aware of. One of them played in the NBA, eventually. I would have been hard-pressed to tell you who played football.

I had bone-straight hair. I wore no makeup and my clothes tended toward chinos and IZODs, bohemian long skirts, with granny boots and layered scarves, Gatsby-inspired drop-waist dresses.

The girls wore sleeves of rubber bracelets, slouch socks, zippers. So many zippers. Boys and girls both wore cut-off sweatshirts. There were a lot of leggings and big sweaters, and leggings with leg warmers and big sweaters. I had a swatch, and jellies, and the leg warmers and the sweatshirts—I was a dancer—but I was out of sync.

In 1983, kids in my school were listening to AC/DC and Led Zeppelin and Pink Floyd. My sister and her friends gravitated to Michael Jackson, the Go-Go's, Bananarama, and lots and lots of Madonna. In 1983, I found Kate Bush, whose existence confirmed that it would be impossible for me to be normal. Ever.

Kids know: you're either one kind of person or another. You're either the kind of person, like my sister, who moves through life with ease and comfort, normal, integrated, justified—in the sense of "made right with." Or you're the other kind: the one who's always a little out of sync, always striving a little too much, or failing, or falling behind, or walking ahead of the crowd. These were the nerds, the geeks, the goths, the druggies, the burnouts, the straight-laced, the queer. And me.

Another way to put it: you're either the kind of person who gets Kate Bush, or you're not.

That summer, I met A—. He was a lifeguard, and with his best friend was teaching the certification course I'd enrolled in. The way he told it later, I came out of the pool, approached him, asked about the class. He said he looked in my eyes and got lost. Everyone knew him. He was fit, athletic, an engineering student at a nearby tech college. He skied and held a black belt in some kind of judo and looked excellent in his swimming trunks. He read science fiction, loved arcade video games, and beat me at chess every time. He kept his blond hair shaved military close, and his eyes were impossibly, brightly blue. We started dating the day I passed the course.

A— had music. In a room off the family room, shelves of vinyl ran the full length of the wall. There was a pristine, shining black stereo, a finely calibrated turntable, a double tape deck, stacks of speakers. There was no dust in that room, even though he had three brothers and the house was full of their noise and sweaty-boy lives.

Were there 500 albums? A thousand? I have no idea. How much room does vinyl take up? The albums were organized methodically and he could pull any one of them—Laurie Anderson, Nena, the Eurythmics, Tears for Fears, Thomas Dolby, the Talking Heads, Echo and the Bunnymen, Siouxsie and the Banshees, Bowie, Martha and the Muffins, the Police—immediately. His collection was eclectic, and veered toward UK artists and obscure (to me) Canadian bands. Every LP that entered that room was recorded on the tape deck, each track recorded on the blank cardboard liner in blue ink, in his perfect block print. The albums remained pristine.

After dinner, or movies, or the arcade, we'd greet his clan and shuffle through the TV room, and shut the glass door, and sink into the sofa, the music, and each other.

And that was where I heard her.

One night, not long after we met, he put on *The Kick Inside*. Twenty haunting seconds of whale song filled that hermetically sealed room, a single deep chord…and then that voice. Her first intonation climbed how many octaves?… Two? Three?… I have no idea, but it was a note that climbed into my throat and burrowed inside me, a sock of deep, dangerous pleasure. It was impossible to resist that sexy, ethereal longing. I let myself go in a kind of wonder. It was like drowning or dreaming. Or both. All around us there was lush, layered instrumentation; drums, guitars—electric and acoustic, bass, piano—also organ and clavinet, mandolin, synthesizer, sax, and something called a boobam. If it sounded like nothing I'd heard before it was partly the impossible, unearthly pitch of her voice, and partly her headlong, relentless slowdive into the lyrics.

Was she *really* singing about Berlin bars and Beelzebub? Urging her lover to *feel it* in an orgasmic post-party union? And was that song really a hymn to the strange, uncanny power of every girl's punctual blues? Here was Gurdjieff and Jesu and Whirling Dervishes. Her unbridled phrasing saved the music from cliché, her weird caterwauling rescued it from its own melodrama. It didn't sound like rock and roll or pop. She was a dancer but it didn't sound like dance music. It wasn't classical, or punk, or new age, exactly. It just sounded like someone had rigged a pipeline to her unconscious, and now it was spilling out.

Until then, I had no idea such people existed outside of books, or my own head.

The thing is, for all of A—'s all-American good looks, his enthusiastic optimism, his polite, cheery way with adults, his steadfast devotion to me, his athletic, sexy ease in his body, he was also not what he seemed. He was, in fact, Canadian. When you listened closely, you could hear the faintest shift in his vowels. His family kept a tub of solid honey in the kitchen that they spread on bread. They were really into hockey. Canada explained his niceness, and the slightly formal, mannered pleasantness of his family. It also explained his gravitation to British musicians. It almost explained Kate Bush. If a guy introduces you to Kate Bush's music, then gives you every one of her albums, he is probably not as normal as he seems.

My attic room was a study in green, with an accent wall papered with abstract clouds. Looking at that wall was like falling into some weird, painted sky. The ceiling sloped down on both sides, like a large tent, or a high-altitude cave. It was private. It was safe. It was mine. I took those albums up to that room, and almost every night in high school I raised the arm of my turntable, the one you used to stack records on to play sequentially, and pulled it all the way to the side so that whatever side I played would repeat, for hours, until I was done and ready for bed. I spread my books, and papers, and pens, and typewriter across my desk and worked while one side of *The Kick Inside*, or *Lionheart*, or *Never for Ever*, played relentlessly. It was like mainlining poetry. It was ridiculous, and addictive, and I couldn't stop.

I scoured the liner notes like they were novels and parsed the lyrics like sacred text, which they sort of were. "I love the whirling of the Dervishes / I love the beauty of rare innocence / you don't need no crystal ball / Don't fall for a magic wand / We humans got it all, we perform the miracles." It was ritualistic, and pagan, and spiritual, and it appealed to the Catholic in me. Like the cover of *Never for Ever*, all manner of beings and beasts inhabited her songs.

Except in Kate Bush's case, they were spilling out from under her dress.

Which is to say, she made me uncomfortable. There was something transgressive about her. Obviously there was that voice, which could be ethereal, angelic, all lace and romance until it dropped off some dark moor of her mind and sent you shivering into a Hammer horror nightmare. Then, there was her subject matter: *Babooshka*, who murdered her husband; an old English incest ballad; a *Turn of the Screw*-inspired pedophilic nanny. When A—and I watched *The Day After*, we'd already been traumatized by the lyrics of "Breathing," which she'd released three years earlier: "Breathing / Breathing my mother in / Breathing my beloved in /

Chips of plutonium / Are twinkling in every lung." I still love that ghastly end rhyme.

She had, too, a penchant for climbing into other people's stories. Her first person ballads are more dramatic monologue than anything else, and they appealed to my bookish, literary soul, as did the Latin, Sanskrit, and French. But she didn't just tell the story of, say, Bess Houdini or Lizzie Wan, she seemed actually to possess her subjects or channel them—like a medium. She inhabited Brontë's Cathy, she took you right up to Heathcliff's window and left you there wandering with your desolate passion. Or she took you to the edge of enlightenment, but no further, and left you suspended there, struggling for transcendence, rigged and tortured, suspended in gaffer tape. In "Houdini," sure, she possesses Houdini's wife at the séance, but she also voices several registers of her experience in that single song: tender lover, angry wife, the dead husband's whisper from behind the grave. And the thing is: you fucking believe her. You kind of stumble with each shift and think: *This chick is crazy*. You also think: *This chick is totally original.*

It helped explain things when I learned her dance teacher was one of England's premier mimes (and also David Bowie's influential movement teacher). It explained her weird, literal interpretive movement that made all the sexy modern leotard dancing just seem, well, so very unsexy. You had to respect that, too, her refusal to be simply sexy, or sexy in a way we understood. She wasn't just dancing to the music, she was enacting the story. On the cover of her first album, she's hanging from a Chinese kite and whether she's happy up there or hanging on for her life, your guess is as good as mine. On the back of her third album, she flew like a harpy across a night sky. On the front of *Lionheart,* she wore a lion unitard and crawled across an attic floor. She had those demons flying out of her skirts, and a few years later, lay down with a pair of hounds in cover art that manages to be romantic and awkwardly literal and bestial all at once.

I liked that she made me uncomfortable. I listened, some nights, in spite of myself, until her music wore a groove into my soul so deep that I still remember every single word of *The Kick Inside,* and more: I listen digitally now, but I still know the exact place where I dropped the needle on "The Man with a Child in His Eyes" and it jumped and scratched the record, a hitch in the song, a thirty-year-old hitch in my heart. My kids, hearing her voice for the first time, ran into the room, began chastising me, *Omygodwhatareyoulisteni gntowhosthatwhydoesshesoundlikethatmomomomwhoisthatwhatist hatsongisthateven*English*Icann*ot*believeyoulistentothis.*

Here's what she showed me: that desire could be my own. My feelings would not kill me. More important: it was okay not to be normal. And a girl could create with abandon. I was seventeen, then eighteen, and I was working so hard, running up the hill of late adolescence to get out and find…what? Something about myself, probably. Something about being a writer, definitely. Something about love, eventually.

Here was the thing: I loved A—, but I loved my singularity more. So I stole orgasms and we found plenty enough mutual pleasures, but there was just no way I was going to fuck up my life by fucking him. There was just no way I would take even the slightest chance of becoming pregnant.

When I finally enrolled in the Ivy League school I'd dreamed about most, I found myself at home in the preppy, bookish days, and the Gothic-towered nights. I dug the gargoyles, the pseudo-Anglican history, and the long, dark nights walking across campus, and the deserted golf course, looking for a friend I loved, who was often out looking for me, and who would sometimes show up, rain-drenched, at my door, or who would have left, while I was out, a cryptic, poetic, Heathcliff-like message on my whiteboard, though truth be told, he was nothing at all like Heathcliff, except maybe in the intensity of his ability to feel. I think he hated Kate Bush. Eventually, I broke up with A—, and Kate Bush faded from my playlist. She'd served her purpose.

Why did Kate Bush become mine in a way no other musician ever would? Other boys gave me albums, and mix tapes, and I fell in love with other bands on my own, but it wasn't the same. I suspect now that it wasn't so much that she was the soundtrack to the end of my childish life as much as she was the foil to everything normal at that time: perfect grades, perfect family, perfectly preppy wardrobe. I wasn't comfortable. I lived in a kind of little girl drag. Except in that room at the top of the house, where I sank, finally, fully into my skin. Kate Bush was the antidote that let me commune with myself, in intimate, wordless conversation. She drove me into myself, which was how I finally found my way up that hill, and out into the rest of my life.

Not Rid of Me

Ian Daly

February 22, 2014
Venice, California

Dear Miss Harvey,

I think I'm supposed to be writing an essay about you. That's off to a bad start, isn't it? As the first three words of this thing would suggest, I appear to be writing you a letter. Well okay, technically it's a letter in a book of essays about powerful women in music—and thus will likely be read not by you, but by those who adore you. In that sense you could say this is more of a postmodern meta-letter. Happily, as the postmodern meta-letter remains an emergent and as-yet undefined genre of epistolary, I'm just going to fucking wing it.

Like most letters I've written to women I've adored over the years, this is hard to write. And as always, the hardest part is knowing where to begin. But I think I found a hook.

I'm going to begin at Bob Dylan's house.

Last week I found myself idling outside the corrugated metal fence of Dylan's Point Dume compound in Malibu—trying to squint past the giant old shipping containers into what I suppose I hoped might resemble his life.

I probably don't have to tell you that I don't know Bob Dylan and had no business idling in front of his property that late mid-February afternoon. I probably also don't have to tell you why I was there: I was lost.

Not in the literal sense, of course. Sadly, it isn't too difficult these days to Google your favorite rock star's address, plug it into your smartphone, and allow the pleasant female voice to direct your creepy ass to within sprinkler distance of his front lawn. I'm talking about the kind of lost that leads otherwise sane and well-adjusted individuals to the base of Salinger's driveway—or the greenhouse that hasn't belonged to Kurt Cobain in twenty years. A spiritual kind of lost that doesn't even require the subject of your pilgrimage to be alive, much less home at the time. The kind that finds you in the question-mark phases of your life and drags you forward, with a sad and lonely gravity, to the doorsteps of your idols. It is there that you will find yourself asking—often to nothing more than a mailbox or a shrub—for help. Spiritual guidance. Answers.

I guess what I'm saying is, writing a letter to you in a book of essays, for which you are the intended subject, not the audience, is a little like idling at Dylan's place. It is at once a meaningful and shameful exercise. And the more I think about it, the more I'm certain that I want you to read this letter about as much I wanted Dylan to come at me that day with a garden trowel, sporting a fresh pair of New Balances and screaming "I'M NOT YOUR PROPHET, MAN!"

There is nothing about the folly of deifying our rock and roll heroes that hasn't been written, so I won't waste your time. Except to say this: to those of us without religion, in the traditional sense of the word, people like you are the closest thing to God we have. And while it is not only unfair but insane to suggest our musical heroes have some kind of duty to save us, the fact remains: they fucking do save us. Just as you, Miss Harvey, saved me. To tell you how, I'm going to have to put the car in reverse, back out of Dylan's driveway, and keep driving all the way to Naples, Florida—in 1992.

***

The sun was setting over the strip malls of Pine Ridge Road when I fed the tape into the cassette deck of my parents' Merlot-hued Acura Integra and felt the mechanism suck it in and click into action. Back then I was a high school junior. If you were a high school junior in Naples, Florida in 1992—especially one who wrote for an underground literary magazine and had only recently been introduced to Thoreauvian ideals of nonconformity via his tenth-grade English class—here is what you most likely were: bored.

I know you understand boredom. Thanks to one of Nick Cave's many breakup songs about you, "West Country Girl," I know you hail from a little nowheresville yourself. But hear me out: at least you had sheep and rivers and, from what I've read, rock stars of the likes of Charlie Fucking Watts crashing at your house. And while our hometowns may be of roughly the same populace, mine was not a postcard of pastoral English life. Mine, rather, was an innocuous coastal utopia for retired insurance adjusters from Indiana and the medical staff who tend to their prostates. A place with more millionaires and golf courses per capita than all but one other American city. A smooth jazz seaside hell of 20,000 people—and a surrounding sprawl of a quarter-million more—tucked away in ant-farm subdivisions adorned with chlorinated fountains and streets named after the flora they razed to make way for. A place where the generally accepted notion of "art" amounted to life-size lawn sculptures of bronze dolphins that cost more than Jaguars. A place where "culture" amounted to Boz Scaggs tributes at the local philharmonic. And the closest thing we had to rock stars crashing at our house was the time my stepfather's cousin's alcoholic boyfriend stayed for a week and played sloppy renditions of Neil Diamond on my electric piano between swigs of Jack Daniel's and falling.

Because of this—and equally, I suppose, because of The State Of Being Sixteen—I was lost then, too. I was a mediocre student— too lazy to excel and too scared to fail, a piano and drum student who never practiced. A noncontributing zombie member of a few academic clubs—not into sports, semi-entrenched in a handful of computer games, done with Dungeons & Dragons but not yet making inroads with girls who weren't fourteenth-level Magic users. I was headed to college but for what, I hadn't a clue. I am pretty sure I wore pleated Hilfiger shorts and ate a lot of Wendy's. And while I definitely listened to Frank Zappa, I have some repressed memories of a Pat Metheny CD, too. In other words, if you're ever asked to paint an abstract of my life back then, just pick up a bucket of beige Glidden at your local hardware store and dump it on a canvas while yawning and eating saltines.

But then it happened. I was on my way home from a drum lesson. I should say, here, that my teacher was no ordinary man— he was a prophet. More accurately, he was the manager of our local independent music store, The Turntable. But that meant he was tapped into the only outside line our town had to truth and beauty. He was a lanky man with a little mustache, prone to wearing black berets and smoking clove cigarettes—all of which earned him the respectfully applied nickname of "Frenchie." Frenchie got me into Robert Fripp and Daniel Lanois. And when Frenchie said things like "you should check this out," you can bet whatever he was holding in his hands when he said it would be life-changing shit. And life-changing shit is exactly what I found on the tape he'd made for me that fateful afternoon in 1992. I hadn't even glanced at his liner notes before I plucked it out of its charcoal gray plastic case and popped it in the Acura's stereo. But it wouldn't have mattered because none of the names made any sense to me back then. Nevertheless, when the magnet met the ribbon, everything changed.

It started off with a low syncopated guitar riff in 5/4 time—detuned and droning up through the sludge of a distorted bass. And the drums—what the hell was going on with those drums? Taut toms beating out some kind of tribal riff over a hissing cymbal metronome in another time signature altogether—all of it colliding in a cyclical, consciousness-altering polyrhythm that seemed to transform the drab suburban landscape outside the Acura into something more exciting. With one last ca-clack-ATA-CLACK-ata, the intro riff faded, and she spoke:

"Samson / The strength / That's in / Your Arms / Oh to be / Your stunning / bride…"

The voice was deep and deadpan. Who was she? She kept the Bible story going—softly, sardonically: "Samson / Your Hair / That's in my hands / I'll keep it safe / You're mine / You're mine…" And then, in a white flash of distortion and drums, the whole thing just exploded.

> *He said waaaait!*
> *said way-haaaaait!*
> *Dee-lilah my babe!*
> *Dee-lilah my babe!*

I had heard Nirvana. And I was a fan. *Nevermind* was right next to Pearl Jam's *Ten* in my small, but growing CD collection. The truth is, I didn't hear the tide-shifting clarion call in *Nevermind*'s guitar riffs that everyone else did—certainly not in 1991, when I was equally amped up about Metallica's "Enter Sandman." But this—this was something from another planet.

I tried to imagine the creature "singing" to me. What was she wearing? Was she grunge or glamor? Was she metal or punk? Was she angry or arty? Was she smirking or serious? I sifted through archetypes in my head but came up blank. I had no frame of reference. So I did the only thing anyone in my position would have done at the time: I cranked up the volume until that voice sliced through the thick Florida air like a steak knife, and this strange woman I now know as Polly Jean Harvey belted out the climax of a song called "Hair."

"You lied in my face / You cut off my hair / You lied in my bed..."

I had no idea who you were or where you came from. But believe me when I tell you that your music was the key that unlocked a door inside of me I haven't shut since. That music was borne of no definable scene or genre. And it sure as hell didn't sound as if it were tied to any zeitgeist other than The Way I Was Feeling At That Exact Moment. That music was special. It had *answers*. It was a map. And those verses and those riffs were the splashes of color I needed to paint my way out of the beige world I'd somehow hemmed myself into. I didn't know it then, but I was making a decision: From here on out, I will devote my life to the discovery of, and assimilation into, the wild and brilliant world that this woman represented. A world of energy, determination, and purpose. A world that, in many ways, I got to define *myself.*

Maybe for our parents it was Hendrix or The Stones, or The Beatles before them. Those were the musical sparks that got their generation fired up about a freer, more meaningful way of living. But for me, you were that spark. And it wasn't long before I adopted the trappings of my generation's equivalent of that freer, more meaningful way of life for myself. I don't mean trading the pleated Hilfiger shorts for Doc Martens, though I did. I'm talking about the intelligence, honesty, energy, determination, and purpose. At the risk of sounding like some shitty self-help testimonial, I'm going to go ahead and say that I wouldn't be who I am without you. I don't know if I would have gone to grad school or embarked on a career in journalism. For me, *Dry* was like an exit ramp off a highway lined only with strip malls and soprano sax factories.

You probably think I'm exaggerating your influence.

That's fine. You're humble. So let me unearth something you may have forgotten. It's what Laura Lee Davies of *Time Out London* said back then, around the release of *Dry:* "This is the beginning of a thinking music that talks to those who don't like to be told what to think." See? It wasn't just representative of something incredible. It was the *beginning* of something incredible.

Allow me also to offer you some broader cultural context, by reminding you of the shit parade marching through the American airwaves in 1992. In 1992, Boyz II Men occupied the number-one slot on the *Billboard* charts. Sir Mix-A-Lot was rapping about the things his anaconda wanted and wanted none of, Eric Clapton was milking "Tears in Heaven," and John Fucking Secada was, well, John Fucking Secada. Meanwhile, Nirvana's "Smells Like Teen Spirit" was barely maintaining its lead above Bobby Brown's thirty-third-ranked "Humpin' Around." As for chart-topping women in rock? Unless you count Madonna, there were none. Scanning the Billboard charts that year, you'd find the likes of Vanessa Williams, TLC, En Vogue, Shanice, Mariah Carey, Sophie B. Hawkins, Cover Girls, and Amy Grant—a family-friendly drugstore soundtrack of big label R&B and crossover country. Hole's black anthem "Violet" was still three years away from becoming a single—and it wouldn't even crack the top one hundred.

If the charts weren't friendly to rockers of the female persuasion, things weren't particularly good for women *off* the charts, either. In 1991, MTV's *120 Minutes,* a show that for six years had been serving up alternative music to cable subscribers across the country, spun off a 2-CD compilation called *Never Mind the Mainstream.* Of the thirty-two tracks, exactly one was the work of a female solo artist: Sinead O'Connor's "Mandinka." Only four others even featured female vocalists (Sonic Youth, X, The Sugarcubes, and the Cocteau Twins, if you're curious).

My point is this: you really did herald something special, Miss Harvey—not just in contrast to the cultural wasteland of my smooth jazz hometown, but within the emerging alternative scene at large. Something important was happening. The lonely trail blazed by Sonic Youth's Kim Gordon was becoming less lonely. You were barely out of college when you found yourself on the frontline of what could only be described as a movement: a movement of powerful, unclassifiable women who were redefining rock music from every direction. And maybe one day you can tell me how the fuck it all seemed to happen during the same magical little window of time: from 1992 to 1994. The range stretched from so-called Riot Grrrl bands like L7, Hole, and Sleater-Kinney to strange and magical wood nymphs like your pal Björk, who seemed to come out of nowhere and resemble nothing. As you know, her first album, *Debut,* was a smash in 1993—the same year former Pixies bassist Kim Deal, fronting The Breeders, had a hit with "Cannonball." The same year Juliana Hatfield of the Blake Babies rose to alterna-stardom with *Become What You Are.* The same year Liz Phair released what is now widely regarded as one of the most important albums of its time: *Exile in Guyville.*

I know you are not so keen on being lumped into any category beyond "women who make incredible fucking music." And you shouldn't be. You even said as much in a 1993 interview on the French television show *Metal Express*.

"I don't think I feel a part of what anyone else is doing," you remarked, then just twenty-three years old and fiddling with the bangs that broke free from your slicked-back hairdo, "whether it's Courtney Love, the Breeders, or whoever—any more than they feel a part of anything I'm doing. I think we should all be seen separately. Unfortunately, we're not. We're always lumped together because we're all women."

But Miss Harvey, please help me make sense of why there was so much magic in the air. As resolute as you all were to be defined as individuals, not a scene, you certainly seemed to feed off of each other's energy. How did you and these women break through at virtually the same time? With such little precedent for the boundaries you were pushing—and such little concern for the world's receptiveness to your pushing them? Were you all sneaking off to the same secret oracle under cover of darkness, to receive the same Golden Gift of Pure Awesomeness? Most importantly—and this gets a little personal—*why did it all have to align so perfectly with my sexual coming of age?*

Look, I don't want to reduce you to an archetype. But it's the only way to shed light on another aspect of your significance. You, like these women, represented a very important first—not just for me, but for many men: it was the first time women in music could be both sexy and *powerful*. If you don't believe me, just refer to that list of chart-topping ladies I gave you a few paragraphs back. With the possible exception of Mariah Carey's high notes, not a drop of power among them. Sexy, maybe, but certainly not a thinking man's sexy. Before you and the Great Wave of alternative rocker girls, who did we have? Joan Jett? Loud and rude, maybe, but in a spiked-wrist-cuff-from-planet-Claire kind of way. Which is *posturing*, not *power*. Before her, who? Stevie Nicks? Grace Slick?

Sure, but back then they seemed like Gonesh-scented caricatures of my mom's generation. So they were definitely out.

The archetype of the alternative female rocker that you helped usher in was another species altogether. You were a laundry list of the seemingly impossible. You were badasses but you were *literate*. You were cultured but a little dangerous. You left the impression that you were far smarter than any man who ever coveted you— and *definitely* more talented. You'd probably driven faster, stayed up later, and felt deeper than any of them, too. You came off as spontaneous and unpredictable—but *always* in charge. You were rock stars, but you weren't reckless. You were vulnerable, too—but you could transform those vulnerabilities into distorted, head-thrashing anthems that made a woman's failings feel as raw and relatable as our own. And that made you *powerful*. Unconfinable. And above all else, fucking sexy.

This much is irrefutable: from the moment rock and roll was first played to another human being, human beings have wanted to emulate their rock and roll idols—to dress like them, to talk like them, to drive Rolls-Royces into swimming pools of similar depth and with similar impunity, even die on the same brand of motorcycle. Rock and roll has always offered an escape from business as usual. A way out. Alternative rock was no different. But my point of entry had an entirely different purpose: I didn't start acculturating into the alternative scene to *emulate* my idols—I did it, at least in the abstract sense, because I wanted to win them over. I guess that's just a reality of opposite-sex idol worship over same-sex idol worship. But until that special time and place, I didn't know it. And now, thanks to you, there's an entire generation out there who's never known life *without* female rock idols who are at once both powerful and sexy. The fact that it feels absurd to even write that is a testament to just how thorough the transition has been. You only have to wade through a few Miley Cyruses and Katy

Perrys to get to the good stuff. The contemporary music scene is positively overflowing with powerful, sexy, free-thinking, and wildly creative women. So many that I cannot, as I did then, simply catalogue the handful of game-changers. There are multitudes. The game is changed.

Now it seems I've gone from thanking you personally to thanking you on behalf of the entire male species. This is some letter. I think I'd better get us back to where we started: Dylan's driveway. I'm taking us back there because it is the underlying metaphor of this letter. Of course, you're better at those than I am, but bear with me.

At this point, as a platinum-selling artist, it shouldn't be too creepy to hear that you've been there for me at various times in my life—not just at that critical point of divergence in 1992, when you helped determine the path I'd take in life, but many others, too. *To Bring You My Love* became the late-college musical backdrop against which some extremely deep and complicated relationship dramas unfolded (and imploded) under the moss-bearded oak trees of Tallahassee, Florida. It was around then, too, that I was introduced to Nick Cave's *The Boatman's Call* by a woman who might have been the love of my life, but whom I never found the courage to be with. I didn't learn until later that those songs were the work of a man whose heart you yourself had just broken— though if you hadn't, I wouldn't have had that tapestry woven into my own heartache, either. At times we've even taken parallel paths. I moved to New York City in 2000, the same year you released your paean to Gotham, *Stories from the City, Stories from the Sea.* All your shout-outs to various Manhattan neighborhoods might have come across as a little naive, had I not been discovering those same neighborhoods and rooftops at the same time you were. And that made it special.

After that, I admit, I lost sight of you. You veered off into some new musical frontiers. I drifted away from journalism and then, after a thirteen-year run, away from the city that enchanted us both at the same time. Now, twenty-two years after discovering you, I find myself here on the lush West Coast, lost. Parking at the barbicans of notoriously private rock stars, walking the streets of Venice, trying to find purpose in the blinding blue sky, writing letters that are supposed to be essays to women who will never know the special province they occupy in my life.

I guess twenty years ago this would have been fan mail. That's not what this is—not even in a postmodern meta-letter sense. This time around, Polly Jean (what the hell, we can be fake friends in a fake letter), I'm thirty-seven, not sixteen. I'm not diving into your mysterious river, eager to be carried fast into the far-most corner of Anywhere Else. This time around, I'm just idling in front of your house, looking for answers. And just like it didn't matter last week, when Dylan didn't invite me in to talk about the ghosts of electricity over what probably would have been fucking scones, it's just fine if you never read this. I feel your presence, just as I felt his. And we don't always talk to God to find answers. Sometimes we just want to say thank you. Sometimes we just want to bask in Her grace for a couple minutes—when the car's idling, when the heart is heavy, when the words won't come, when the cursor flickers, when we can't find the bridge, when purpose and perspective eludes us, when we're worried that the choices we've made in life are probably all wrong and we wonder what the hell it's all about and if we ever really got it right. But we can always always, always turn up the stereo, roll down the windows, and go home.

In That Dark Room: Aretha, Loretta, and a Microphone

Ada Limón

One member of the group never sang. She sat with us and made song requests. One member, who was going though a divorce, was all knee-slapping bawdy talk until it came to her singing, then she transformed into the tenderest Karen Carpenter tenor, smooth and pretty as a canary's coo. One member could only rap or scream. But she could do those things amazingly well, so that people would stand up and shout with her when she reached a particularly tongue-twisting riff. One member would only sing Nancy Sinatra or be the man in any duet, but she could do the dude well and stood in for the fact that men were rarely allowed.

There were more of us some nights and less of us others. But for better or for worse, and without really trying, we had formed a reckless kind of word-obsessed roundtable in the dank air of an underground Brooklyn karaoke club, with a microphone set in the middle of us like a mascot.

Before I wanted to be a writer, I wanted to be a singer. That's probably not unusual. Most writers want to be rock stars. Rock stars trump everything. They're like the nuclear bomb of artists. I wrote short, ethereal songs at a very young age, highly sensitive and weird; I sang them to the Calabazas Creek water in my Northern California home of Glen Ellen. One of my earliest memories is when I learned to work the record player by myself without ever damaging the delicate needle that made the music magically come out.

I didn't know then that the records I played would be an essential part of my early studies of the word. I sat on my knees on the thick, cream-colored carpet in the one patch of oak-leaf-patterned sun that streamed in like a poor-man's spotlight, and listened to women of the words: Joni Mitchell, Janis Joplin, Bonnie Raitt, Aretha Franklin, Rickie Lee Jones, Stevie Nicks, Dolly Parton, Loretta Lynn, Patsy Cline, Carole King, Odetta, Big Mama Thornton, Etta James, Billie Holliday, and the ladies that made my grandparents sing, the Andrews Sisters, Doris Day, and Patti Page. Even now, just saying their names feels like a witchy spell, something made for incantations, something curative.

At the age of twelve, I sang the torch song "Cry Me a River," poorly and with lots of dramatic hand gestures, at Dunbar Elementary School. I wanted badly for my voice to turn amazing and grow deeper. I wanted to be taller and wear a floppy brown beret and smoke a cigarette like Rickie Lee Jones on the cover of her debut album. None of that ever happened. I managed to don a loose-fitting beret now and then, and smoke occasionally while trying to grow up, but I never became a singer. I became a listener. And that listening led me to an obsession with two very different, but distinct female singer-songwriters: Aretha Franklin and Loretta Lynn.

***

WHEN I FIRST MOVED to New York to become a poet, I had an angry twisted knot in the middle of my chest. You couldn't see it under the forest green, secondhand corduroy coat I had brought from Seattle, but it was there. It wasn't sadness, or guilt, or shame, but rather a raging kind of panic that held me down at nights and mostly felt like someone was squeezing my sternum in a vise. To this day, I'm not sure if that painful weight that took my air away was due to my fear of failure or my fear of success; all I know is that very little helped to relieve it. Even describing it now, I can feel it sneaking under my shirt like a familiar fist. Panic attacks were so regular for me that I didn't even talk about them. I'd get dizzy. I'd sit down. And then I'd get back up again.

Once, I went to the doctor at NYU and said I was having "most likely a heart attack or something," but the very nice doctor, a woman, assured me that maybe I had just pulled a muscle doing too many pushups and, she thought, I might be having some anxiety issues. The weight on my chest only seemed to go away when I was doing two things: writing or drinking. A cheap cold beer in the afternoon—preferably in a bar that had both equal parts dark and light and a good jukebox—seemed to clear the volcano-like pressure right away. And writing, even bad writing, seemed to help, too.

Like many who move to New York, I was struggling through a heartbreak; I was far away from my small hometown, and I had no idea what I wanted to do with my life other than write some poems and generally create stuff that meant something. I routinely missed my family. I would imagine my mom's black rotary phone in the kitchen, the answering machine, the wide low oak tree out the windows. But I didn't like to call her too often because I was afraid she'd feel my panic through the phone lines, or the satellites, or the atmosphere.

Luckily, I had the benefit of moving to the city around the

same time that a lot of brilliant women also moved there. Give or take a year or so, somehow, a group of quick-witted, liver-hearty, kindred spirits gathered at the same bars around the city and took to calling each other family. My best friend T, a playwright whom I lived with and who was the much-needed armor to my thin skin, my dear friend J, who was a fellow poet and made everyone die laughing with her smart and idiosyncratic storytelling. My dear friend H, who we once determined, through a game of random questions, could do everything and do it well (skiing, waterskiing, speaking French, etcetera). None of us knew what we were doing with our lives, but we'd liquor ourselves up until that was fine by us. We'd take to the streets and barhop until we finally ended up in the karaoke bar.

The bar, which was underground and smelled like industrial cleaners and the sticky-sweet, almost-burnt odor of buttery nipple shots that came in waves to the red lounge-style couches where we sat, became the ultimate cave-like hideout of the literary girl gang. The group was sometimes fifteen deep, sometimes just a twosome, but it was, make no mistake about it, the absolute VIP gathering place for anyone craving less gossip and more straight talk and some sweet stolen time on a microphone.

At first I didn't know how to sing karaoke. I had taken voice lessons at the Sonoma Community Center, when I was fourteen, from a straight-out-of-a-movie woman named Dusty who looked like Janis Joplin and thought I had a bigger gift for songwriting than I did singing. And she was right. Still, singing in public made my throat close up. Not unlike the weight of anxiety in my chest, my tongue would turn to glue when I thought of singing the first note. Cheap white wine was tossed around like crucial scuba gear for going under, and soon I was able to give it a go. When I was done, to my surprise, both that nasty knot that perched in my chest like a building's gargoyle, and the pasty thick tongue I had from fear, were gone. I'd found a cure; it was song.

***

THE FIRST TWO SONGS I took on at karaoke were an Aretha Franklin hit, "Dr. Feelgood," and Loretta Lynn's signature classic, "Coal Miner's Daughter." In the beginning, calling these songs up to the giant karaoke screen, with their strange eighties music videos that seemed as if they had been made in someone's basement, felt almost sacrilegious, but when the words began to roll I felt like I was tapping into something bigger, something wider, a deep ocean of proto-feminist anthems that had been composed by two women who had, for different reasons in different times, been through the wringer and come out queens. Tucked away in the pre-utopian Williamsburg in the early 2000s, this karaoke bar was the perfect hiding place; it was an unconventionally cheesy choice for us. In that neighborhood, everyone was a musician. Everyone was happily couch-surfing. Everyone was making choices for themselves, trying to be an artist, and living freely off their parents' money or the small bartending jobs they could manage between hangovers, band practice, and threesomes. This was a place where everything was all right, even when it clearly was not. Not one of these hipster cowboys would be caught dead in a karaoke bar that catered to large groups, drew a highly diverse crowd, and carried every song you'd ever heard in numerous black binders. In that enclave of budding artists, designers, fuzzy-brained fakers, and honest-to-goodness wannabes, we had found a safe place to be fully ourselves.

It was a world away from the Memphis where Aretha Franklin was born in 1942, or her papa-preacher's Detroit church where she learned to sing gospel and made an early name for herself for both her voice and her piano skills. And it was a far cry from the Butcher's Holler of Van Lear, Kentucky, where Loretta Lynn was born in 1932 and learned to sing on the front porch while watching her seven siblings. Still, there in Williamsburg, these two were with us. When their songs were invoked in our contemporary world it did more than just celebrate the roots; it exposed the very infrastructure of female artistry. They were the knights of our roundtable.

Aretha Franklin, heralded by many as the Queen of Soul, went from singing gospel at her father's church to eighteen Grammy awards and forty-five top hits. Melissa Etheridge famously said, "You can hear Aretha Franklin in any female who makes the hair stand up on your neck." But what has always drawn me to Aretha, as an artist, is her ache—she is not scared of her pain, nor is she ashamed of sharing it. The loneliness, and the sheer intimacy she has with her audience when she sings, make her not weak but extremely powerful. When her hit "Respect" (written by Otis Redding) became an anthem for the Civil Rights Movement, I wasn't even born yet; still today I can hear the vigor and intensity in her performance, and she still makes the room spin.

Loretta Lynn, born ten years earlier than Aretha, is one of the most important female artists of the twentieth century. Writing songs for women and about women, she was speaking honestly and wryly about subjects that women everywhere knew to be true. Songs like "Fist City," "The Pill," "Rated-X," and "Don't Come Home A-Drinkin' (With Lovin' On Your Mind)," all spoke of the real life of a woman who was married at fifteen, a mother at sixteen, and a grandmother by the age of twenty-nine. Raised in the poor village of Van Lear, where the only options were, "coal mine, moonshine, or move it on down the line," Lynn went on to win four Grammy Awards and propel ten number-one albums. In that dark room under the bright lights of the Williamsburg bar scene, we were getting to know these women in the way they were meant to be known: not through biographies, gossip, or awards, but through their songs.

***

BEFORE LONG, WE STARTED calling it Karaoke Therapy. You came in with your job anxieties, your impossible boss, your money woes (we all had no business buying rounds in a bar when we could barely afford our weekly MetroCards), your creative blocks, your jealousy, your shame, your oh-man-I-should-not-have-slept-with-him, and you sang it out. You picked a song that fit the kind of healing you needed and you burrowed into it. When you were done, more than likely you were a bit drunk, a bit voiceless, a bit foul-mouthed and wild, and feeling a whole lot better.

Aretha once said that her homecoming concert in Detroit was "too fantastic." That's what the feeling was—ecstatic and frenzied and fueled by our failures. We took to the microphone and learned what it was to be our most gigantic selves, our biggest bravest selves, the selves that didn't have a weight of fear on our breast bones, that didn't question what we were doing or who was going to love us next or hurt us next, or who we were going to hurt next or love next. Instead we lifted ourselves up to the low, sparkling, stucco ceiling that looked like upside down waves, and we sang about it. Aretha taught me what it was to sing an anthem. A real, get-down-on-your-knees-and-scream-like-you-mean-it anthem. Loretta taught me what restraint was, with the cool tongue-in-cheek, "I've got this" songwriting that sounded like she had a tornado of power tucked inside her boot just waiting for the right wailing time.

We went on like this for years: kids in the underground closet of song. Once, when a bearded man (they were all bearded then in the hairy hipsterville) broke up with me in that way that felt shattering, and stupid, and freeing all at the same time, I went down to the basement of the battering microphone and sang two songs. With Aretha's "Don't Play that Song for Me" I got to shout "He lied, he lied, he lied!" at the top of my lungs and dance and whoop and get fixed. Then I sang Loretta's "You Ain't Woman Enough (To Take My Man)," but that night, surrounded by all the feminine fierceness of my tribe, I changed the words to "You ain't woman enough to *be* my man." And even though he had left me, and cheated on me, and made me feel like I was no one, by the end I felt like it was I that had had the last word—not just my last word, but *our* last word. We were the league of women in the service of language. This was the boat we were in. These were the oars we used to get to the other side.

I remember reading once that Aretha Franklin said, "I sing to the realists. People who accept it like it is." Maybe that's why her songs spoke to me so clearly during those dark and delirious days when I was working hard to write honestly and make rent. Loretta Lynn said once, "I write about whatever's bothering me at the time." That's what made it work. That's what made her songs lifelines. They were true. And they encouraged the truth.

But truth can be such a vague word. What I mean is something bigger. What I mean is that those songs, those women I was singing them with, those nights underground in the cavern of sound—it was all about being okay with the truth. Aretha's endless ache was okay. Loretta's cheating husband was wrong, but she was okay. This was the new part. This was where that pain in the chest loosened, or rather exploded into something new. All of us in those stinky red lounge chairs getting ready for our next song were alone; we were unsure of our future, we were messy and screwed up, but we were learning how to live with it, be okay with it, and talk about it—and write about it.

I never had sisters, and for many years in my life, I didn't feel all that close to the girls my age. I didn't know what it was like to tell the truth the way you can tell it to women when they're all listening and when you really trust them. In that musty dim room below the too-cool streets of Brooklyn, I told nearly every secret I had. And in telling them, I was making steps toward writing the way I wanted. This, in many ways, was one of the most important writing lessons I ever learned. To be brave. To tell it honestly.

I remember those nights and I can't help but think we were being schooled. A real old-fashioned schooling. We weren't reading academic papers, or studying poems on the page, we were crooning the songs that allowed us to be writers in the first place. We were mimics and butchers and fools, but we were part of a tribe much bigger than us. And there were Loretta and Aretha, our heroes of the howl, guiding us to get the words right. Telling us we're all alone in the dark with our stories. And to this day, if I feel that terrifying fist of panic pressing against my chest, I begin, almost automatically, to sing.

A Vision of a Daughter of Albion

Rosie Schaap

"How can I be defil'd when I reflect thy image pure?"

—William Blake, *Visions of the Daughters of Albion*

Sandy Denny has been on my mind, and she does not rest there easily. Her grave is unquiet, as the Child Ballad goes. My head is unquiet, and I love her too much, and like many of my best loves, it doesn't feel like a healthy love.

I started thinking about this essay last autumn. Autumn: Keats's season of mists and mellow fruitfulness; my season of spooky folk ballads and brown liquor and willful melancholia; my season of Sandy. To listen to her sing "Late November" (among the most strange and powerful of her own compositions, from the 1971 solo record, *The North Star Grassman and the Ravens*) over and over, thirteen times (it had to be thirteen), on a dark and cold and lonesome night in late November: that alone can trouble an already fretful mind. For all of its opaque weirdness and queer prophesizing, it knows its season:

> *The wine it was drunk, the ship it was sunk*
> *The shot it was dead, all the sorrows were drowned*
> *The birds they were clouds, the brides and the shrouds*
> *And as we drew south the mist it came down*

I have been spending so much time with her music these last four or five months, even more than usual, and I have been relearning the mostly unhappy details of her short life. I have come to feel too close to the greatest folk-rock singer of all time. So close that I will continue to call her "Sandy" here, and mean no disrespect. On the contrary, I expect that calling her by her first name (her nickname, short for Alexandra) says that I would have wanted to be her friend (chronologically not possible; *North Star Grassman* came out the year I was born). She has come to feel like a friend to me, a beloved and lost friend. A ghost friend. It is hard to gather together my thoughts about her. I am feeling crazy for her, and certain she would understand. Near the end of "North Star Grassman," she sings to me:

> *The methods of madness, the pathos and the sadness*
> *God help you all, the insane and wise*
> *The black and the white, the darkness of the night*
> *I see only smoke from the chimneys arise*

***

OUR RELATIONSHIP STARTED LONG before I ever heard her voice. A poster of the monarchs of England took up much of one wall in my brother's boyhood bedroom in Manhattan. It was festooned with crests and seals and crowns and other regalia, rendered in one of those *ye olde* typefaces, the kind a child instinctively knows is gorgeous before some adult, or adulthood itself, tells her it's distasteful and fucks everything up. And the names: Æthelred (the Unready) and Æthelbert, Harold Harefoot and Harthacnut, a passel of Plantagenets. I devoted hours every week to gazing upon it, transfixed. It was given to my brother by our maternal grandfather, the sort of unrelenting Anglophile who held seasonal subscriptions to a Gilbert and Sullivan repertory company and knew the lyrics to every Noël Coward song.

In time I would come to appreciate the Wodehouse, the Coward. But that poster, and the sounds of those names inscribed on it, in that lettering, got me right away. It was still fixed to the wall when John Boorman's 1980 film *Excalibur* came out and which, within a couple of years, my brother and I watched compulsively on our Betamax; at age ten or so, there was no one in the world I wanted to be more than Helen Mirren's beautiful, bitter, cursing and accursed Morgana. "Your eyes never leave me, Merlin," she says to the magician, her mentor, and the same is true of anyone who watches the movie. As with the fanciful typeface, someone came along and told me that *Excalibur* was a very silly movie and not to be taken seriously. Well, I love it to this day, and, if pressed, I'm afraid I can still recite "The Charm of Making"—the spell spoken in some make-believe pseudo-Celtic language that Merlin teaches Morgana and with which she imprisons him—but, no, not with a straight face.

Anyway, this was so not the England my grandfather loved; this was not high tea at Fortnum & Mason. This place that I glimpsed in *Excalibur,* then extrapolated in my sweaty adolescent imagination, was murky and mythic, sexy, strange: one vast dark wood, broken up now and then by a remote village full of dreadful secrets, a pestilence-benighted city, a werewolf's dark moor, a lightning-blasted oak on a dreary plain. Of course, this was not England, not exactly. This was Albion, even if it would be more than a decade before I learned its name from William Blake.

Watching *Excalibur* now, as an adult, I don't appreciate its dreamlike, hallucinatory effect any more or less than I did in my youth. But, I suppose, from the perspective of experience rather than innocence, I am better acquainted with its kind. And it doesn't surprise me at all that the notions of mythic Albion it first impressed upon me would be reawakened—more than that, would be deepened, would find their most mesmerizing expression—when I was on LSD and listening to Led Zeppelin. The very first time I heard "The Battle of Evermore," I knew this much: *My ears will never leave you, Sandy.*

Nevermind the inscrutable, Tolkienist lyrics. Nevermind, too, that Robert Plant manages to sound filthy and sexy even singing a line like, "The apples of the valley hold the seeds of happiness." But when Sandy sings, "War is the common cry, pick up your swords and fly," that's exactly what I want to do, even though I hate the idea of war and had no sword. If Sandy had sung, *sacrifice virgins and eat the shit of dragons,* I'd probably want to do that, too.

Sandy is the thing that makes the song great not good, its excellence owed to the otherworldly harmony, to that voice that sounds as though it, too, was handed to us by the Lady of the Lake along with the Sword of Kings.

This is the Sandy I heard: The High Priestess. The Empress. The queen of faerie; daughter of Titania and Oberon. Handmaiden of the elements, of earth and air, fire and water. Daughter of Morgana and Merlin. This is who I thought she was, and had to be. A dream woman, a creature hybridized from Blake drawings and Tarot cards.

***

SANDY WAS A MIDDLE-CLASS girl raised in the suburbs of London by parents who'd met when both were in the British Army. She trained to be a nurse. She liked very much to drink and smoke. She liked men, too; sometimes crazy ones, sometimes ones who treated her badly. She had misgivings about her appearance. She had a wicked sense of humor. She drew well. Consider this account from Joe Boyd, a frequent producer of both Fairport Convention and Sandy's post-Fairport band, Fotheringay, in his memoir, *White Bicycles: Making Music in the Sixties:*

> She was entertaining company…her laugh was the loudest thing in a room. She had a way of jerking her cigarette to her mouth so that the ash scattered everywhere and she was very adept at knocking over drinks. I once saw her upend three mugs on one trip to the kitchen to freshen up the teapot. When playing the guitar, she would stare at her left hand, keeping a wary eye out for the inevitable slip… She was clever and quick and a brutal punisher of fools, but she wore her neediness and her heart very much on a sleeve.

How far all this is from my Arthurian vision of Sandy. How very familiar it all sounds. Except I can't sing.

And Sandy is her singing; her singing is Sandy. The two cannot be separated. Hers is the prettiest voice I've ever heard. (I resist using the word "purest," because it means next to nothing, but I resist it with effort). My mother, who sang wonderfully in a barely-trained, smoke-and-gravel alto, always said: "Every church choir is full of pretty voices, but most have only one good singer." There is no one who sounds like Sandy, and many have emulated her. Most of them sound pretty, and little else.

Peter Ackroyd issues this solemn warning in *Albion: The Origins of the English Imagination*:

> ...*the Druids were supposed to believe that Albion, the spirit or embodiment of the English, was an original portion of the lost continent. It is a very rich, not to say heady, brew. Any attempt to drink it will inevitably lead to numbness and disorientation.*

Drink of Albion's murky waters and sing long enough like its daughter, and maybe you will become one after all. She was not a devoted scholar of the folk tradition, not like Martin Carthy or Shirley Collins in that way, no purist like Ewan MacColl. But Boyd (who came around to the singular beauty of Sandy's singing) is on to something when he says that he initially dismissed her taste as too American. In the early days in London's folk clubs, Sandy sang Dylan covers and American spirituals and the like. Her voice was always beautiful, but it belonged not to these songs but to Albion and its tradition, and to the weird English ballads she would have to write herself.

***

A FEW YEARS AGO I got very, very drunk one night with a long-lost high-school friend who had lived many years in India and wound up teaching yoga in Milan. I had complained to him about the arthritis afflicting my right knee. He gave me a few pointers. When I got home, I locked the door to my building behind me, and faced the stairs that lead to my apartment. As my yogi friend advised, I took the stairs up two at a time. My foot landed in the empty space between them and I fell forward. I heard my head slam against the tread and my first two thoughts were:

> *I am going to get a blood clot in my brain and die.*
> *I will die as Sandy Denny died.*

My head was bruised and swollen and the edge of the stair had sliced a small, jagged strip of skin from my forehead. My head hurt badly for a couple of days. And then I recovered.

Sandy tumbled down a staircase in late March, 1978. A few weeks later, after suffering from terrible headaches since the accident, she fell again. She died in a coma on April twenty-first. She was thirty-one.

***

TODAY IT IS THE sixth of January, in the year 2014. Sandy would have been sixty-seven years old today. I read this morning that Linda Thompson, her friend and contemporary, called Sandy's recording of "The Banks of the Nile" with Fotheringay "the best vocal ever." I have listened to it six times in half as many hours, enough almost to agree with Linda Thompson. But I can't pick a favorite. After hearing "The Battle of Evermore" as a teenager, I found my way to Fairport Convention's *Liege & Lief,* a perfect record, one I have not stopped listening to since I was sixteen.

Today my favorite Sandy vocal is not "The Banks of the Nile." Today it is "Fotheringay." Tomorrow it could be "Reynardine," sung with such emotional force that I suspect she encountered the rakish man-fox more than once in her time. And while there are other singers of British folk ballads who give me deep and stirring pleasure, too (Shirley Collins, Maddy Prior, Anne Briggs, among many), it was Sandy singing "Matty Groves" on *Liege & Lief* that almost made a folklorist of me. (That dream died during an internship at the Library of Congress's American Folklife Center in 1993, but I wouldn't have gotten even that far were it not for

Sandy.) And when autumn comes around again, "Late November" will once again supplant all other songs.

Listening to "The Banks of the Nile" at my breakfast table, I toasted Sandy's birthday with a small glass of stout.

***

RICHARD THOMPSON WROTE A song about her. So did Jackson Frank. And Dave Pegg, too.

Bert Jansch (one of Sandy's lovers, as was Frank) wrote a particularly sad and bitter-sounding song about her, "Where Did My Life Go?," its title a grim echo of Sandy's most famous composition, "Who Knows Where the Time Goes?" Unlike Jansch or Thompson, Frank or Pegg, Nick Talbot, the gifted songwriter, singer, and guitarist of the band Gravenhurst (essentially his one-man operation), never knew Sandy personally; he's also too young for that. But he wrote a song for Sandy, too, and these are all of its words:

> *Then she dances*
> *Skirt swaying in the half-light*
> *She dances*
> *White blossom in the black sky*
> *I need new clothes, she thinks*
> *New skin, a mind I can bear to live in*

Capturing her not as changeling, not as fairy princess, not even exactly as a rock star, nor klutz, nor drunken party girl, but as a harder and richer being, the most important, the most relatable; a real person, who lived a real life. A real person, who may have wanted a new skin, and may have needed a more bearable mind. A real person—still illumined, magical, and in motion.

Soul Survivor

Kate Christensen

Watching early performance clips of a twenty-one-year-old Tina Turner on YouTube, I said out loud to my dog, "Where the hell did she *come* from?" He had no answer. Maybe no one has the answer.

The young Tina seems to have sprung fully-formed from some magical hybridization—of a panther and an Amazon, maybe. She's hybridized in general: female and masculine, black and white and Cherokee, superhumanly spectacular and approachably girl-next-door, and her style is a synthesis of R&B, rock and roll, and soul, a secularized blend of the Southern black church gospel tradition she came from.

Other performers seem to have a carefully thought out stage persona, a nuanced layering of deliberately displayed attributes, but Tina is TINA. There's no apparent gap between who she is offstage and on, except that quite possibly, she is more at home onstage, more fully herself. Onstage, she perfectly inhabits her own skin. Onstage, she looks as if she's happier there than anywhere else. Given her life story, it's not hard to fathom why.

In the clip, which was shot in the early sixties, she's skinnier than she is now—in what in anyone else would be called "old age," for Tina is more like ripeness, fruition. But she's already a kinetic force. Her powerful voice, once described by a producer as "screaming dirt," seems fueled by some lava pit in her chest. Supple, rippling, powerful, rangy, dynamic, tireless, she tears up the stage in her micro-miniskirt, with the amazing, taut legs of an elite athlete, tossing her manelike straight wig, windmilling and farmer-hoedowning her arms, which are ropey with muscle and elegantly long. Then she turns to the mike and lets loose with her unique brand of shredded, smoky vocal heat, not even breathing hard. She looks like she's having a blast. She looks like the distilled essence of what used to be called rock and roll—its absolute embodiment. The seeds of her later conversion to Buddhism are as evident as her Baptist roots: she's holy rolling, and she is one with the music.

Meanwhile, her husband, Ike Turner, that emaciated proto-hipster with his Brilliantined hair and villain's mustache, wearing peglegged pants and holding his guitar like a weapon, lurks Svengali-like in the background, watching her with burning eyes, no doubt readying his post-show critique, his slaps over missed notes, his teardowns and corrections.

It's almost impossible to believe, watching her onstage, that this powerful and magnificent creature was ever subjected to such treatment, let alone for so many years, and so brutally. But we all know the Ike and Tina story.

Born Anna Mae Bullock in Nutbush, Tennessee in 1939, the daughter of a sharecropper overseer and an African-American mother who was also part Native American, she'd grown up singing in the Baptist church choir and being shunted from one grandmother to another as her parents moved around and eventually split up. Her childhood was hard and tumultuous and full of loss and upheaval, but she always loved to sing.

As a teenager in St. Louis, Anna Mae (who was working as a nurse's aid and dreaming of becoming a nurse) hung out in nightclubs with her older sister. One night, Ike Turner, the leader of the local band the Kings of Rhythm, invited various audience members to come up and sing with the band. When her sister, who was dating the drummer, demurred, Tina seized the mike, and that was that. Ike instantly recognized her potential and kept her onstage, made her sing every song she knew. She was sixteen. After training and coaching her, he hired her to replace the lead singer. He also changed her name, first to Little Ann, and finally to Tina—allegedly because it rhymed with Sheena, his favorite TV character, but changing a name is one of the hallmarks of a super-controlling relationship. Tina was Ike's ticket out of St. Louis.

Their act, "Ike and Tina," shot to international stardom after their first single, ironically titled "A Fool in Love," became a hit in 1960. After Ike split up with his wife and Tina broke up with the Kings of Rhythm's sax player, with whom she'd had a son, they eventually became sexually involved, although both of them described the relationship as sibling-like rather than romantic, and agreed that neither was the other's type. And Ike always had other women, some of whom even slept in the same bed with Tina and him. Even so, they got married in Tijuana in 1962; she was his sixth wife.

Ike physically abused and controlled Tina for almost the entire time they worked together, almost eighteen years. The first time he hit her was after Tina mused aloud about possibly leaving the group; he bashed her in the head with a shoe stretcher. And then his paranoia, criticism, and controlling rages became the norm. When she was eight months pregnant with their son, he forced her to perform. Shortly after she gave birth, he forced her onstage;

she sang sitting down and bled during the high notes. She often sang through busted lips, heavy makeup hiding black eyes and bruised cheeks. When she got bronchitis, Ike wouldn't treat it, so her damaged lung plagued her for years afterward.

His violence aside, they were totally unsuited for each other. Ike was an alcoholic cokehead womanizer; Tina, who was steady and grounded and sober, mothered their four sons as well as she could, given her work schedule (in addition to her first son, they had a son of their own, and Ike had two sons from a previous marriage). In 1969, in Los Angeles before a show, after a particularly severe beating, she tried to commit suicide by swallowing fifty Valiums; when she came to after her stomach was pumped, Ike was berating her for trying to screw up his life. She became a Buddhist in 1974, chanting "Nam-myoho-renge-kyo" to help her "get through hard times."

As the story goes, after the last beating she would ever take from Ike, Tina finally left the marriage in Dallas in 1976, sneaking out of their hotel room during a tour while Ike was asleep. She threw a cape over her bloody clothes; her head was too swollen for her usual wig. She had nothing but thirty-six cents and a Mobil gas card in her pocket. She also had four sons to support, which she did, at first, by cleaning houses. She hid from Ike by staying with various friends; he hunted her down and threatened her, but she was finally through with him.

The tour promoter held Tina responsible for repaying the money the tour had lost by Tina ditching Ike, but she got to keep her stage name. After the divorce, she had surgery to correct her septum, which had been damaged by Ike's frequent hitting. Meanwhile, her career skidded sideways and stalled. At thirty-seven, she had to start all over again, from the bottom.

***

IN THE SPRING OF 1987, I was living in Portland, Oregon, cocktail-waitressing at a blues club called the Last Hurrah. I had graduated from Reed College the year before and had stuck around town because I had no idea what else to do. I paid 160 dollars a month for a little apartment up the hill from campus with hardwood floors and high ceilings. French glass-paned doors separated the tiny bedroom from the tiny living room, which had a huge multipaned casement window. The place smelled strongly of mold and was always chilly, even on the hottest days, but I loved the romantic architecture, the proximity to campus where the guy I had a seemingly hopeless crush on was still a student, and the cheap rent.

My best friend at the time had worked at the Last Hurrah with me until she'd quit to be a stripper. Danielle, who'd majored in English at Reed and played classical guitar and was an accomplished painter, also had huge boobs and a tiny waist and long legs and a catlike, French face, and silky blonde hair. Raised Catholic, an army brat, she was uninhibited, provocative, and exhibitionistic. Stripping came naturally to her. She and I had in common the fact that we were both headstrong, independent, ambitious young women who allowed ourselves to be treated badly by unattainable men we obsessively pined over. We fought a lot. She was hilarious, bright, impossible, bitchy, needy, self-involved, and possibly certifiable. We were incredibly close.

Danielle was always giving me cassette tapes: Eurythmics, Simple Minds, Cyndi Lauper, Lloyd Cole. Before I caught the number nineteen Tri-Met bus downtown for my nightly shifts at the Last Hurrah, I blasted music on my tape deck, loud, to pump myself up for a night of dealing with drunk customers, mostly men, to whom my job was to serve even more alcohol. I spiked my short hair with gel, put on a lot of eye makeup, ran fishnets up my legs under my miniskirt, adjusted my boobs in a push-up bra under a strategically ripped T-shirt, then slid my feet into spiked pumps. My feet would be aching about two hours into my shift, but the shoes made me feel powerful.

"Tina Turner?" I said one day when Danielle handed me a tape labeled *Private Dancer*. "Wait, wasn't she the one who sang 'Proud Mary' a million years ago? My parents listened to her in the sixties. She was married to that guy who beat her."

"She's amazing," said Danielle. "She's back."

After Danielle left, I put the tape in, pushed "play," and went into my little bedroom to get dressed for work.

Instantly, "I Might Have Been Queen" filled my apartment—a kickass, thrilling, inspiring song, Tina's voice rasping and shrieking with defiant pride, an almost-unearthly triumph, her band bouncy and tight as a trampoline underneath her, musical proof that she had survived, and to hell with anyone who didn't believe it.

The air crackled. My blood beat in my veins. That song made me whoop with joy and dance around like a banshee, half-naked. I loved the rest of the album, too, but "I Might Have Been Queen" was the song I played from then on when I needed bucking up, a reminder that even if Kip didn't love me back, I would survive just fine because look at Tina. She was glorious.

She growled her way through "I Can't Stand the Rain," which Ann Peebles arguably sang more hauntingly, more beautifully, but without Tina's idiosyncratic feline screech and don't-mess-with-me bravado, over-enunciating words as if her native language were European, with the slightest hint of a laugh at the back of her throat.

"At first, I thought it was 'I can't stand Lorraine,'" Danielle told me, "'against my window'. Like some obsessive, weird lost girl who stands outside scratching at the glass, trying to get in. 'There's just one sound… I can't stand Lorraine.'"

I almost fell over, laughing. From then on, that's what I heard when I heard the song. Some obsessive weird lost girl trying to enter Tina's life. I could sort of imagine Tina going to the window and opening it and letting her in, sitting her down, and telling her what was what. Her voice had that kind of weary, fearless, warm survivor's confidence: Honey, if I can do it… Now you go out there and get yourself together.

So I went out there and got myself together. I socked away packs of money at my job at the club, which was, I confess, augmented by all the brazen stealing I was doing. I stole from customers and the Last Hurrah alike: serving trays of drinks in the deafening honk and crash and thud of the live bands, I shortchanged drunk letches who kept a pile of money on the table and never counted it. I used my creative writing skills to alter the food tickets to fool the kitchen and the bartender, my pal Jeff, who must have known what I was up to but never squawked. We all did it, me and the other "girls." We made out like pirates, all of us tough and young and gamine in our barely-there skirts with our long, lean legs. We felt we deserved it.

And so my bank account fattened. And then, by some miracle I never understood, I got into the Iowa Writers' Workshop, and then lo and behold, Kip told me he wanted to move to Iowa City with me and live together. We bought a mustard-colored 1977 VW hatchback, and off we went. As we drove out of Portland, I put Tina into the tape deck and turned it up and rolled the windows down.

I was going to marry him, and we'd have babies and live happily forever; I was going to be a famous writer. My future was in the bag. As I sang along with "Private Dancer," I thought about Danielle. I was sure she'd be a famous writer, too. I was sure we'd succeed together. She was unstoppable, she was brilliant. I was really going to miss her.

Danielle, it turned out, would never leave Portland, would be a stripper for years and then decades. We would lose touch in our mid-thirties because I couldn't deal with her self-destructive craziness anymore. Kip would break my heart at least twice more before it was finally over for good, and I wouldn't publish my first novel until 1999. But I didn't know any of that yet. I sang along with Tina, "I want to make a million dollars, I want to live out by the sea, have a husband and some children, yeah I guess I want a family..."

Tina, meanwhile, would make a terrifying stripper. Trying to imagine her giving a lap dance to anyone makes me laugh: those powerful thighs, that mouth, half-pout, half-sneer, always with the hint of a smile, the fierce muscularity of every move she makes, those arm-swiveling, frog-marching dance moves that are all hers... She submits to no one, not even momentarily, not even for Deutschmarks or dollars. And any old music *won't* do, not for the Queen of Rock. In "Private Dancer," her frank, unhurried, passionately strong delivery of Mark Knopfler's lyrics seem to me, at least on some level, to be acknowledging and leaving behind her past with Ike.

***

Post-Ike, Tina performed with many other male singing partners: David Bowie, Mick Jagger (watching them perform together, I feel as if they're soulmates, as if she taught him everything he knows, taught him to be Mick Jagger), Eric Clapton, Bryan Adams, Barry White, Elton John, Tom Jones, even Bruce Willis. They're all white, which strikes me as not a coincidence. Along these lines, she made her comeback not in the United States but in Europe, at least at first; vast, adoring, mostly-white audiences in Britain and Germany embraced and supported her. She recently married her boyfriend of twenty-seven years, a much-younger (he's fifty-eight; she's seventy-four) German music producer named Erwin Bach, and relinquished her American citizenship for Swiss. She lives on Lake Zurich and speaks fluent German.

Despite her no-holds-barred stage presence and her flamboyant movie appearances as the Acid Queen in *Tommy* and the Queen of Bartertown in *Mad Max,* Tina is by all accounts a straight arrow in her personal life, private and quiet and modest, no diva, no troublemaker at all. She's never been much of a drinker, never used drugs, never been involved in a scandal except for her abuse at the hands of Ike, which was not exactly her fault. Wholly committed to Buddhism while still observant of the Baptist faith she was raised with, she told Oprah Winfrey, "God is a way of life." By every account, she's lived her life as a mature adult: responsible, true to herself, kind to others, and humble.

Her latest and possibly (never say never) final tour was in 2008, to commemorate the fiftieth anniversary of the start of her career in 1958, the year she joined the Kings of Rhythm. The tour was sold out in thirty-seven North American cities and went on to near-equal success across Europe. She soared over the crowd on a cherry-picker wearing stilettos, sweating, dancing, singing her heart out. She was sixty-eight; fans and critics alike went nuts over her. Jonathan Cohen wrote in *Billboard,* "The point: this woman defies so much conventional wisdom that being in her presence for two-plus hours is a bit of a head trip." The *Sunday Telegram's* Tom Horan wrote that Tina "showed why she is a goddess in Germany. If you had to say what that feeling is with Turner, it's a feeling of triumph: I've come this far, I've done it—I'm still standing."

Watching clips of her exuberant performances on this tour, shot fifty years after the early performance clips I'd watched earlier, I looked at my dog, silently repeating the question, "Where the hell did she come from?" and he looked back at me, as if to say, "I still have no clue."

Anna Mae Bullock, Tina Turner, heroine, star, soul survivor, Queen of Rock—whatever you call her, she's the only one of her kind.

Punk Nerd Grrrl

Felicia Luna Lemus

I.

t was 1994. I was nineteen, and, things—as I would have
so eloquently said then—pretty much totally sucked. The
simplest part of this story is that I was a punk nerd, at least five
kinds of Other, and…ominous drum roll or maybe the Darth
Vader song if you prefer…I lived in Orange County.

Yes, Orange County, as in "The OC." And like so many
other nineteen year olds in Orange County—punk, nerd, and
otherwise—I really, really, *really* wanted to leave the stifling mix
of stuff that was my hometown. But it wasn't my time yet. I'm
not suggesting one has to petition for formal permission to leave
Orange County, à la an outtake from *Battle Royale* or some other
dystopian narrative, but, honestly, that's kind of what it felt like.

It is a tightly controlled place, Orange County. And the
town I grew up in, the City of Orange—Orange County's proud
eponymous heart—is among the most staunchly conservative parts

of the county. Ours was a town where segregation-era placards that read "No N-----s, No Dogs, No Mexicans" were sold as charming kitsch in antique malls. Seriously. I first saw one of those signs when I was six. It was on display right next to a country kitchen-style hand-painted sign that read: "Home Sweet Home."

And that's the thing—even though Orange County was a bastion of questionable politics and fixed horizons, it was also my home. My family had been in the City of Orange for nearly a hundred years. It took time to build up the courage to leave. But still, there was never any question that Orange County didn't like the likes of me. I was of color. I was a feminist liberal. And I was punk. Nope, Orange County and I were not a match made in heaven. One thing about that, though…

When considering why punk runs in my veins, it's worth mentioning that my neighborhood was the barrio: el OVC (Orange "Varrio" of Cypress Street). Mexico is the motherland of my people. Well, my maternal people, that is. My other half hails from Flanders and Sweden, by way of San Bernardino County. Anyhow, contrary to what some may assume, I'm here to tell you that it's entirely possible to be both from the hood and punk.

Exhibit A: La Llorona, the Weeping Woman.

Long story short, a favored old school tactic for keeping little kids in line in the neighborhood of my youth was to tell them terrifying stories about La Llorona, the Weeping Woman. "Who is she?" you may ask. Well, imagine a phantom who flies through night skies and steals bad children. And then make said spooky ghost lady really scary. Okay, now *scarier*. There, that's her. So why does she go around stealing kids? Because she's wicked. (Duh.) Oh, and she wails and wails and wails as she steals children. Like a banshee straight out of H-E-double-hockey-sticks, mija. You know all those creepy sounds old houses make in windstorms? Well, when the Santa Ana winds—aka the "Devil Winds" (ask any So

Cal old-timer)—come and slam stuff around, that's the Weeping's whisper. *Better run and hide, little ones!*

Let's just say this childrearing tactic backfired on me. Big time. I thought La Llorona sounded cool. Way cool. I wanted to meet her. Damn, I wanted to *be* her. She was fierce, she didn't take crap from anyone, and that girl knew the power of a good wail. She was the Original Gangsta' Riot Grrrl, yo.

In thinking back to my early days crushing on La Llorona and the origins of my hunger for punk, I realize I should mention that I was raised by pilgrims.

In our home, austerity and self-denial were lauded as the highest of values. Work came before pleasure. Pleasure was vain. Vanity was unbecoming. And, maybe the most punk-making belief of them all, children were to be seen, not heard. There were a lot of secrets in our house, a lot of loud silences; even the most unbearable loss and hurt was never to be addressed. Add to all this: for the first ten years of my life, I was the only child in our four-generation household; my family didn't like me leaving the house any more than necessary; and I wasn't allowed to play with other children from the neighborhood. I read. A lot.

But even as bookish as I was, school wasn't the welcome escape you might think it'd be. Classmates called me a "martian" (a nuanced spin on illegal alien); wrote on the bathroom stalls that I was a "beaner bitch" (fifth grade); and threw pennies at me while chanting "Mexican whore" (seventh grade). Representative example of how this stuff played out: when the principal refused to paint over the slurs written about me on bathroom stall walls, I scrubbed them clean myself. Orange County. As for the crushes I had on girls other than La Llorona? Forget it. There was only so much a kid could take.

Is it any wonder that all through my teens I mainlined a steady diet of punk and goth? The Clash, The Ramones, Sex Pistols, Blondie, Lou Reed, Patti Smith, Siouxsie and the Banshees, X, Bauhaus. These bands were the ticktock of my inner workings. Their cacophonies and laments were my sweetest comfort and nourishment.

And then there was The Day that It All Came Full Circle.

II.

I knew this girl who was seriously cool, so cool that she was transferring to UCLA. She was Big City in all the ways I was still Orange County. And she called herself a Riot Grrrl. "A *what*?" I distinctly remember asking, fully aware I was going to get razzed for my cluelessness but wanting so badly to know that I didn't care. By way of explanation, she lent me a tape. No, not a mixtape, dear Retro-Sentimentalists. An actual tape purchased at a gig. A tape-tape. Remember those?

Bikini Kill. I'd never heard of them. (Or I'd probably already know what a Riot Grrrl was, right?) The title of the album made me bristle involuntarily. *Pussy Whipped.* What the…?! Wasn't that like totally misogynistic? I mean, were we really allowed to say that?

"Listen to the B side first," Cool Girl said.

Tape in hand, I got in my car to wander off to who knows where, as young adults in Orange County are wont to do. Car in reverse, I popped the tape in. And there it was, all cued up: B Side, Track 4.

"B4." So fitting. Because there was *before* "Rebel Girl." And then there was *after*.

Holy freaking punk wow!

Feedback. Throbbing bass. Guitar *rat-a-tat-tat* drumming like a machine gun. A soldier's strut. A battle hymn. Then this throaty, dare-you-to-listen voice kicked in. Kathleen Hanna. She sounded young, like maybe just a few years older than me. And she sounded like a girl I could imagine hanging out with. She was, I immediately understood, a Riot Grrrl. I just sat there—car idling, my foot still on the brake—completely transfixed.

Just to contextualize, this wasn't totally my first time at the rodeo. I had heard plenty of fierce fight songs before. Nina Simone's "Mississippi Goddamn" was queen of them all as far as I was concerned. And Patti Smith's hella transgressive "Gloria" sparked my brain every time. But the first time I heard "Rebel Girl" I felt it in a way I'd never felt another song before. Immediately, viscerally, it coursed through my veins all hot mercury liquid fire like my own boiling blood:

> *When she talks, I hear the revolution*
> *In her hips, there's revolutions*
> *In her kiss I taste the revolution*
> *Shut the eff up! Did she just say…?!!*
>
> *That girl thinks she's the queen of the neighborhood*
> *I got news for you: she is!*
> *They say she's a dyke, but I know*
> *She is my best friend*

I crashed my crappy Plymouth Horizon. Right into a totally obvious concrete column in a stupid parking structure I'd parked in probably a zillion times before. *Crunch,* there went my back bumper. Apparently Orange County policed cultural infractions via all sorts of means. I put the car in park, got out, hitched my dangling bumper up onto my jenky car, drove very slowly and carefully to the hardware store, bought a roll of black duct tape, and put my automobile back together again. Sort of. Like me, that little car was forever changed. I kept listening.

Song after song, Bikini Kill rocked the fiercest punk beat and Kathleen Hanna snarled and whispered and screamed smartly about love, fear, pain, lust, about being a girl in a boy's world. Those songs were a license to profess, to protest, to scream. And so I did. I screamed. Did I ever.

Actually, my first scream was kind of quiet. This was predictable, really. Orange County and my family's ethos of Politeness Above All Else still had a grip on me. If I had nothing nice to say, I knew it was better to say nothing at all. But no more. Windows rolled up, cruising down the freeway, I screamed again. And this time it was a scream Weeping Woman would have been proud to call her own. Loud. Fierce. With purpose. As catharsis. As vindication and validation. As a map for future plans. I screamed until my throat was raw and the screams turned to laughter. It felt good. Really, really good.

For weeks (okay, maybe for *years*), I listened to Bikini Kill on heavy rotation—practically *exclusive* rotation, actually. I just couldn't get enough. It was like they'd seen the inside of my brain. I liked the company.

And, yes, Punkologist Careful Reader, the start of all of this did take place in *1994*. Indeed, that does mean I was unfashionably late to the Riot Grrrl party. I'll claim the excuse that I was up to my nerd neck in coursework, research papers, and other related academic miscellanea. Punk or not, I was still an Honor Roll kid. Hell, I was a *Peer Academic Advisor* as an undergrad. Don't know what that is? Exactly. Let's just say it's so transgressive that it's not. (Like, really *not* at all.) But that is neither here nor there; one taste of what Bikini Kill promised and I was starving for more. The second I graduated from college, I packed up my car. The 55 to the 405 to the 605 to the 101. Off at Silver Lake Blvd. I broke free.

III.

LA, that mythical town that may as well have been planet Mars for how different it was from Orange County—oh how I adored my new home!

Silver Lake. K-Town. Eagle Rock. I was an East Side Grrrl. And I went out almost every night.

Spaceland. The Echo. Silverlake Lounge. The Smell—back when it really *did* smell and developers hadn't "discovered" the loft-potential of Skid Row yet. Ah, those were the days. I hung with the coolest of the cool queer punk kids, and over time, I learned about plenty of Riot Grrrl and queercore bands. My most favorite to see was The Need. Rachel Carns—Sharpie Ultra Fine drawn-on eyebrows and wild eyes, operatic punk trill, and maniacal stand-up drumming—was a mesmerizing Maria Callas/Bertolt Brecht love child. So good. But, at the end of the day (or night, or whatever) it almost didn't matter. I always came back to Bikini Kill. They were my first. There was something special, something unmatchable, magnetic even, about that.

Funny thing is, I never even saw Bikini Kill live. It's not like I didn't have the opportunity to, but deep down I worried it would be like getting to Oz and finding the sad little Wizard behind the curtain. I couldn't risk possible disappointment. As Mr. Nobel Prize Isaac Bashevis Singer once said, "...if Tolstoy would live *across the street*, I *wouldn't* go to see *him*." Amen.

Life marched on. I went to grad school. I wrote a novel. Bikini Kill stayed with me in all those long nerdy days at my desk. They'd become the sound of my brain in neutral. Their chaos was my calm. Their screams kept my voice strong. But, like so many good love stories, things inevitably changed...

IV.

2004. A decade after I'd first heard Bikini Kill, I moved to NYC. I didn't listen to much punk in the five years I called Manhattan home. In retrospect, I actually didn't listen to much music of any sort when I lived there. And I could count on one hand the gigs I went to during those years. Downtown was such constant noise that I needed silence whenever I could get it.

Still, Bikini Kill held a special spot in my punk nerd heart.

Like, there was that one time I saw Kathleen Hanna walking down Avenue B on the east side of Tompkins Square. If she had been alone, I might have approached her to thank her for her part in Bikini Kill. But she was with her Le Tigre bandmates. They were wearing zany, neon-hued coordinated outfits. The era I'd been so touched by was distinctly over. I kept walking.

Oh, and then there was that time in 2007 when I toured my second novel and Tobi Vail, Bikini Kill drummer fantabulist, came to dinner after my reading in Olympia. "Tell Me So" is included in a pivotal moment in that book. Vail wailing, "Get out a piece of paper / write everything down"—it's the epitome of punk nerd excellence. I told her as much. She was very gracious and kind. And I was delighted to meet her.

But something had shifted.

In 2009, right before I left NYC to move back to LA, I imported all my CDs to my computer and sold them at a little shop in the East Village. Yes, even my cherished Bikini Kill CDs. The liner notes were thin as rice paper for how many times I'd unfolded them and smoothed them out to read them like holy scripture. The CDs' plastic cases had cracked corners that held stories. They'd gathered some dust, but they'd been with me through so much. I can't articulate why I sold my collection exactly. It was sort of like shedding old skin. Reptilian. Evolutionary. But I kept Bikini Kill with me where it really counts. In spirit. They are with me in who I am.

V.

Bikini Kill recently celebrated their twenty-fifth anniversary. Kathleen Hanna was interviewed in *Bitch* as saying that the band wants to start its own label. I know this because I shared the article with students in the advanced fiction course I was teaching at the time. The course was titled Punk Nerd Revolution! and, among other exercises, we'd examined Bikini Kill lyrics as models of compelling and transgressive creative writing. My students thought it was cool that Bikini Kill was starting their own label, in a "history comes alive" sort of way. The Big Four-Oh is nearing on my horizon. And as much as I know my nineteen-year-old self would cringe at the thought, at this point you'd be hard pressed to get me to blast Bikini Kill at eardrum-busting volume, let alone go to a club to watch a gig—*especially* to the dive joints where the really good stuff used to go down…always well past midnight, if I recall correctly. It's just not my thing anymore. I've come to like quiet. I like waking up before 8:00 a.m. and not feeling like I have sandpaper for a tongue. Trust me, I really do understand that there's something incomparable about being part of an enraptured crowd, about witnessing an amazing band transgress all sorts of boundaries, musical and otherwise, and that oftentimes that punk *je ne sais quoi* simply cannot translate to downloaded MP3 enjoyed privately in the comfort of one's own home. I guess that'll be my loss at this point. It's okay.

So, yeah, there was once a kid from Orange County who really, really needed to scream. Loudly. Publicly. In a most riotous fashion. But time has passed, she's gotten space from the things that compelled her to scream that way, she's made her own home, and plenty of people would probably look at her now—prim sweaters and such covering her tattoos, her piercings long gone, her face fresh-scrubbed, and her hair showing silver but not a sign of blue-black—and not realize how very punk she is.

Exile in Godville

Bart Blasengame

Snot, and sweat, and grease ride sidesaddle atop Sid
Bream's magnificent mustache as he rounds third base.
His body heaves, and huffs, and spasms like some shit-
pile jalopy gagging on Interstate 40. It's the bottom of
the ninth inning of the 1992 National League Championship game
and the Atlanta Braves' gangly, oft-injured first baseman is headed
for home, arms shadow-box wildly for momentum like a Rock'Em
Sock'Em robot. It's as if he thinks the Pittsburgh Pirate trying
to throw him out—an unswollen, pre-'roid Barry Bonds—has a
gun. Bream scores and the Atlanta Braves go to the World Series.
A pinpoint laser to the plate and the most enduring symbol of
Dixieland futility since Antietam—a team with just eight winning
seasons since 1966—would limp back to their suburban palaces,
leaving their fans to shrug, mutter, and gaze longingly toward deer
season.

At that exact moment, 600 miles away, in the modestly attired
family room of an upper-middle class home in a nondescript
Arkansas sprawl, I am about to come. I *will* come. And after I *do*

come my brain will disconnect from its housing hunched over my high school girlfriend and blissfully implode into a vaselined constellation wash of X-Men comics and Nintendo cheat codes. Somewhere in that postcoital haze, there will be a faint pinch of Christian guilt—the familiar stink of brimstone in the air—signaling that all this beautiful agony will eventually send me to hell. It will be ignored, but will eventually grow into an enormous smothering hand and I will go to bed that night, like many nights before, praying for the salvation of my eternal soul and promising with tears in my eyes that I will never sin like that again. But I will. I always do. A blowjob in my red Toyota Celica. A handjob on her parent's pontoon boat. Desperate, awkward sex in her closet. The pantry. The balcony.

Like any other seventeen-year-old boy living in 1992 or any other year with a digit in it, I am a fiend, scratching and pacing and chewing the inside of my mouth, prowling around the tastefully wreathed front door of my girlfriend's house like a wolf. I am full of "yes ma'ams" and "no ma'ams," I will hold car doors open, I will say and do whatever it takes to get her alone and fumble around through her underthings. Unlike most other seventeen year olds, though, I have no clue what I am doing when the clothes come off on even the most basic molecular level. My parents, three-times-a-week worshipping, nondrinking, noncursing Christians, hoped their combined prayers coupled with my own fear of eternal damnation would be enough to ward off my most primal of urges. It didn't.

As I'm wriggling my pants on that night back in Arkansas, I am momentarily at peace. Sure, my girlfriend and I didn't use rubbers. And, sure, I did ejaculate inside her. But while that's not a *great* thing, any moron knows that in order for a man and a woman to make a baby the man and woman have to come together. *At the same time.* This is what is inferred when sex is awarded such a sinister shadow on the sin scale that your parents just assume you would never deign to do it. In fact, to that point, everything I knew about sex I learned from the fuzzy, soundless Shannon Tweed softcore flicks on Cinemax that I could just make out by mashing two buttons on the cable box together.

But since my poor girlfriend never came, how was this a problem? Unless…unless of course, the idea of mule-kicking orgasms as species propagation was a fallacy. Which makes a lot more sense, right? Because otherwise why are rubbers even necessary. Could Skinemax be wrong. And if so…shit! I'm gonna have a baby and my mom is going to be mortified, and Jesus is going to hate me and banish me to hell where my offending genitals (*especially* my offending genitals) are going to burn forever and ever on a spit.

I came and my girlfriend didn't. No condom. Which is how two eighteen-year-olds with no business wielding sperm and ovum ended up on the phone with her aunt in Louisiana having a very awkward conversation about mutual orgasms the night Sid Bream came sprinting home. "Oh honey…no," my girlfriend's aunt drawled disappointedly over the phone, the receiver facing open air so we could both hear the death sentence. "That's just in the movies. If he, uhm, *finished his business* with no protection, then you two might have a problem." There was a pause. "But did you see the Braves won, hon?"

All of which is a roundabout way of saying that if Liz Phair had been rasping in my ear about sex and blowjobs and the novel ideal of indie rock feminism in 1992 instead of a year later, I would've spent a lot less time loitering around my girlfriend's locker before homeroom waiting to hear whether or not she'd started her period.

Alas, Phair's *Exile in Guyville* was released in 1993 and nobody in my red neck of the woods gave two shits. If it wasn't on Kasey Kasem's Weekly Top 40 or wafting from the pews of the local

Church of Christ, it wasn't important. The only music venue in town was a rodeo arena that attracted the likes of Starship—that abominable iteration of Jefferson Airplane that poisoned the well with *Knee Deep in the Hoopla*—Molly Hatchet, and Stryper. My pinnacle rock and roll moment was holding the door open for a haggard looking Grace Slick as she shuffled from her tour bus to the local Holiday Inn. Oh, and I met The Outfield once. My desperate attempt to discover anything "alt" was to subscribe to *SPIN* and *Rolling Stone,* whose year-end best-of list is where I first heard about *Exile.* I can still remember leering at the album art like it was porn. Here was this grainy picture of a girl floating out from under some black shroud, frozen in the act of a no-doubt salacious perversion. Her mouth was open wide for…something, and there was the faint suggestion of her pale nipple hanging off the bottom right corner. That slightly dirty come-hither image buoyed by song titles like "Fuck and Run" and "Girls, Girls, Girls," were all I needed to know. I must possess this album.

In Nowhere, Arkansas, there was no record store, only Walmarts and Kmarts and general stores with a few CD racks flush with Reba, Billy Ray, and Garth. If you fancied your music sans mullet, you had to have it special ordered. It was easy to be ahead of the curve in a place like Arkansas, where we were consistently at least one year behind whatever cultural zeitgeist folks in real cities were already disavowing. I'm still righteously convinced I was the only Arkansan listening to Radiohead's *Pablo Honey* in February of 1993. Conversely, I still feel guilty being the first person in town to own a copy of Stone Temple Pilots' album of date-rape classics, *Core,* in late 1992. Ordering *Exile* was simultaneously an effort to right that wrong, as well as an early permutation of my burgeoning music snobbery.

When I arrived at Hastings—Walmart wouldn't carry the album because of the appearance of the F-word on the back cover—

to pick up my copy of *Exile in Guyville,* the woman with pudding jowls working the music counter looked at the cover, loosened a couple deep, long frown lines, then stared at me: "Your momma know you listen to this filth?" she said. I was told I would need to place the CD in a brown paper bag, like I was carrying a copy of *Juggs* out of the Kum & Go.

There are two lightning strike musical moments in my youth, bolts of pure reckless energy where I was shown that music could be more than the trifling FM love songs and Motown pantomimes I was raised on. It could be dangerous. Sexy. Shocking. It could rearrange the way you thought about right and wrong. The first was in 1987, on the way to a round-robin church social, listening to a clandestine copy of *Appetite for Destruction,* headphones cupped hard to my ears as W. Axl Rose droned, "turn around bitch I gotta use for you." The second was idling in my car and hearing Liz Phair's "Dance of the Seven Veils," with this tiny, pale, blue-eyed blonde cooing orders and questions to a lover she has apparently shot and whose dead body is now rolled up in a tarp with the repeated refrain of, "I only ask because I'm a real cunt in spring / You can rent me by the hour."

The hell? Twenty-two years later and I still don't know what that line means (I don't know what that *song* means) but I know that four tracks in, Liz Phair's sexuality was overpowering. It was a muscle—a weapon—I had never heard brandished so powerfully, if at all. Her voice was deep, often struggling to remain in key, and frequently in danger of bottoming out, but her scalpel-sharp words sold the conviction. Phair was spitting fire: calling bullshit on both delicate feminine wiles and bullying man-child machismo, plotting revenge on exes, reigning down sex and murder from above and below, and promising to destroy anybody who got in her way. "I take full advantage of every man I meet," she sings in "Girls, Girls, Girls." "I get away, almost every day, with what the girls call murder." She was pumping herself up, singing the words before she actually believed them, and gaining traction and pluck with every song. She was only five-foot-two, but she was talking shit like she was six-one.

I suppose if you didn't grow up in an Arkansas cow town you might actually have known a Liz Phair. Someone who played a Fender Mustang and smoked Camels and had wants and desires that spanned the width and breadth of the MPAA ratings system and could, if they wanted to, use the hypnotizing empowerment of cleavage and a hip shake to manipulate men, because men are just that stupid. She laced big, female-centric ideas about sex and love and relationships through bedroom production values and shimmering guitar lines. She spoke the word "fuck" with the same conviction most girls I knew reserved for coda-ing their prayers with "In Jesus' name, Amen." And she did all this without forgetting the hook.

For somebody who fetishized every sludgy lick and mumble of the early nineties grunge scene, hearing Liz Phair give voice to feminine longing in such explicit detail was like being let in on a secret. It also helped rewire those weird sexual thoughts I was beginning to have about Eddie Vedder. Grunge was great. I *still* love Pearl Jam. But when boiled down, much of the Seattle sound I obsessed over was wounded man-children hemming and hawing and flailing themselves into mosh pits over their daddy issues (That and heroin. Can't forget the heroin). But the former was right in my wheelhouse. I still consider grunge the last great worthwhile musical movement we will ever see. But did it help us get laid? Did it help us understand women? Did it help level the sexual playing field in a way that took away the stigma of sluts and whores and loose women? If a guy could sleep around for shits and giggles, why couldn't a gal?

And it's usually somewhere in a piece like this where one would doff the ball cap and pledge their solemn allegiance to the pussy. But this is not that piece. At eighteen, I already held a marrow-deep respect and awe for strong women. I owed my life to one. My mom had pulled us out from under the work boot of an abusive redneck and scrubbed strangers' toilets in order to get us free of an apartment complex where drunks liked to sleep it off in the back of our Buick. We went without heat sometimes. We loaded the washer and dryer in the basement together, by flashlight, to stave off our fear of the dark. And we sang Marvin Gaye and Tammi Terrell songs at the top of our lungs when nobody was watching. I knew a *lot* about strong women. I knew nothing about what a girl my age might be hiding behind her chastity belt.

Phair wasn't trying to be Gen X's Dr. Ruth, of course. History tells us the album was a screed against the cock-stuffed leather trousers of the Chicago rock scene. The line "Temper my hatred with peace, weave my disgust into fame, and watch how fast they run to flame," from "Help Me Mary," remains one of modern rock's greatest fuck you lines. But nobody living outside of Chicago in the early nineties cared about that. They were lining up to hear songs about blowjob queens, being fucked like a dog, and blue dicks. At first I was no different.

Speaking as a sexually repressed Christian teenager growing up in the South, hearing that kind of filth coming from the mouth of a woman was goddamn novel.

In a never-ending rush to get *my* rocks off, I'd never even stopped long enough to consider what the girl underneath me might want. For a girl to have a sexual appetite was for the girl to be a whore. It meant shame. I knew a drill team member at my high school who made a joke about masturbation and got stuck with a rumor about jerking herself off with a frozen hot dog. It ruined her. Another girl got caught having sex in the parking lot. The administration kicked her out of school; the student body labeled her a slut. A couple members of the cheerleading squad got pregnant. This was not abnormal.

Phair, whether being filthily, comically over the top like on "Flower," or almost uncomfortably vulnerable like on "Fuck and Run," was singing about sex as this many-faceted thing. It could be sport. It could be fun. It could be filthy. It could be boring. It could be a chore. It could be meaningless. It could be a means to empower, or to render one powerless. For the first time in my life I was hearing a girl say that, sure, nice boys with their "yes ma'ams" and "no ma'ams" and ladies first door opening were quaint, but sometimes a girl just wanted her hair pulled. Or to be on top. Or to be left alone with her thoughts of putting a bullet in her man's brain and wrapping his corpse in plastic.

Not that she was an expert on any of this. Underneath the bravado and blue dicks was the very real sound of a twenty-five-year-old woman trying to convince herself of the things she was singing. The bellows of *Exile* laid in less steady, knee-weakening songs like "Canary," "Divorce Song," and "Shatter," songs about, in order, a miserable, kept woman who views herself as nothing more than a receptacle; a relationship turned to shambles in the middle of a road trip; and the dizzying, sickening possibilities of new love. "The license said you have to stick around until I was dead," she sings nearly deadpan over an otherwise jaunty guitar part in "Divorce Song," "but if you're tired of looking at my face I guess I already am." "Flower" is funny if it comes up on shuffle; those other songs still get played on my stereo twenty-two years later. And they still carry a lot of weight.

Which is why for me, Liz Phair was the first fully formed woman of the indie era. Up until Phair, with her filthy mouth and feelings, female musicians tended to be either one thing or another and neither of those things involved sex. Aretha was soulful. Patti was militant. Loretta was a belligerent baby factory. Debbie Harry was a careerist. And Joan Baez was a tuneless lummox who made a career out of the fact that she once blew Bob Dylan. And it's not like I'm trying to compare someone who is basically a one-album wonder to certified legends, but her embodiment of sex and grit and heart was important. I can't speak for female Liz Phair fans because, honestly, I've never met one. And maybe that's kind of the point. To guys like me, who would grow up to create worlds and fashions and ideals and opinions based almost solely on the music they loved, she was the template: the bookish, slightly mousey every-babe who could talk about Big Star and screwing around with equal amounts of passion.

She was my ideal woman. I may have sprouted my first boner watching Erin Gray in her tight, white Buck Rogers leotard as Juice Newton's "Angel of the Morning" played on the radio, but it wasn't until Liz Phair that somebody got me thinking about where, and at whom, I was pointing the thing.

I just wish I could say I put those lessons to good use back in 1993. But much like Phair herself, I just kind of reverted to a rut of what I knew best. Her second record—a couple of very high highs surrounded by plateaus and filler—was my three years wasted at a Christian college, not having sex, not drinking, engaging in some perilously homoerotic, usually naked shenanigans in an all-boys dorm. Her third album—a poppier, breezier Phair, fangs filed down by marriage and childbirth—was my own marriage at twenty-one to my virgin college sweetheart and the first job, first home, and first years of pleasant married missionary sex back in Arkansas.

And then I got divorced.

My wife and I had bounced from Arkansas to North Carolina to New York City trying to bang out a spark that would keep us going. But by 2000 we both realized that neither of our hearts was into it. Apparently all the experimental drinking, drugging, and unbridled sex at your typical non-Christian college turns out to be not only fun, but also a good way to work out your social and sexual kinks. We may as well have been married with blindfolds on. After four years together, we didn't know whom the other was, each of us branching off in different directions hoping that the roots would hold. They didn't. She was secretly racking up massive credit card bills; I was secretly slipping off my wedding ring when working out of town and pretending I might actually do something.

Eventually she left New York for some deserved fuck-you European bacchanalia before holing up back home with her parents in North Carolina. I stayed in the city to try and make a living as a writer. The night I found out she'd cleaned out my bank account I was standing at an ATM in a bodega on First Avenue. I had never wanted to kill another human being until that moment, but just then the thought of driving 700 miles to North Carolina in order to commit first-degree murder with a claw hammer seemed like the only thing that might unclench my fists and jaw. Maybe I'd even roll her body up in plastic. Too bad she had taken the car. Instead, I bought a six-pack of High Life, went back to an empty apartment, and happened upon my cracked CD copy of *Exile in Guyville*.

And sure, the first song I played was "Divorce Song," and the second song I played was that big, weepy number, "Shatter," and then maybe I played that one again. But after that? Then I remembered 1993 and the allure of blue-eyed, blonde girls with guitars and dirty mouths. I was a single man in a big city, a twenty-five-year-old who had yet to see a pair of thong underwear in the flesh. Or had a one-night stand. Or gotten a blowjob in the back of a cab. I hit play on *Exile* and let my mind throttle at the possibilities. I gathered up my courage.

This time I vowed to make Liz Phair proud. I was alone in a big city and that didn't seem like such a bad thing. I was already six-foot-one, but I had room to grow.

Wreckage

Phyllis Grant

1990

Dear Madonna,
I will fuck you if you want.
Love,
Phyllis

2014

At least once a week, my husband will turn on the car and Air Supply, Whitney Houston, Peter Cetera, or Mariah Carey will pour out of the speakers. There is only one person in the house to blame.

Lite FM? Really?

Really, my love.

There is something seriously wrong with you.

My husband thinks we have a bit of a parenting crisis on our hands. He believes our kids need a crash course in good music. Like yesterday. Fine. This can be his job. For me, music has always been more escapist than cerebral. I'm borderline snobby when it comes to abstract expressionism and French cheese, but with music, I'm unapologetically mainstream.

Like every single episode of *Parenthood* or all of the Nancy Drew books, music enters my body at an easy-listening frequency. There's a satisfying build, the requisite yanking of my heartstrings, and then bam, I'm mainlined with pure emotion. I rarely listen to lyrics. In fact, most music misses my brain entirely.

> *We clawed, we chained, our hearts in vain*
> *We jumped, never asking why*
> *We kissed, I fell under your spell*
> *A love no one could deny*

I am on the edge of my desk chair watching Miley Cyrus' video for "Wrecking Ball."

> *Don't you ever say I just walked away*
> *I will always want you*
> *I can't live a lie, running for my life*
> *I will always want you*

I'm not really following anything she's saying.

> *I came in like a wrecking ball*
> *I never hit so hard in love*
> *All I wanted was to break your walls*
> *All you ever did was break me*
> *Yeah, you wreck me*

I am drooling.

I want my twenty-year-old breasts back, Miley.

My desk is in the hallway. Six years ago, this was a strategic move.

And by the way, why exactly are you licking a mallet?

I was able to write and still keep an eye on my one-year-old son while he upended the living room.

Who fucked you over, Miley?

Or I could bolt up just in time as he tried to climb out the window.

You didn't really need to get naked, did you? I just worry about my daughter. Will she think she needs to get all sexytown in order to accomplish anything? Because that's hella fucked up.

One room removed from parenting. A mini vacation.

I love pubic hair. Yours is basically gone. Please help me understand. Don't you want to look like a woman?

But now my desk feels like Grand Central. A husband or a child or dog is always sneaking up behind me.

HEY!

What?

My daughter's eyes get big. I quickly close the browser window.

What's that you're watching, Mom? Why isn't she wearing any clothes?

I'm a fairly chill mother. But I have my limits. Watching Hannah Montana rub her inner thighs and roll around in bashed-up cinder blocks is just not appropriate for my eleven-year-old daughter. It's barely appropriate for me.

I am Miley's mother. I am her lover. I am her critic. I am a mixed-up hormonal monster.

I'm mesmerized. The white tank. The combat boots. The aggressively-mascaraed, neon-blue eyes. That little bit of springy saliva. The perky pre-breastfeeding breasts. The power. The destruction. The tears. The youth. The breasts. The breasts. The tight ass. The breasts. Did I mention I'm perimenopausal and certain times of the month anything will turn me on because my body is in overdrive saying *make one more baby before all of your eggs are dead and gone just one more baby please.* Even Miley Cyrus' landing-stripped pussy can rile me up.

I go underground with my Miley. To protect my sanity. To protect my children. No more watching. I only listen with my headphones. Five times. Ten times. Then I just put it on YouTubeRepeat.com.

For three weeks straight, "Wrecking Ball" is my writing song. While I bang out the section in my book that examines young love and hormones and angst, I listen to Miley frothing at the mouth about how fucked up love is. No matter that she was born in 1992, the year I graduated from college.

1981

Eleven years old. My body was just starting to wake up. All was heightened. In a matter of weeks, I went from being a voracious reader to a sullen dreamer. I would stare at the wall for hours. Volume down in my brain, volume up in my heart and vagina. I was so blindsided by hormonal shifts that I lost my appetite. I was fifteen pounds underweight. I was shy. I was a wreck.

Despite some early *Joy of Sex*-inspired role-playing with other girls my age—*let's try this position, you pretend to be the woman, I'll be the man, she sits on top facing away, one leg is stretched back, she arches her chest up and her head rests in her arm, like that, now bounce, wait, stop, that's not right, let me get the book*—my love for boys was clear as day. I just didn't know what to do with them. And they didn't know what to do with me.

First there was the eleven-year-old who chased me with the scissors and showed his love by cutting off a chunk of my hair. His mother forced him to call and apologize. I did all of the talking. *You cut my hair. What was that about? You. Cut. My. Hair. I don't understand. Why?* Silence.

And then there was the dreamy French boy with perfect curls and striped nautical shirts. Even after he punched me in the stomach, I still dreamed of kissing him at night.

And Guillaume. French again. During an afterschool session of Truth or Dare, he found out I was into him. He attacked hard by telling everyone I had a thing for a dork named Dirk. My sixth grade social life was ruined. Poor Dirk. Poor me.

P.E. class. Seventh grade. I was dancing with a group of friends and trying to catch the eye of a gangly, blond surfer dude. I pas-de-bourréed pas-de-bourréed step-kicked jazz-melted to the ground thinking *please look over here please this is all I've got I don't know how to talk to you but I can do this.* He didn't glance up. Not even a quick peek.

As I got older, it just got harder. I wanted a boyfriend so badly that I felt the ache of a phantom heart. As if I had experienced love once but couldn't seem to find it again. I was a throbbing bundle of heartbreak and I had never even held a boy's hand. A hardwired notion of where I should be on the romantic spreadsheet of life was so heavily reinforced from books and television shows and movies that I convinced myself there was something deficient in my girlness and I should be returned to sender.

For my teenage years, I perpetuated this unattainable fantasy by locking myself in a padded room of cheeseball love songs, Harlequin romances, and John Hughes movies. I had the Thompson Twins blasting through my head as I tried to daydream my true love into fruition. There he was on the other side of the street, à la *Sixteen Candles*, wearing Levi's and a sweater vest, leaning against his red sports car.

Me? I'd say, pointing to my heart.

Yeah, you. He'd reply all slow motion-y.

But there was no Jake Ryan loving my silent goofiness. Turns out, if you don't talk to boys, they don't talk to you either.

The music I was listening to didn't help. Corey Hart and his sunglasses at night, Lionel Richie and his hellos, Bryan Adams and his heaven, Michael Jackson and his crotch, Prince's "Darling Nikki." They all seem old and odd. They didn't help me relax. I needed a guide.

I started listening more and more to Madonna. In her early days, there was an awkward old-school Hollywood veneer to her whole package. The diamonds-are-a-girl's-best-friend of "Material Girl." The pregnancy drama of "Papa Don't Preach." The bebop of "True Blue." Not my stories. Not my groove. I couldn't even get a boy to talk to me. What did I care about abortion and engagement rings? I didn't know it yet, but Madonna was stirring something up inside of me. It was just a slow build.

In high school, friends tried to help me out.

Phyllis. You can get over your awkwardness with boys.

I was already turning red.

You can do it. You can say it. Penis. Say it. Peeeeennnnniiiissss.

I can't do it.

Yes you can. I'm going to write it down. Phyllis. Just read the word.

No.

Once you can say it, then maybe you can touch one. Pass me that banana. Let me show you.

Considering my epic list of hang-ups, I still managed to lose my virginity before going off to college. It was a two-minute affair, sponsored by Budweiser, with a soundtrack by John Cougar Mellencamp. I remember the cracks on the ceiling, the nicotine on his breath. But my heart and mind were closed. It was like prison.

I went off to The Juilliard School to study modern dance. I dated a series of actors. They came out of the box in four categories. 1. Crazy. 2. Crazy with girlfriends back home. 3. Crazy with girlfriends all over New York City. 4. Crazy in love with themselves. They entered me, but only with their very busy and distracted penises. No love connections. No orgasms. No. Nothing.

Then 1990 changed everything. It was a big year all around the world. Saddam Hussein invaded Kuwait. Nelson Mandela was released from prison. East and West Germany reunited. I turned twenty. I saw Madonna's "Cherish" video for the first time and I melted from the crown of my head down to my pelvic floor.

She rolled on the beach in her black dress, waves splashing up her body, laughing as she arched her chest up to the sky. She was perfect, elegant, playful, graceful, beautiful. I wanted to jump inside her body. I wanted to be Madonna. I wanted to be held by Madonna. I wanted to fuck Madonna. My gay male dance friends also wanted to be Madonna. So much so that they auditioned for her world tour. I placed the proposition note in my friend Stanley's hand, making him promise to deliver it to Madonna.

I gave up on straight men. I fell for gay men. They were so easy to love. I mothered them. They took me downtown to the Limelight and the Pyramid Club. They were so uninhibited with their bodies. With their words. So dirty and sassy and brave. We embodied Madonna. We moved. We breathed. We sweated. For the first time in my life, I didn't care what anyone thought.

Two months later, I fell in love with a straight man. Like the shaking-all-over kind of love. The unhinged kind. The multiple orgasms kind. Ten years later, I married him. And while this man still doesn't approve of my music choices, he remembers the moment we first met. On the dance floor. There I was. Dancing like a motherfucker to Madonna. Open, comfortable, and free.

2014

I only corrupt our children with bad music when he's not around. What he doesn't know won't hurt him.

Mom. Can you change the song?

Why?

Madonna makes me yawn.

Dash, that is unacceptable.

What? Why? She doesn't do that to you?

She makes me want to dance.

Oh.

Come on. Sing with me. I was never satisfied with casual encounters—

Dash yawns. I yawn contagiously. We yawn together uncontrollably. I continue singing.

I can't hide my need for two hearts that bleed with burning love that's the way it's got to be—

Mom. Come on. Hearts that bleed? Burning love? What?

Don't listen to the lyrics, my love.

Just spin.

Just spin.

Just spin.

P.S. I just learned that Madonna never got my note. My friend Stanley saved it. It's tucked away in his apartment in Williamsburg. He plans to give it to my children someday.

About the Authors

CHARLOTTE DRUCKMAN is a journalist and food writer whose work has appeared in various publications, including *The Wall Street Journal*, *The New York Times*, and *Bon Appetit*. She is also the author of *Skirt Steak: Women Chefs on Standing the Heat & Staying in the Kitchen* (Chronicle, 2012). She's also the proud cofounder of Food52's Tournament of Cookbooks, and lives in New York City. She hates writing these bios.

ALLISON GLOCK, a magazine journalist of twenty-five years, has been published in *The New York Times*, *The New York Times Magazine*, *Esquire*, *Rolling Stone*, *Food & Wine*, *Elle*, *O: The Oprah Magazine*, *Men's Journal*, *GQ*, and *The New Yorker*, among many other publications. Her poetry has appeared in *The New Yorker*, *South Writ Large*, and the *Portland Review*. Glock was the recipient of the Whiting Award for her book, *Beauty Before Comfort*, (Knopf, 2003) a memoir of her grandmother's life in West Virginia and a *New York Times* notable book. Glock is also coauthor of the Young Adult book series *Changers*, and has written for television.

ADA LIMÓN is the author of three collections of poetry, *Sharks in the Rivers*, *This Big Fake World*, and *Lucky Wreck*. Her fourth book,

Bright Dead Things, is forthcoming from Milkweed Editions. Her work has appeared in *The New York Times, Poetry Daily, The New Yorker*, and elsewhere.

MARISA SILVER is the author, most recently, of the novel *Mary Coin*, a *New York Times* bestseller and winner of the Southern California Independent Bookseller's Award. She is the author of two previous novels, *No Direction Home* and *The God of War*, which was a finalist for the *Los Angeles Times* Book Prize for fiction. Her first collection of short stories, *Babe in Paradise,* was named a *New York Times* Notable Book of the Year and was a *Los Angeles Times* Best Book of the Year. When her second collection, *Alone With You,* was published, *The New York Times* called her "one of California's most celebrated contemporary writers." Silver made her fiction debut in *The New Yorker* when she was featured in that magazine's first Debut Fiction issue. Winner of the O. Henry Prize, her fiction has been included in *The Best American Short Stories, The O. Henry Prize Stories*, and other anthologies.

ALINA SIMONE is a singer-turned-writer whose work has appeared in *The New York Times, The New York Times Magazine, The Wall Street Journal,* and *Slate* among other publications. She is a regular contributor to BBC's *The World*, and the author of two books: the essay collection *You Must Go and Win* (Faber & Faber, 2011) and the novel *Note to Self* (Faber & Faber, 2013).

SUSAN CHOI is the author of four novels. Her first novel, *The Foreign Student,* won the Asian-American Literary Award for fiction. Her second novel, *American Woman*, was a finalist for the 2004 Pulitzer Prize. Her third novel, *A Person of Interest*, was a finalist for the 2009 PEN/Faulkner Award. In 2010 she was named the inaugural recipient of the PEN/W.G. Sebald Award. Her most recent novel,

My Education, received a 2014 Lammy Award. A recipient of fellowships from the National Endowment for the Arts and the Guggenheim Foundation, she lives in Brooklyn, New York with her husband, Pete Wells, and their sons.

Isabella Alimonti is a recent graduate of Barnard College. She lives in New York City.

Bart Blasengame has written about foot fetish whorehouses, bastard celebrities, and Midwestern virgin cults for the likes of *Details, Rolling Stone, SPIN*, and *The New York Times*. He owns a bar, The Fixin' To, in Portland, where he lives with his wife and daughter.

Felicia Luna Lemus is the author of the novels *Trace Elements of Random Tea Parties* (FSG, 2003; Seal Press, 2004) and *Like Son* (Akashic Books, 2007). Her fiction and essays have appeared in publications including *BOMB, The Believer, Latina*, and *ZYZZYVA*, and have been anthologized in collections such as *Lengua Fresca: Latinos Writing on the Edge; Fifteen Candles: 15 Tales of Taffeta, Hairspray, Drunk Uncles, and other Quinceañera Stories*; and *It's So You: 35 Women Write About Personal Expression Through Fashion and Style*. She lives in Los Angeles.

Kim Morgan has written for *Playboy, The Criterion Collection, The Los Angeles Review of Books*, and *The Michael Jackson Opus*, among other publications. She's presented movies for Turner Classic Movies, sat in for Roger Ebert, and was once Guest Director of the 2014 Telluride Film Festival. Read more at her blog, Sunset Gun. She lives in Los Angeles.

Katell Keineg was born in Brittany and was brought up both there and in Wales. In the mid-nineties, she went to live in New York and was quickly embraced by the buzzing café scene around St Mark's Place's Sin-é. In 1993, while building her reputation for "conveying a nearly beatific sense of joy in performance" (*Los Angeles Times*), she released a seven-inch single on Bob Mould's SOL Records label. That same year, Katell sang on Iggy Pop's *American Caesar* and, following his passing of her single on to Elektra, was signed and released two albums now regarded as cult classics; *O Seasons, O Castles* and *Jet*. She has gone on to release several more albums and EPs, most recently *At The Mermaid Parade* on English indie label Honest Jon's Records.

PHYLLIS GRANT still doesn't know what she wants to be when she grows up. In her twenties in New York City, she was a dancer, a chef, a birth doula, and a yoga teacher. Her thirties were a blur of birth, breastfeeding, tantrums, and sleep deprivation. Now, almost halfway through her forties, she is the proud mama of a popular blog called *Dash and Bella: Cooking with Two Kids*. Her writing, photos, recipes, and parenting advice have been featured numerous places including *Oprah*, *The Huffington Post*, *Saveur*, *Williams-Sonoma*, *Food and Wine*, *Apartment Therapy*, *The New York Times*, and *The San Francisco Chronicle*. She writes a column for Food52 called "Cooking What I Want" and is hard at work on a food memoir called *This Dinner Will Not Kill Them*. She lives in Berkeley and can't stop making tarts and ice cream for her husband and two kids. She loves all music, but when John Cougar comes on in the car, right after carpool drop-off, she cries like a motherfucking baby.

IAN DALY is a freelance writer living in Los Angeles with 2,439 LP records, an upright piano, a synthesizer, eight guitars, a set of finely-crafted British drums, several excellent rock and gem specimens, various antique test tubes, vials, and Erlenmeyer flasks, five unplanted mangosteen seeds, an original drawing by Wayne Coyne featuring lasers genitals and fangs, two actual lasers, three Balinese masks, and a closet full of clips from *The New York Times, Details, Esquire, Glamour, Wired,* and *The Poetry Foundation.* He makes a mean penne and is never out of bourbon. You should probably visit.

Jennifer Nix is a writer and activist-designer based in Sausalito, California. Over the years she's been a political activist, a fellow at the Washington-based think tank NDN/New Politics Institute, a co-founder of the international school-building non-profit BuildOn, and the publisher of Pulitzer Prize-winner Glenn Greenwald's first book, the *New York Times* best-seller, *How Would a Patriot Act?* Nix was also editor-at-large for Chelsea Green Publishing, a producer for National Public Radio's "On the Media" and a staff writer for *Variety.* Her freelance work has appeared in *New York, The New York Observer, The Nation, The National Law Journal, The Village Voice* and *Wired,* as well as on Salon, Huffington Post, Poetry Foundation, The Rumpus, Alternet and many political blogs. She is currently finishing a novel and is a producer of the 2015 documentary, "Robert Bly: A Thousand Years of Joy".

Kate Christensen is the author, most recently, of *Blue Plate Special: An Autobiography of My Appetites,* as well as six previous novels, including *The Epicure's Lament* and *The Great Man,* which won the 2008 PEN/Faulkner Award for Fiction. She has published essays and reviews in numerous publications, most recently *The New York Times Book Review, Bookforum, Cherry Bombe, Vogue, Food & Wine,* and *The Wall Street Journal,* among other anthologies. Her second nonfiction book, *How to Cook a Moose,* will be published by Islandport Press in September 2015. She blogs about food and life in New England and lives in Portland, Maine and the White Mountains. She is currently at work on a new novel.

DAEL ORLANDERSMITH is a playwright/poet/performer best known for her play *Yellowman*, for which she was a finalist for the Pulitzer in 2003. She has worked extensively in theatres around the country and throughout Europe. She is currently working on a play for the Goodman theatre in Chicago called *Lady in Denmark*, and another play, *Antonio's Song/ I was dreaming of a son*.

TAFFY BRODESSER-AKNER is a contributing writer to *GQ* and *The New York Times Magazine*. She lives with her husband and two sons in New Jersey, where she just bought Taylor Swift's new album at a Starbucks as God and country intended.

LISA CATHERINE Harper is the author of *A Double Life: Discovering Motherhood* and co-editor of *The Cassoulet Saved Our Marriage*. She writes and teaches in the San Francisco Bay Area, and she recently took her daughter to see Lorde for her first live show.

DANIEL WATERS broke into the world of screenwriting in 1989 with the thunderbolt that was *Heathers*. He has gone on to write *Batman Returns, Demolition Man*, and many cult films with very small cults.

ELISSA SCHAPPELL is the author of two books of fiction, *Blueprints for Building Better Girls*, which was chosen as a Best Books of the Year by *The San Francisco Chronicle, The Boston Globe, The Wall Street Journal*, and *O, The Oprah Magazine; Magazine*; and *Use Me*, a *New York Times* Notable Book and runner up for the PEN/Hemingway award. She is co-editor of two anthologies, and her fiction, nonfiction, and criticism have appeared in many publications including *The New York Times Book Review, SPIN, The Paris Review*, and *One Story*, and numerous anthologies including *The Mrs. Dalloway Reader, The Bitch in the House*, and

Lit Riffs. Currently, she is a Contributing Editor at *Vanity Fair* and a founding editor, now Editor-at-Large, of *Tin House.* She teaches in the MFA program at Columbia and in the low-residency program at Queens in NYC. She lives in Brooklyn.

MARGARET WAPPLER is the author of the novel *Neon Green* (Unnamed Press). She has written features and criticism for *Elle, Rolling Stone, NYLON, Salon, The Believer,* and the *Los Angeles Times,* where she covered music and pop culture for several years. Her fiction and essays have appeared in *Black Clock, Another Chicago Magazine, Public Fiction,* and the anthologies *Yes Is The Answer* and *Joyland Retro.* She currently teaches fiction and creative nonfiction with Writing Workshops Los Angeles, and can be found online and @ MargaretWappler.

ROSIE SCHAAP is the author of the memoir *Drinking With Men,* named one of the best books of 2013 by NPR and *Library Journal.* The drink columnist for *The New York Times Magazine* and a contributor to *This American Life,* she has also written for *Bon Appétit, Gather, Lucky Peach, Marie Claire, Saveur, Slate, Travel + Leisure,* and many essay anthologies. A native New Yorker, Schaap lives, writes, and tends bar, in Brooklyn.

Acknowledgments

MARC WEINGARTEN: Thanks to all the wonderful writers who contributed to the book and made it such a pleasure to edit. I was blown away by everyone's insights and personal impressions of the performers whose music has touched us all. Jeff Gordinier is about as sharp as they come, folks, and I'm grateful to have edited beside him. Tyson Cornell, Julia Callahan, and the rest of the gang at Rare Bird worked their magic on the book, as usual. Thanks, Lee Ranaldo, for the blurb. And thank *you*, reader.

JEFF GORDINIER: I would like to dedicate this book to my daughter, Margot Jane Gordinier.